Cross-Cultural
Human Development

Cross-Cultural Human Development

Robert L. Munroe
Ruth H. Munroe
Pitzer College

JASON ARONSON, INC.
New York, New York

Originally published as a quality paperback edition by Wadsworth Publishing Company, Inc., Belmont, California 94002

ISBN: 0-87668-322-7

Library of Congress Catalog Number 77-74733

Manufactured in the United States of America

Preface

This book, through a consistent emphasis on cross-cultural materials, attempts to cast human development in broad perspective. It is intended for undergraduate courses in child or human development, and can be used as a supplement to a text for a course in which the instructor wants students to be aware of development in other societies. In addition, the book can be used in courses on cross-cultural psychology, culture and personality, and psychological anthropology.

The first chapter traces development in three representative societies from the traditional world. The succeeding seven chapters are devoted to standard developmental topics—that is, physical growth and motor skills; affect; language and perception; cognition; dependence, aggression, and sex; sex role; and social motives. At the end of each of the seven topical chapters, the three traditional societies are briefly reconsidered in terms of the major points that have been made in the chapter, thereby inducing a thread of continuity among the disparate sections.

We wish to thank several of our colleagues at Pitzer College for reading and commenting on parts of the manuscript: Donald Brenneis, Ronald Macaulay, Ronald Rubin, and David Thomas. Valuable bibliographic contributions were made by Leah Light, John Lucy, Judith Piette, Sara Schurr, and Jeffrey Wilde. Preparation of the manuscript was carried out by Stella Vlastos, Rose Schneider, and June Charles, all of Pitzer College. The Research and Development Committee of Pitzer College generously contributed encouragement and funds.

Douglass Price-Williams and Beatrice B. Whiting kindly read the entire manuscript and made suggestions that materially improved it, as did Freda Rebelsky and Lynn Dorman, the editors of this series.

We are also strongly indebted to the many of our former teachers at Harvard—especially John and Beatrice Whiting—who instilled in us a strong and abiding faith in the merits of an interdisciplinary orientation.

The book is dedicated to our parents—to our mothers and to the memory of our fathers.

Robert L. Munroe
Ruth H. Munroe

Contents

Cross-Cultural
Human Development

Introduction

Students of psychology have been exposed largely to research findings and generalizations made on a special breed, Western man. The value in studying people with the same cultural heritage as our own is obvious: our hunches are more likely to be correct because we have the advantage of insight into our own behavior. But other approaches are valuable too, and in this book cross-cultural materials are used to construct a systematic commentary on some of the main research findings in human development. The focus of the book is on what can be learned from the peoples most different from us—the tribal groups of the world.

The most important benefit conferred by a cross-cultural approach is that it allows us to ask whether any given relationship is valid only in the Western world or whether it appears to hold universally. The knowledge that a certain aspect of development creates predictable behavior for all societies stands as an ultimate goal of behavioral-science research. A second benefit of a cross-cultural approach is that we can avoid assuming too much about human nature. A whole set of questions arise that simply do not appear when we confine ourselves to the West. For instance, we can ask: What are the effects on growth of daily baths in scalding water? What are the perceptual effects of growing up in an environment that consists mostly of natural objects rather than man-made objects? What are the cognitive effects of growing up in a bleak, almost featureless environment? Or what are the effects of puberty rites on sex typing? A cross-cultural perspective allows us, in short, to extend both the kinds and the range of variables available to investigation (Whiting, 1968).

There are also disadvantages to using a cross-cultural approach. The very breadth of the materials usually precludes intensive probing in any one area, so that we know the general course of development in a large number of traditional societies, but we seldom know the precise details. Even where intensive work has been carried out, the difficulty in measuring variables accurately and the lack of experimental control in the field setting have raised questions of validity. Because of these problems, a single piece of negative cross-cultural evidence should not be enough to overturn or bring seriously into question a Western relationship that has been based on careful research and numerous replications. Further, an anomalous cross-cultural finding that fails to make sense in terms of what is already established from Western research would not usually present sufficient reason to reinterpret all previous work in that area. More generally, the evidence stemming from cross-cultural work cannot form a foundation for the study of human development; for this basic undertaking, the cumulative findings of Western research over a period of decades are more adequate. But the cross-cultural evidence can yield valuable modifications and checks on the validity of our presumptive knowledge.

A few of the authors' biases are reflected in the preceding paragraph; however, other major ones should be stated explicitly. A theoretical eclecticism dominates in the book, except for the authors' guiding convictions that adult behavior is influenced to an important degree by early experience and that individual characteristics become increasingly resistant to change as they reach mature status. Methodological considerations, though seldom a point of direct comment, have dictated fundamental decisions about the inclusion of material. The authors adhere to the standard canons of behavioral science with respect to issues such as rules of evidence, formal testing of hypotheses, inferential statistics, and the desirability of replication, and have accordingly been inclined to report work abiding by those canons. Within these limits, however, and with the reminder that Western research findings are used as a touchstone for discussion, the authors tend toward what some have called the *strong inference* approach (Willerman, 1972)—that is, making as strong a case as possible from the data at hand. Rather than stopping "a little short of the present," as Margaret Mead (1972, p. *x*) advocates, the approach involves going beyond the core of consensual knowledge to consider problems that are only partially answered. In many instances the interpretation in this book will prove in the long run to be wrong, but it is in this gray area of indeterminacy—"where the next step and the next answer are nowhere given"—that the essence of scientific activity lies, and the certainty of error should not dissuade us from providing the best interpretation we can at this time.

As in most discussions of development, this book includes a combination of developmental *stages* (for example, infancy and early childhood) and developmental *topics* (such as physical growth and cognition). The first chapter focuses on the life stages as differentially defined by three traditional societies, and the seven subsequent chapters are devoted to a topical treatment of development. Within most of those chapters, a broad division into stage characteristics is attempted. In general, the topics differ little from the set that would be found in any presentation of developmental materials, but several areas (for example, morality and interpersonal competence) are omitted or barely touched on because so little work involving non-Western peoples has been done. The topical coverage begins with areas that are probably more closely controlled hereditarily, such as physical growth, and ends with those that are more completely determined by learning processes, such as social motives. Thus the earlier chapters contain more instances of developmental universals and the later chapters more of developmental variability. Characteristics such as the adolescent growth spurt, the basic perceptual abilities, and language acquisition (which are discussed in the first few chapters) appear in relatively unvarying form among children in all societies, while characteristics such as aggressiveness and achievement orientation (which are discussed in later chapters) may appear everywhere, but their levels of expression vary sharply from one society to the next.

The first chapter traces development in three very different traditional societies and thus exemplifies the great diversity of cultures around the earth. For many developmental topics, however, the traditional societies of the world (including those located geographically in the western hemisphere) are more similar to one another than they are to the West, and, conversely, Western and other modern urbanindustrial societies contrast sharply with traditional groups. Accordingly, wherever this dichotomy occurs on a developmental topic, the presentation has been organized in terms of a comparison between modern and traditional patterns. The dangers of oversimplification and stereotyping are clearly present in any such comparison, and the problem is heightened by the brevity of treatment required in a book of this length. But it is the conclusion of the authors that in several areas of development the findings justify an emphasis on the differences between modern and traditional societies. The validity and usefulness of that conclusion will be for the reader to decide.

Methods in the Cross-Cultural Study of Development

Two main approaches have been used to study human development outside Western society: the descriptive and the experimental. The first approach involves studying the descriptions of other cultures provided by anthropologists, explorers, travelers, missionaries, colonial officials, and native members of the cultures. Taken together, these observations make up a vast corpus of library material, a kind of natural history of the species *Homo sapiens*. To facilitate the use of this ethnographic material, a portion of it has been codified in the following systems.

1. The *Human Relations Area Files (HRAF)*—a reproduction of the original texts on some 200 societies, with the data distributed into more than 700 cultural categories (Murdock, Ford, Hudson, Kennedy, Simmons, & Whiting, 1967). If we were interested in breast feeding, we would look under category *853,* "Infant Feeding," for each society of interest. We would find reproduced there all the information on infant feeding that ethnographers had written—data on sucking, initiation of sucking in neonates, stimulation of the flow of milk, feeding problems, communal nursing, fosterage, supplementary feeding, and so on.

2. The *Ethnographic Atlas*—a series of over 100 codes on more than 1000 societies (Murdock et al., 1962). For instance, an *Atlas* code on "Post-Partum Sex Taboos" yields information on taboos that require a lactating mother to abstain from sexual intercourse. Each society in the *Atlas* receives a score on a six-point scale in relation to the duration of the taboo.

Of course, rather than work with the data systems of the *HRAF* and the *Atlas,* some investigators choose to go back to the original ethnographic sources for the selection of sample societies and use of materials.

Studies using the *HRAF* and *Atlas* ratings, in which cultures instead of individuals are taken as the units of analysis, employ *the cross-cultural method* (Whiting, 1968). Because of the breadth of sample, this technique is especially valuable for answering questions about the general validity of relationships and about the incidence and distribution of specific customs. However, there are four clear drawbacks to the cross-cultural method with respect to the study of human development. First, there is a problem of data accuracy (Naroll, 1962). Many ethnographic reports have been written by individuals untrained in the behavioral sciences; therefore the error factor is great. Second, the relationships discovered through the cross-cultural method are all of a correlational sort; that is, variable x may be associated with variable y, but no means exists to demonstrate that x has caused y (Whiting & Child, 1953). Third, because published ethnographic material reports the typical behaviors and beliefs of a culture but seldom focuses on the individual differences among members of a culture, highly indirect measures of personality and motivation are often used. For example, the incidence of witchcraft accusations may be used as an index of the typical level of aggression among individuals within a society. And, finally, studies of this type usually make the somewhat questionable assumption that cultural practices, particularly those involving child training, have remained stable over at least one generation. What the ethnographer actually describes in his or her work are the current child-training practices and the current adult customs and behaviors. If these are to be tied together, it is necessary to assume that today's adults were subjected to today's child-rearing practices when they themselves were children. Perhaps in traditional societies this assumption is not far off the mark.

The other main approach to the study of development in non-Western societies is more familiar, being an adaptation of the standard psychological experiment to field conditions. (See Brislin, Lonner, & Thorndike, 1973, for a detailed explanation of the approach.) This standard approach has been used primarily to amass data about known psychological variables for comparison with data from Western samples and to investigate hypotheses drawn from research in the West. Although the adaptation to field conditions generates some special problems of its own, such as equivalent translation and the high artificiality of a standardized situation, most of the advantages of the experimental approach are retained, and the four major difficulties of the cross-cultural method are either reduced or eliminated. The cross-cultural experimenter may use several different ways to measure a phenomenon of interest (for example, tests, interviews, observations, and ratings of behavior and traits made by other members of a society). But the precise measurement of just a few variables to the exclusion of others may create a major problem—a loss of the sense of context. When the cultural context is unknown or is treated sparingly, possible alternative explanations for findings (or nonfindings) are hard to come by, nuances of interpretation are unavailable, and even the central import of a finding can become moot. The criticism of lack of context is also sometimes made about the cross-cultural method, but it applies much less broadly, and the ethnographic sources necessary for aiding the understanding are always available to the interested party. However, these sources are often not available in the case of an experimental cross-cultural study.

In recent years an increasing number of studies have blended the two approaches by taking findings from the cross-cultural method and retesting them in specially designed field research or by combining experimental designs with long-term, intensive ethnographic work. One important discovery was that the original findings, made with one approach or the other, were relatively robust. Reliable relationships emerged despite methodological problems. These results can give us confidence that both approaches are fruitful and that many findings obtained with only a single approach are likely to be upheld as research proceeds in the future. Nonetheless, the points of difficulty with each type of approach continue to apply, and the reader should keep the problems in mind as findings from research using the cross-cultural and experimental methods are presented in the succeeding discussion. Every chapter except the first presents findings from both types of research.

Chapter One

Life Stages in Three Cultures

This first chapter describes the life stages in three representative societies from the traditional world—the Ainu of Japan, the Trobrianders of Melanesia, and the Gusii of East Africa (Figure 1-1). Although succeeding chapters largely forego consideration of specific societies and instead concentrate on developmental topics like physical growth, cognition, and sex role, at the end of each chapter the Ainu, Trobrianders, and Gusii are briefly reconsidered in terms of the major points that have been made.

The Ainu

The Ainu (ī'nü) lived in Japan even before the forefathers of the present Japanese reached there some 2500 years ago. They are a racial puzzle, because with their light brown skin, brown or hazel eyes, hairiness, and general facial features, they differ markedly from all their Asian neighbors and resemble more the Caucasoid races of Europe (Figure 1-2). Today they live primarily on the northern island of Hokkaido, and they have been strongly assimilated into Japanese culture (Hilger, 1971). The following description depicts their way of life as it was in Hokkaido before major inroads had been made by Japanese customs.[1]

The sea is the main source of food for the Ainu, and settlements are located on the coast and along banks of rivers (Murdock,

[1]For convenience, the cultural descriptions are given in the present tense. More complete descriptions of the three cultures may be found in the following sources, from which the present sketches are drawn: Ainu—Batchelor (1895), Hilger (1971), Kindaiti (1941), Landor (1893), and Murdock (1934); Trobrianders—Malinowski (1929, 1935, 1955); Gusii—LeVine and LeVine (1963).

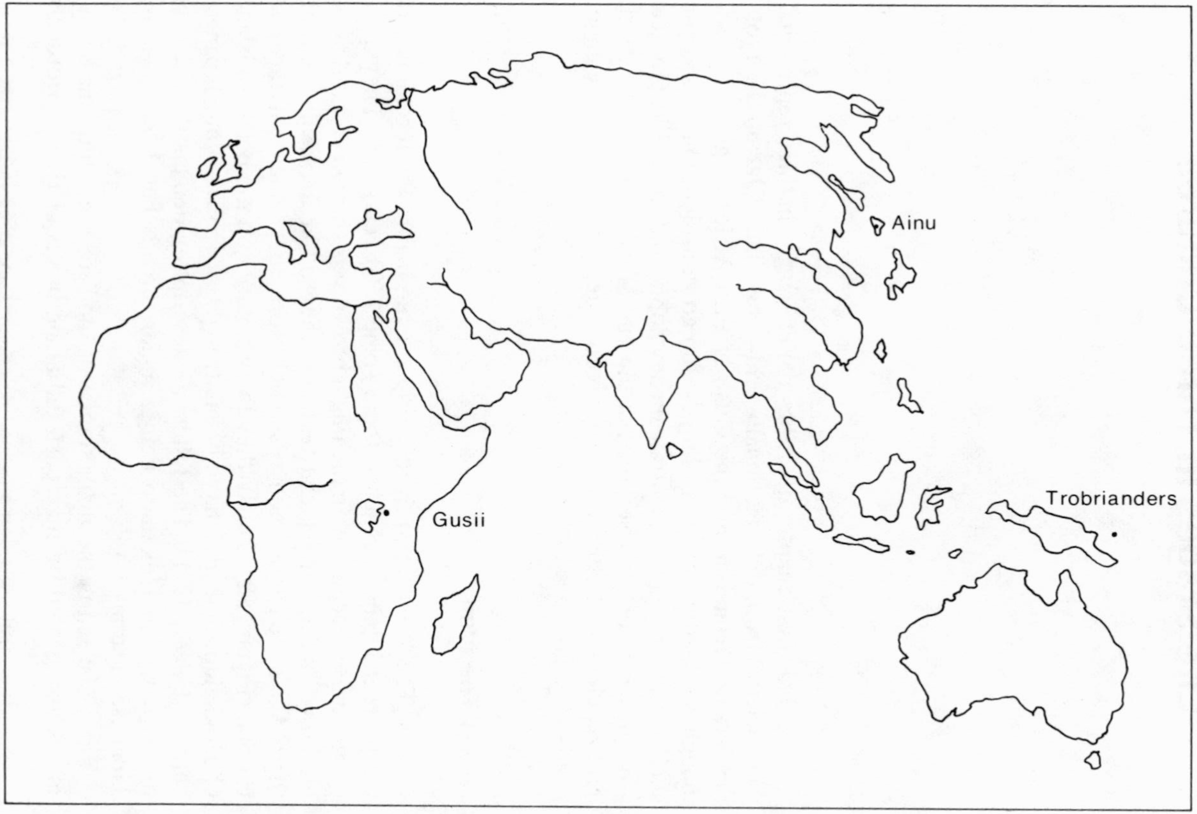

Figure 1-1. Location of the three cultures: Gusii, Ainu, Trobrianders

Figure 1-2. Ainu man and woman. Courtesy of the American Museum of Natural History.

1934). More than a hundred wild plants are gathered, and bears, deer, wolves, and smaller animals are trapped, or hunted with a bow and arrow, to augment the food supply from the sea. Villages are ruled by a chief and a council of elders. Descent is matrilineal—that is, traced through the female line. The typical social unit is the small extended family, in which a married couple may reside with the parents of either the groom or the bride, though most frequently they build themselves a new house near the bride's father. Polygyny (a man's having more than one wife) is common but not universal.

The newborn Ainu is given small doses of an herbal extract for a few days and then is breast-fed. Suckling may continue until the fourth or fifth year. From the age of one month, the infant is tied to a cradle suspended from the ceiling of the hut (Figure 1-3), and no attention is paid to his crying. "Babies," according to the Ainu, "are like talkative men and women; they must have their say" (Batchelor, 1895, p. 43). Outdoors, the infant is transported by means of a *tumpline,* or

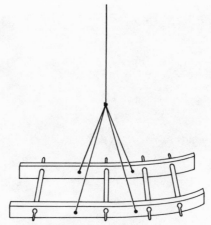

Figure 1-3. An Ainu cradle. (Batchelor, J. *The Ainu of Japan.* Fleming H. Revell Company, 1895.)

carrying strap (Figure 1-4). Some time after the birth, the father reports the event to the Ainu deity, and kinsmen, friends, and neighbors are invited to a meal of celebration.

The Ainu recognize a series of developmental stages in babies and young children: in some areas, a young infant is called by a derogatory name (*shiontek* or *poishispe*—that is, a lump of dung or dung-covered) to discourage evil spirits; when the infant can inflate its cheeks and make sounds like "poo-poo," it is said to be *ai-ai;* when another child is born in a family, the former infant becomes *ahushikore* (it is older now); when a child begins to eat the food of adults, it becomes *yaian ibe* (it eats food independently of its mother now); later it becomes *ki yakka pirika* (it can eat with adults now) (Hilger, 1971).

The child is given a name by the chief of the village in a brief ceremony. At some point in childhood, also, the ears are pierced for both sexes. Small children play with carved fish, boats, leaves, and animals made by their fathers (Hilger, 1971). Older boys receive miniature bows and arrows (Figure 1-5) and spears. Older girls play with dolls carved from wood or made of rags. Children receive explicit instruction in economic duties, proper etiquette, religious customs, and traditions, and it is considered most important that they learn obedience and respect for their parents and older men (Murdock, 1934). A boy of 5 or 6 is allowed to sit in a boat and watch his father make fishing preparations, and at 12 or 13 he can go to sea with the men. A girl is taught domestic duties by her mother beginning at age 5 or 6. If a child habitually lies, steals, or is lazy, a rite is performed to drive away the offending spirit.

Figure 1-4 Modern Ainu woman using tumpline to carry infant. Photograph by Eiji Miyazawa, Black Star. Reprinted through the courtesy of Black Star and Sister M. Inez Hilger.

Puberty is celebrated with a feast and drinking bout (Murdock, 1934). At age 13 a girl undergoes the first stage of complex tattooing around the lips. Small meshes are made with a razor, and the cuts are

Figure 1-5. Ainu boys fishing in the old way. Photograph by Eiji Miyazawa, Black Star. Reprinted through the courtesy of Black Star and Sister M. Inez Hilger.

filled with ashes to effect the darkening (Kindaiti, 1941). A few years later, when the final stage of the mouth tattooing is completed, the girl puts on a woman's dress. A boy has his hair dressed as an adult when he is about 15, and he thereafter wears men's clothing.

Ainu young men and women carry on their own courtships without parental supervision. Marriages frequently grow out of trial unions. The usual age of marriage is 16 to 17. The wedding ceremony itself is arranged by the parents of the couple. At the conclusion of the ceremony, there is a feast, with drinking and dancing. Not long after the wedding, the bride and groom indicate satisfaction with their new status by exchanging gifts that they have made for each other (Murdock, 1934).

A pregnant woman observes food taboos. She and her husband abstain from intercourse for two months before childbirth and for a month or two after. The mother rests after delivery for six days; then she resumes household duties. The husband, in the meantime, observes the *couvade,* a custom involving a father's abstention from normal activities after the birth of a child. In the Ainu variant of the *couvade,* the father is required to rest for 12 days, and, for the first six, he observes taboos and stays wrapped up near the hearth (Batchelor, 1895; Murdock, 1934).

Marriage continues at the convenience of both parties, and the wife as well as the husband is able to terminate the relationship. If divorce occurs, sons live with their fathers, and daughters live with their mothers (Murdock, 1934).

Older persons among the Ainu enjoy a comparatively high status, and children are taught the importance of caring for them. Grandparents have an absolute right to assist in child training. In the evenings, they often tell folk stories and cautionary tales to their grandchildren. Grandfathers observe their grandsons and teach the ancestral history to the most capable one (Hilger, 1971). Upon a death, children are not allowed to attend the ceremonies, and no child is ever named after a dead person.

The Trobrianders

The Trobrianders (trō' brē an'dərz) are Melanesians who inhabit coral atolls northeast of New Guinea. Their aboriginal culture, much changed today, is described in the following paragraphs as it was in 1920.

Garden products, especially yams, make up the bulk of their food supply, and they traditionally produce enough to maintain a dense population and even to yield a surplus (Malinowski, 1935). Fishing also provides a substantial supply of food. Trobrianders have headmen, or chiefs, who if powerful have as many as 60 wives. Descent and inheritance are matrilineal. A husband and wife and their small children reside together near the home of the husband's maternal uncle, who, in a matrilineal system, is a close kinsman of the husband.

The Trobriander infant spends its first month with its mother on a raised bedstead that has a small fire underneath as a health measure and as a guard against magical illness (Malinowski, 1929). During the second month, they remain in seclusion in the house. The baby is breast-fed, but almost from the start it is given additional food in the form of a mash. Weaning takes place when the child is about 2 years old, and, to effect the process, the child is separated from its mother and sleeps with its father or paternal grandmother.

Trobrianders distinguish the following prepubertal stages of development: a fetus and an infant until it can crawl are classed together and called *waywaya;* an infant until it can walk is called *pwap-*

wawa; a child until it reaches puberty is called *gwadi* (the sex of the child can be designated with a prefix) (Malinowski, 1929).

When children reach the age of 4 or 5, they begin to associate with the highly independent children's group (Figure 1-6), of which they remain a part until puberty. As the mood strikes them, they remain with their parents during the day or join their playmates. If the children make up their minds to go for a day's expedition, the adults, and even the chief himself, will not be able to stop them (Malinowski, 1929). After their entrance into the children's group, the children initiate one another into sexual play, unrestrained by their elders. Often, however, boys and girls will be found in groups comprising only their own sex. Always, a brother and sister will play in separate groups, and they must at all times refrain from intimacy, never consorting freely together socially and never showing the slightest suspicion of interest in each other's sexual affairs.

Despite the freedom given Trobriander children, the family does a great deal of work together, particularly in the gardens. The children are shown by the parents how to break the ground (with

Figure 1-6. Trobriander children's group. Used by permission of the Estate of Bronislaw Malinowski and Routledge & Kegan Paul, Ltd. From *The Sexual Life of Savages* by B. Malinowski. Copyright 1929, 1957, by the Estate of Bronislaw Malinowski.

miniature digging sticks) for planting and how to place a yam in the right position. A boy's relationship with his father is close in the early years, and the two remain emotionally tied to each other. But, after the age of 6, the boy comes increasingly under the authority of his maternal uncle, who now solicits him to come on expeditions, to work in his gardens, and to assist him in the carrying of his crops (Malinowski, 1955).

From puberty until marriage, Trobriander young people are called by a new, sex-differentiated term (Malinowski, 1929). Although a boy continues to eat at his parents' home and still does some work for the household, he now sleeps in a "bachelors' hut" with three to six other bachelors of his age (Malinowski, 1955). Each boy is joined in the special house by his sweetheart. Because the relationships are not stable, a girl sleeps at several of these houses during her adolescence, returning home during the day and occasionally sleeping at home for a night.

As the boy passes to manhood, he begins to take a more active part in economic pursuits and tribal occupations, but mainly as a freelance. At this stage, his maternal uncle has come to be important to him in teaching traditions, magic, and arts and crafts. The girl, at the beginning of puberty, acquires a new freedom from her family but then gradually starts to do more work and carry on the duties entailed by womanhood.

Adolescents, after a few years of casual affairs, ultimately pair off in protracted relationships (Malinowski, 1929). When they begin to appear together outside the bachelors' hut, they indicate readiness to marry. If the consent of the girl's family is forthcoming, one morning the girl will remain at the hut instead of going home. This informal acknowledgment of the marriage is followed by an exchange of gifts between the families. The boy has his own hut built now. The couple may reside for a time near the groom's parents, but eventually they must live near the home of the boy's maternal uncle.

The Trobrianders recognize no connection between intercourse and pregnancy; they believe that a child is inserted into the mother's womb by the spirit of one of her dead kinswomen and that the father therefore has nothing to do physiologically with the child (although the child is thought to resemble the father physiognomically because it is "molded" by continued association between the father and the mother). There are fewer premarital pregnancies than might be expected in a culture that allows early and frequent premarital intercourse and that recognizes no connection between intercourse and pregnancy. Malinowski (1929) gives several possible reasons for the low incidence of "fatherless children." Intercourse practiced at a young age, frequently, and with many different partners is somewhat biologically incompatible with pregnancy. The few pregnancies that do result may end in abortion, or more likely, the baby may be adopted by the mother's kinsmen, with no mention made of its illegitimacy.

Midway through a woman's first pregnancy, she participates in an elaborate ritual and dons a ceremonial robe, which she wears for two months then and again after the birth. During all pregnancies, she observes food taboos. In the seventh or eighth month of pregnancy, she leaves her husband's house and goes to her father's or maternal uncle's home to await confinement. For a two-month period following the birth, she and her husband may not eat together, and, for more than a year, they are prohibited intercourse.

Divorce occurs frequently among the Trobrianders, and it is more often the wife than the husband who seeks dissolution of the marriage. Children always follow the mother in instances of divorce.

Beyond the grandmother's role, mentioned above, of helping the mother to wean the baby, Trobriander grandparents have little to do with child rearing; it is almost entirely the responsibility of the parents and the maternal uncle. Middle-aged Trobrianders are called by terms meaning "old man" and "old woman." For men of rank or importance, there is an additional honorific term that translates literally as "tabooed man." Trobrianders sharply contrast the attractiveness of youth with the repulsiveness of old age; for example, their term for old women conveys a tinge of scorn or ridicule. The complex mortuary ritual is less extensive for departed females than for departed males (Figure 1-7).

The Gusii

The Bantu-speaking Gusii (gü′ sē′) of Kenya live near the equator in a green, well-watered highland area of rolling hills. Their culture today closely matches that of 1955 when the main ethnographic work was carried out (LeVine & LeVine, 1963). Aboriginally stateless, the Gusii were divided by the British colonial administration into chiefdoms, which still operate at this time. There are no villages, only contiguous, extended family homesteads occupied by a homestead head, his wives, his unmarried children, and his married sons and their wives and children. The patrilineal extended family tills the land of its own homestead. Cultivation of maize and eleusine (a grain), together with limited animal husbandry, forms the backbone of the subsistence economy, but coffee is grown as a cash crop, and most men work at wage labor in urban areas during some part of their lives.

Figure 1-7. Trobriander widow in mourning, wearing seed beads, balls of deceased husband's hair, and deceased husband's jawbone. Used by permission of the Estate of Bronislaw Malinowski and Routledge & Kegan Paul, Ltd. From *The Sexual Life of Savages* by B. Malinowski. Copyright 1929, 1957, by the Estate of Bronislaw Malinowski.

The Gusii neonate is called *Mosamba Mwaye* ("the burner of his own home"); that is, he has left his previous home, the womb, and cannot return (LeVine & LeVine, 1963). When the umbilical cord

Figure 1-8. Gusii mother nursing infant. From Nyansongo: A Gusii community in Kenya, by R. A. LeVine and B. B. LeVine, in B. B. Whiting (Ed.), *Six Cultures: Studies of Child Rearing.* Copyright 1963 by John Wiley & Sons, Inc. Reprinted by permission of John Wiley & Sons, Inc.

drops off, food is prepared for guests, the child's head is shaved, and the child is named by its paternal grandmother. Breast feeding (Figure 1-8) begins immediately and is supplemented with gruel when the baby is about 6 months of age. Weaning starts within two months after the mother again becomes pregnant, so the infant may be anywhere from 1 to 2½ years old; the average age is just under 2. An unweaned child sleeps with its mother at night and is carried on its mother's back for long trips. But during the daytime, when the mothers are working in the fields, the babies are usually cared for by child nurses (Figure 1-9).

Children are largely restricted in the range of their friendships and associations to other homestead children and near neighbors (LeVine & LeVine, 1963). Unless the family owns a herd of cattle, children are expected to stay close to home. When there are cattle

Figure 1-9. Gusii child nurses carrying their charges. From Nyan-songo: A Gusii community in Kenya, by R. A. LeVine and B. B. LeVine, in B. B. Whiting (Ed.), *Six Cultures: Studies of Child Rearing.* Copyright 1963 by John Wiley & Sons, Inc. Reprinted by permission of John Wiley & Sons, Inc.

(about half the families have cattle), the oldest uncircumcised boy is in charge of the herd, and the younger children tag along to the pastures, which are contiguous to the residential area. Unlike the Trobrianders, Gusii children are strongly discouraged from early sex play. A child is given tasks and errands at a very early age, sometimes immediately after its displacement as the baby in a family by the birth of a sibling. By the age of 5, girls are left at home to care for infants, and, by the age of 6 or 7, both boys and girls do hoeing in previously cultivated fields. Although certain tasks are sex-differentiated, if there is no older boy in a home, the herding assignment will be given to a girl, and, if a home is lacking a girl of the appropriate age, the caretaking of infants will be assigned to a boy.

While the mother-child relationship is relatively informal and the relationship between grandparents and children is warm and often even jovial, the father is seen by the child as a frightening and awesome person. The father is a severe and inflexible disciplinarian; he does not play with, fondle, or praise his children; and he is away from the home much more often than the mother. As children grow older, they are excluded from sleeping at home due to the parents' sexual embarrassment. Girls are sent when they are 5 or 6 years old to their paternal grandmother's house, and boys are sent when they are 7 or 8 years old to a children's house erected on the homestead. Gusii children between weaning age and initiation are referred to by sex-differentiating terms that denote their uninitiated status, and even the children themselves consider the terms insulting and look forward to initiation and circumcision.

The Gusii girl is initiated when she is 8 or 9 years old—two to three years before males (LeVine & LeVine, 1963). A girl shows her eagerness and readiness to be initiated by attempting demonstrations of womanly competence at domestic duties. On the appointed day, the initiates are taken to a specialist, who performs on each a clitoridectomy (Figure 1-10); that is, the head of the clitoris is cut off. As each girl is led homeward, the adult women who accompany her engage in a joyous rowdiness, lifting their skirts high, using obscene language, and expressing desire for prohibited sexual relationships. The women engage in wanton theft and destruction of crops. In the afternoon, the girl is placed in a month-long seclusion in her home, and the men present for the seclusion ceremony are jeered at and embarrassed by explicit sexual references. There is a sexual theme to rituals conducted during seclusion, but the initiate does not engage in actual sexual activity. A ritual marks the end of seclusion, after which the girl is decorated and goes to promenade around the marketplace with other new initiates. She begins (for the first time) to pay close attention to personal appearance and spends hours each day washing herself and her clothes. As she reaches adolescence. she goes to the marketplace with other girls to be seen and eventually approached by boys and young men. Her parents try to continue controlling her, but all girls have sexual relations before marriage.

The boy of 10 to 12 demonstrates his readiness for initiation by attempting to behave in accordance with adult expectations. The day before the initiation ceremony, he shaves his head. The next morning, before dawn, he and the other initiates are taken to the circumciser. The boy is told that he will be killed if he moves or shows pain, and, throughout the operation, older men and boys aim spears and clubs at his head (see Chapter Seven). In the afternoon he is led into seclusion by his kinsmen. who are much less bawdy on this occasion than the

Figure 1-10. Gusii clitoridectomy. From Nyansongo: A Gusii community in Kenya, by R. A. LeVine and B. B. LeVine, in B. B. Whiting (Ed.), *Six Cultures: Studies of Child Rearing.* Copyright 1963 by John Wiley & Sons, Inc. Reprinted by permission of John Wiley & Sons, Inc.

kinswomen in the female initiation. The boy stays in a newly built house with one or two other initiates. While in seclusion, he is hazed by older boys and is warned against divulging the initiation secrets to women. He is expected to leave the seclusion hut to do minor hunting. Traditional ceremonies of emergence from seclusion include a mutual oath of "respect" taken by the boy and his father. The initiate can now begin to assume adult responsibilities. He lives in a separate hut within the homestead and is free to bring girls to his house.

Following initiation the Gusii boy is called by a new term meaning "circumcised man" or "warrior" (LeVine & LeVine, 1963). The initiated Gusii girl also is called by a new term, which she will relinquish for another term when she becomes a married woman. Girls marry at about 15 years of age, and boys at 18 to 20. After several years of brief premarital liaisons, a young man chooses a girl whom he considers attractive but with whom he has not had sexual relations. He sends an intermediary of his own age to inquire about the girl's background. The intermediary also discusses with the girl's father the amount of cattle bridewealth that would be expected from the father of the boy. (A shortage of pasturage in recent years has put cattle in short supply, however; so many couples have begun to elope first and to hold the bridewealth discussion later.) If agreement is reached, the cattle are transferred. A month later, the bride is taken from her homestead to the home of the groom. She is expected to resist leaving home and is dragged away forcibly by the groom's kinsmen. On the wedding night, she continues her resistance, and her husband (aided by his clansmen) physically overpowers her to achieve penetration. The bride remains at the home of the groom for a month or so and then returns to her father's homestead for about two months. Should she be unhappy, this visit allows her the opportunity to plead termination of the marriage.

A pregnant woman is not treated specially and is not subject to any restrictions. She performs normal domestic and agricultural duties until about a week before the baby is due. The birth takes place in the home of the husband's mother. Afterward the new mother rests for four or five days and then goes back to her own house on the homestead. Within a month, she is performing even the most arduous chores.

The woman has little to say about the original marriage contract made by the two sets of parents and the prospective groom, but she is likely to leave her husband if she is highly dissatisfied or if she does not become pregnant within the first year or so. The husband may initiate divorce on grounds of adultery or sexual dissatisfaction. Whatever the cause of a divorce, the children legally belong to the father because of the patrilineal principle in Gusii society. They would not be welcome at the wife's natal homestead should she return there.

As the head of a homestead, an older Gusii male enjoys high status. However, his grandchildren learn that they need not respect him in the inhibited and deferential way that his wife and children respect him. In fact, insults and sexual jokes flow back and forth between grandchildren and both sets of grandparents. But a child must never strike his grandparent, and sometimes he is expected to obey a grandparent's imperious commands.

At death, a Gusii joins the ranks of the ancestral spirits who sporadically plague their living children with demands for funerary and other customary sacrifices—demands that must be met if disaster is to be averted.

Life Stages and Developmental Issues

During a human infant's first two years of life, physical growth is particularly rapid, dependent and affective relationships are beginning to develop, and environmental factors may be critical to later cognitive development. The mother's physical condition and her proximity and responsiveness to the infant may influence these aspects of development. Mothers in all three societies—Ainu, Trobriander, and Gusii—nurse their infants throughout the first two years, with supplementary feeding introduced at birth for only the Trobriander infant. Severe physical restraint is not imposed on infants from any of the societies, although Ainu infants are confined in cradles and Gusii infants are occasionally tied to their mother's back. Opportunities for social exchanges between infant and mother seem most frequent for the Trobrianders, both during the infant's first two months when there is a day-and-night constancy in the relationship, and later, when the infant continues to sleep with his mother. The Ainu pattern of infant care appears to provide some exclusive contact between the mother and infant, especially at night when the infant sleeps with the mother. The Gusii infant is separated from his mother fairly frequently during the day, when the mother returns to work in the fields. Ainu infants, in closer confinement than infants in the other two societies, may be exposed to less non-human environmental experience—especially visual—than infants in either of the other two societies.

The childhood years are most important for the growth of language skill, the development of specific motives, the refinement of social and cognitive skills, and the learning of appropriate sex-role behavior. Markers used to indicate the end of infancy vary from society to society and vary in the extent to which the infant's developmental accomplishments are used as criteria. Among the Gusii, the impending birth of a sibling forces an infant into childhood status. The Ainu infant is reclassified as a child on the basis of both an external event (the birth of a sibling) and his own competence in eating adult food. A Trobriander infant becomes a child when he is able to walk.

The method each society uses to judge the termination of infancy seems somewhat related, in this small group of three societies, to the treatment and expectations in early childhood. Gusii children are expected to remain close to home, sometimes in the absence of an adult. Very young children are expected to begin independently performing simple household tasks. Ainu children remain near home, but other family members are usually there. The earliest tasks and proper social behavior are directly taught by parents and other family members. Trobriander children remain close to their parents' home at first but may join children's play groups when they are as young as four. Tasks come later for the Trobriander child and, even then, are shared by other household members. The development of language and cognitive skills, social-interaction techniques, and independence are undoubtedly influenced by the pattern of interaction and expectation. The Gusii child has little task training but high task expectations. Ainu children are expected to conduct themselves properly and to contribute to the family work needs, but they are, apparently, directly trained in task performance. Trobriander children experience the fewest restrictions and the highest level of peer interaction, and they perform tasks as part of a family group in which training is more or less constant. As in the boundary decision between infancy and childhood, the Gusii appear to take the child's development most nearly as a matter of course; the Trobrianders appear to consider the child more as an individual, with his own development influencing some of the behavior toward him.

Differential sex-role expectations are evident in all three societies. Gusii child tasks are frequently sex-typed. Ainu children are provided with sex-typed toys and, by the age of 5 or 6, participate in tasks performed by the same-sex parent. Trobriander children sometimes play in children's groups composed of one sex only, and, by the age of 5 or 6, boys, especially, may be drawn into adult activities through the maternal uncle. There are no indigenous formal educational systems for either boys or girls in the three cultures.

The anticipation of adult status is marked by a ceremony, a shift in sleeping arrangements, or a change in dress for males and females in all three societies. Formal circumcision ceremonies and shifts in sleeping arrangements are both present for Gusii males and females. Ainu females are tattooed, and both sexes are permitted adult dress and hair styles. Trobriander males move into bachelors' quarters, and females are free to visit them there during the night. With the exception of the transmission of some tribal lore, there is little direct achievement training in the three societies—that is, no long period of education for specific occupations (except for certain selected individuals). The transition into adulthood is largely social: a change from living in close family quarters as a child to living under less supervision or wearing dress that clearly indicates adult status.

Marriage partners may be self-chosen in all three societies, but, among the Gusii, family approval and arrangement making are formalized. Young couples in all societies must gain parental approval for marriage. They must live near the groom's father in both the Trobriander and the Gusii societies and usually near the bride's father in the Ainu society. After the initial years of marriage, this living arrangement changes for the young Trobriander couple, with the tie to the maternal uncle cemented by close living and cooperation in work.

The transition from infancy to adulthood for the Ainu and the Trobrianders is marked by a steadily increasing distance between the male child and his parents. Gusii boys, who eventually must share their fathers' land, seem to move only short distances from their parents throughout the transition period and, at the end of childhood and adolescence, begin their own families and their adult work on the land of their fathers.

Development for all three groups, as described, progresses within the bounds of a limited group, with adult occupations highly visible to children as they mature and with strong family ties made apparent at many junctures. In these ways, children in non-Western groups share experiences unknown to the child growing up in a complex, highly mobile society. The differences among the Ainu, Gusii, and Trobrianders, though great, will often be minimized in the chapters that follow, as the non-West and the West are compared with respect to specific areas of development.

Chapter Two

Physical Growth and Motor Skills

The higher animals produce rather helpless young—a trend that reaches its peak in the human neonate, who cannot walk, talk, or otherwise exert much control over his environment. A human infant is completely dependent during the first year, is partially dependent for many years after birth, and is never fully independent in any society until past puberty. The slowness in growth and development of skills in the human being does not eventuate in an individual who is notably competent physically. Quite the contrary. Humans are without the physical advantages, such as massive size or fleetness of foot, and the specialized mechanisms, such as sharpness of claw or strength of jaw, that characterize so many other animals. But the entire process of delayed maturation among higher species is evolutionarily entwined with a second trend that peaks in *Homo sapiens*—a heightened learning capacity and the ability to use prior experience as a basis for adapting to the exigencies of existence.

In the history of evolution a kind of trade-off has occurred, with progressive "infantilization" and lowered physical capabilities being the price of ultimate adaptive superiority. Because humans represent simply an end point on this scale rather than some unique organism, close physical developmental continuity should be evident between them and their nearest animal relatives. The similarities are indeed basic. They include, for example, the *growth curve* (found in primates), which shows rapid early development followed by a slowdown, then a spurt at puberty, and full growth soon thereafter; the *cephalocaudal*, or head-tail, *trend* in development in which the parts of the body near the head become coordinated earlier than the parts near the feet; and the *reflexes,* such as sucking and rooting (turning toward tactual stimulation applied to the cheek). Many early behavioral responses also seem to belong to the wider animal heritage of the human being. The cry of the infant acts as a distress signal to caretakers among most mammals. The smile, which appears in humans around the second month, may have evolved from the grinlike response that some higher primates display in anxiety-producing social situations (Freedman, 1968). And play in children is part of a common mammalian pattern. These shared behaviors demonstrate not only the strong affinity between humans and other animals but also the important hereditary component in a few behavioral and many biological processes.

Many societies use biological markers to define life stages and to identify the appropriate developmental points for carrying out social rituals. As we saw in Chapter One, the Ainu, Trobrianders, and Gusii each divide pre-adult life into a series of culturally prescribed stages, but, among the three, the particular stages differ. And some peoples fail almost completely to make discriminations according to physical development (for example, the Cree Indians, who classify all pre-adults as *small men* or *small women*). The same is true of social rituals and age: while a significant proportion of societies center their rites of passage around clear developmental points such as the Gusii male's initiation ceremony, which takes place near puberty, numerous other groups hold their ceremonies at times that are unrelated to obvious developmental events, and still other groups have no ceremonies of this type. Chapter Seven, on sex-role development, considers some of these rituals and the reasons why they occur in certain kinds of societies.

Normal Development

Despite the dependency of the neonate, his visual, auditory, tactile, and olfactory systems all become functional immediately, thus beginning the extremely rapid physical development that continues throughout his first year and, to a lesser extent, through early childhood.

Overall growth and sensorimotor development are demonstrably similar in infants and children everywhere, but important racial, ethnic, and sex differences do emerge, and some are present from the start. Male neonates are slightly larger in all body dimensions than female neonates, but females show a greater skeletal development—a difference that increases with age. Immediate postnatal examinations showed Euro-American newborns to be more perturbable and less easily calmed than Chinese-Americans (Freedman, 1971), a tantalizing discovery that accords with rough national-character stereotypes about emotionality and inscrutability. Birth weights differ between Western and non-Western neonates, the former being slightly heavier (Achar & Yankauer, 1962; Cravioto, Birch, De Licardie, Rosales, & Vega, 1969). The body size of 1-year-old Western infants is greater in such respects as mean body weight, stature, and head and chest circumference than that of non-Western infants (Meredith, 1970). But Western infants typically score lower than non-Western infants on tests of psychomotor development, including examinations conducted at birth (see Chapter Five). Oriental and black infants also have an earlier tooth eruption than whites. Occasionally a standard Western developmental pattern seems to be violated, as when the sitting-creeping-crawling-standing-walking-squatting sequence (true for most Western children) is not followed in a society. For instance, the Balinese infant goes from sitting to squatting to standing (Figure 2-1) (Mead & Macgregor, 1951). Hopi Indian children begin walking about a month and a half later than Anglo children (Dennis & Dennis, 1940)—a result somewhat at variance with the advanced motor development referred to above for members of traditional societies (Geber, 1956). In the second year of life, children in traditional societies begin to lose their advantage on tests of motor development, and, by the age of 2, their mean scores have fallen below the scores of children in the West (see Chapter Five). The differences in physical growth continue, however, and 8-year-olds in Euro-American societies are taller and heavier than their traditional counterparts (Meredith, 1969a). At this age, for example, American whites stand 4'2", New Guinea Marind-Anim 4'0", and Bantu Wadigo 3'10". The weights are even more discrepant—59 pounds, 49 pounds, and 44 pounds, respectively. Growth proceeds at a much slower rate in this middle childhood period. Of course, as in all phases of growth, there are not only marked differences among individuals but also in the developmental rates of various body characteristics. The 50% point of mature development for American males is reached for height at age 3, but for weight at age 10, and for strength only at age 12 (Bloom, 1964).

At adolescence, the growth spurt involves practically all skeletal and muscular dimensions and leads to significant changes in size and strength for both sexes, but particularly for males (Tanner, 1961). Changes also occur in numerous physiological systems, including the reproductive system. The emotional turmoil experienced by adolescents was once thought to be a concomitant of the biological changes at puberty, but Margaret Mead's Samoan research (1928) suggests that hormonal changes alone do not produce the turmoil. Strong and conflicting role demands placed on adolescents in complex

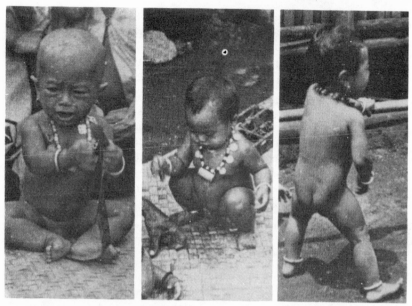

Figure 2-1. (a) Balinese boy (25 weeks) sits erect. (b) Balinese boy (10½ months) squats and maintains balance without support. (c) Balinese boy (13½ months) at right stands alone and takes steps holding walking rail. Photographs by Gregory Bateson from *Growth and Culture,* by M. Mead and F. C. Macgregor. G. P. Putnam's Sons, Inc. Photographs cropped. Copyright 1951 by Margaret Mead and Frances Cooke Macgregor. Reprinted by permission of Margaret Mead.

societies such as our own may intensify any effects of the physiological changes.

Aside from development of organs related to the reproductive system, the main body change at puberty is in size. An important change in shape occurs too. Boys develop the wide shoulders and muscular neck typical of men, and girls develop the wide hips typical of women (Tanner, 1961). In the West, pubertal changes begin about two years earlier in girls than in boys, with the onset of the growth spurt occurring at about age 11 for girls and age 13 for boys. However, *menarche,* the first menstruation, takes place after most of the growth in height has been completed, around age 13. Over the past half-century Euro-American adolescents have each decade grown taller by about one inch and heavier by four pounds. Further, puberty has come at progressively younger ages; girls now experience menarche approximately three years earlier than girls a hundred years ago. The same historical trends are found in Japan and in at least parts of China

(Tanner, 1968). Adolescents in other traditional societies apparently have not been experiencing similar gains. The data on this subject, however, are quite scant (Roberts, 1969).

Earlier maturation might mean simply that people are reaching their final heights at a younger age but that they are no taller than people of a century ago. However, it is true *both* that Western adults are taller than they used to be—about one inch per generation—and that they stop growing sooner. A man today seldom grows more than a fraction of an inch after the age of 19, whereas, at the turn of the century, full height was not reached until around the age of 26 (Tanner, 1968).[1] Records indicate that final height and age of maturation may finally be stabilizing in the United States, but elsewhere the gains continue.

Nonhereditary Factors Affecting Development

Until this point, the course of growth and motor-skill development has been discussed as if it were entirely the result of hereditarily determined processes. Undoubtedly a large degree of hereditary control exists. It can be seen, for instance, in the correlation in times of menarche for related and unrelated women: between identical twins there is only a two-to-three month menarcheal difference, between nonidentical twins and sisters there is a year's difference, and between unrelated women there is a year and a half's difference (Tanner, 1955). Special training in motor skills in the early years tends to yield only temporarily advantageous effects. Two-year-olds who were given 12 weeks' instruction in ladder climbing, buttoning, and the use of scissors showed substantial improvement, but, at the end of the experimental period, a matched group of control subjects reached the same level of competence after only one week of practice (Hilgard, 1932). Thus neuromuscular maturation seems to predominate over instruction. Again, evidence for the power of maturational factors is found in a study of Hopi Indian infants. Some Hopi infants are subjected to considerable physical restraint by being bound to a cradle board during much of the first year of life, while others are not placed on cradle boards, but the age of walking is the same for both groups (Dennis & Dennis, 1940). The lesser freedom of movement for those on cradle boards does not affect the onset of walking.

[1]As part of the same trend, height and weight at birth have also increased during this century (Tanner, 1961), and infant motor development is advanced over that of 1935 (Werner & Bayley, 1966).

The influence of experience can readily be shown even though the development of motor skills seems to be guided strongly by genetic factors. Very complex motor skills, especially those involving fine manipulations, show modification with special attention (Cratty, 1970). Lack of opportunity to practice certain skills may result in lack of development. Extreme deprivation was found to affect the emergence of basic locomotor functions in a sample of institutionalized Iranian infants (Dennis, 1960). The infants were kept lying supine and were thus unable to practice sitting or creeping. By the second year, these confined infants were greatly retarded in sitting, standing, and walking. The cradle-boarded Hopi infants (Dennis & Dennis, 1940) evidently received sufficient freedom of movement (by being taken off the cradle board several hours each day [beyond the early months] and by being taken off the boards completely at nine months) to avoid the Iranian outcome. Differences in the way parents handle a child or in socialization practices also may alter the normal sequence of development, as in Balinese infants who "frog" ("arms . . . either flexed or extended symmetrically and legs . . . flexed symmetrically *in abduction*") throughout late infancy (Figure 2-2). Mead and Macgregor (1951) suggest that the typical carrying pattern (infant's legs spread wide apart over the carrier's hip) "may contribute to the maintenance of this frogging posture" (p. 104).

Socioeconomic condition is a fairly reliable indicator of both nutritional status (Metheny, Hunt, Patton, & Heye, 1962) and general living standards; good socioeconomic condition has been overwhelmingly associated with favorable physical growth patterns. The historical trend toward increased height and earlier maturity is tied to concomitant changes in the standard of living and may be importantly a result of nutritional improvements. (Part of the trend might be accounted for by *heterosis*, or hybrid vigor, resulting from the increased outbreeding due to new forms of transportation, beginning with the bicycle [Tanner, 1968].) Within racial and ethnic groups at a given point in time, a higher living standard also results in growth- and maturation-rate gains. For example, at every age level, Japanese-American children and adolescents are taller, heavier, and more advanced skeletally than children born in Japan (Greulich, 1957); 8-year-old American blacks are taller than 8-year-old West Indian blacks (Meredith, 1969a); and menarche is delayed for Chinese and Bantu girls of low socioeconomic status (Hiernaux, 1968). The Western standard of living exceeds all others, and it is Euro-Americans who are among the tallest and heaviest people in the world (Meredith, 1969a, 1969b). Some of the Western advantage may be genetic, of course, just as the Rwanda Tutsi male's one-inch height superiority

Figure 2-2. Balinese boy (10½ months) "frogging." Photograph by Gregory Bateson from *Growth and Culture,* by M. Mead and F. C. Macgregor. G. P. Putnam's Sons, Inc. Copyright 1951 by Margaret Mead and Frances Cooke Macgregor. Reprinted by permission of Margaret Mead.

over American men is probably genetically based. But, in the case of the Tutsi, the effects of environment also show clearly because, at age 15, the well-nourished American boy is six inches taller than the Tutsi (Hiernaux, 1964; Meredith, 1963). The influence of environment is much more marked for height, however, than for some other aspects of body growth. Permanent tooth eruption, for example, occurs later in Caucasoid populations, despite the nutritional advantages, than in any other major racial group (Roberts, 1969) and can therefore be taken as largely under genetic control.

Other experiential factors affecting growth include season of the year, physical illness, and psychological stress. The height increase rate in spring is about twice the rate for autumn, and weight follows the opposite course (Tanner, 1961). Major illnesses often cause a growth slowdown, but recovery usually results in a catch-up phase that leaves the child unaffected in the long run. When seasonal effects are controlled, children grow at a slower rate during school terms than when they are home for holidays (Tanner, 1961) (this may or may not be attributable to emotional factors). In New Guinea, Bundi children in an eight-grade mission boarding school experience growth retardation for the first four years but then apparently reach an adaptive plateau as they undergo a catch-up phase during their second four years (Malcolm, 1970).

Among traditional peoples, nutrition and other growth-relevant variables were seldom optimal yet generally sufficient prior to the disruptive effects of Western contact. Sometimes the maintenance of adequate growth conditions took a form that Westerners would consider harsh—for instance, the practice of twin infanticide in societies in which the mother's role was too demanding to allow her to rear two infants at once (Granzberg, 1973b). With acculturation has come the falling away of many customs, and one of those that seems to be declining with devastating effects is infant breast feeding. As maternal milk, the "major source of consumer-tested protein infant food" [Jelliffe, 1969, p. 165], has been replaced by adult foods or easily contaminated cow's milk, the rise in nutritional *marasmus*, the "wasting-away" disease, has been significant.

Then too, the classical second-year protein/calorie malnutrition problem, *kwashiorkor*, has been exacerbated rather than helped by the Western world's charitable shipments of dried milk to the developing nations. The ability to assimilate lactose, a primary constituent of milk, is at a high level during infancy but falls rapidly following weaning in almost all races except Caucasoid. Ingestion of lactose by weaned Negroids and Mongoloids often gives rise to cramps, bloating, and diarrhea (McCracken, 1971).

Environmental stress factors, including diseases or traumatic experiences, stimulate glands to secrete hormones and also, usually, to slow growth (Landauer, 1972). However, if the stress occurs early in life, the effect may be reversed. When rats are handled roughly or electrically shocked during the first few weeks after birth, they display lasting changes in endocrine responses to novel stimuli. At maturity they handle stressful experiences well and are more resistant to psychosomatic illnesses such as ulcers. They also grow heavier and longer than unstressed rats. It appears that early stress acts to "immunize" the animal against later stress (Landauer, 1972). But what about humans? Can the same effects of early stress be detected? Two cross-cultural studies on worldwide samples have attempted to answer this question by looking at practices affecting infants (up to 2 years of age) and eventual adult height attained (Gunders & Whiting, 1968; Landauer & Whiting, 1964). In societies in which infants experience immediate postnatal separation from the mother or are tattooed, scarified, or bathed daily in scalding water, adult height is greater. The average height of adult males in the infant-stressed societies exceeds that in societies without these customs by more than two inches. The association between stress and height was statistically independent of other factors that might be thought to influence stature, including race, climate, mode of subsistence, and estimated diet.

Beyond these cross-cultural studies, two U. S. samples showed that adults differed in terminal stature according to whether they had received infantile inoculations—another hypothesized stress inducer (Whiting, Landauer, & Jones, 1968). The group of subjects who had been inoculated achieved greater height at maturity. The subjects had been infants during the 1920s and 1930s, prior to the advent of universal vaccination programs. Parental height was controlled statistically, and inoculation was not associated with general health in infancy. It is true, though, that parents who had their children inoculated may have also provided better growth conditions in some undetermined way. Questions like this may be resolved by experimental research now under way on the subject (Whiting & Whiting, 1970). Pending the outcome of this research, it can be said thus far that the findings fly in the face of one current belief about growth: positive care produces positive development.

High socioeconomic status—along with presumably good nutrition—is associated with both favorable growth and superior intelligence (Deutsch, Katz, & Jensen, 1968; Herrnstein, 1971). The growth is usually attributed to nutrition, but the intelligence is usually attributed to environmental advantages and heredity. Why not make the simplifying hypothesis that the nutrition also causes intellectual superiority, at least in part? In research terms the question has been turned around to become: does malnutrition cause intellectual deficiency? The issue is important and the answer seems to be a qualified *yes*. Infants who died of marasmus in their first year had a decreased number of brain cells (Winick & Rosso, 1969), children malnourished in early childhood showed a reduced brain weight (Stoch & Smythe, 1963), and malnourished children 1 to 3 years of age were deficient on various cognitive tasks (Brockman & Ricciuti, 1971; Ricciuti, 1970). But, since malnutrition occurs under unstable home conditions, it is difficult to isolate nutritional deficits as causal (Scrimshaw, 1967; Scrimshaw & Gordon, 1968). The same point may be made about traditional societies; malnutrition is most likely to appear in detribalized areas that are marked by poverty and social disorganization, and, again, the priority for any intellectual deficiency could not be assigned with confidence to a single factor.

Patterns of physical growth and motor-skill development in human beings closely parallel those found among near animal relatives, and the inference may be correctly drawn that hereditary factors play an important role. Normal development in all humans involves a characteristic growth curve, acquisition of relatively unmodifiable basic motor skills, and some mostly hereditarily timed biological phenomena, such as tooth eruption and menarche. Nonetheless, the important influence of environmental factors can also be demonstrated. At one extreme, severe deprivation retards growth and motor-skill development, and, at the other, the provision of optimal conditions apparently can effect both earlier maturation and greater overall growth, as seen in the 100-year trend in the West toward taller people at all stages of development.

Three Cultures

Only minimal materials are available on physical growth for the Ainu, Trobrianders, and Gusii. Adult-height comparisons show the typical Western advantage over traditional peoples: as against the U. S. white male mean of 5′9″, Ainu males average 5′2″, Trobriander males 5′5″, and Gusii males 5′7¾″.[2]

[2]The Gusii average is based on authors' data on 19 well-nourished and perhaps atypical Gusii males, 19 to 25 years old.

The Ainu and Trobrianders have been included in the worldwide samples used to investigate the effects of infant stress on height. Members of societies that expose babies to stress-inducing practices average slightly above 5'5" as adults (Gunders & Whiting, 1968; Landauer & Whiting, 1964), and both the Ainu and the Trobrianders, who *fail* to stress infants, fall below this mark, just as they, theoretically, should.

Chapter Three

Affect

Attachment, or the focused interpersonal relationship (Yarrow & Pedersen, 1972), is an observable part of the social life of all mammals. Neither we nor our close evolutionary kin distribute interactions randomly, but instead we create strong ties with some individuals and not with others. Affective relationships have the adaptive advantage of bringing and keeping individuals close enough to facilitate cooperative undertakings and mutual learning. A phenomenon as pervasive and significant as this might necessarily seem based on heredity, and perhaps it is. But mounting evidence indicates that the immediate causes of and conditions for mammalian affective development are to be sought in our common developmental histories of infantile helplessness and resulting dependence upon others.

Affect and Early Experience

From theoretical formulations as diverse as psychoanalysis, social-learning theory, and ethology, there are grounds for believing infantile experience to be critical in the development of the affective system.[1] These theories achieve unusual consensus in assigning great

[1]Freud (1938) argued that the infant cathects the mother, developing intense positive feelings toward her due to her association with the gratification of instinctive needs, and thereby becomes capable of taking "love-objects." Among neo-Freudians, Erikson (1950) thought that the infant's basic degree of trust in others was founded primarily in its experience with its mother as a source of security. In most social-learning views, the physically dependent infant acquires emotional dependency on and social responsiveness to the mother by associating primary rewards with biological drive reduction (Dollard & Miller, 1950).

importance to the first relationship formed between an infant and another human. In one way or another they are all saying that either a child develops positive affective relationships, or he fails to "join the human race" (Ferguson, 1970, p. 38). The extension is generally made that affect must be developed early if it is to be developed normally. As the child grows older, early affectlessness not only becomes increasingly difficult to modify but eventually may become irreversible.

The theoretical agreement concerning affective relationships is fully justified by empirical evidence from numerous sources. Dogs raised in isolation during certain critical periods in their early lives show a permanent fearfulness of others (Scott, 1968). Rhesus monkeys fed mechanically by bottle and not given access to their mother or to peers become highly fearful animals in infancy and childhood. At maturity they are excessively aggressive and uncooperative, sexually infantile, unable to engage in ordinary grooming behavior with other monkeys, and defective in maternal behavior (Harlow, 1961, 1971; Harlow & Harlow, 1965). Deprived of ordinary stimulation and social contact, both monkeys and dogs display emotional impairment.

A comparable degree of isolation for human beings cannot be produced experimentally for ethical reasons. But human society has made some natural experiments, and the outcomes have been similar if not so extreme. Occasional reports of children reared in semi-isolation or by animals, while not fully reliable, yield a picture of shy, fearful creatures who are unused to people and incapable of affection unless exposed to human company for months or even years (Brown, 1958).

The institutionalized child represents another natural experiment. There are many kinds of institutions, and those that supply a level of physical and social stimulation approximating home environments turn out children not very different from the ordinary (Brackbill, 1962; Rheingold, 1961). But in institutions where caretaking is restricted to physical needs, where infants spend long hours with little environmental stimulation, and where a low level of care continues

For ethologists, the human infant is like the other highly social mammals and displays species-specific instinctive behavior (for example, sucking, clinging, smiling, and crying) that releases nurturant responses from the mother. Discrimination among individuals and emotional attachment to those who care for him lay the foundation for later affective relationships (Bowlby, 1969; Scott, 1968). The cognitive-developmental view extends the ethological view by integrating Piaget's (1953, 1955) interactionist theory with biological explanations of early social behavior. The developing infant engages in perceptual interactions with his environment, guided, at least in part, by apparently innate stimulus preferences. Since the human face has many of the preferred characteristics and since the nurturing role demands fairly frequent interaction, the infant learns early to recognize the nurturing agent, to discriminate her from others, and, finally, to form a representation of the nurturing agent that may be recalled when she is absent. Responsive, stimulating persons in the environment (not always the mother) are those with whom the infant seems most likely to develop attachment (Schaffer, 1971).

over a period of years, the adverse effects include apathy, unresponsiveness, and even general retardation in extreme cases (Goldfarb, 1943; Provence & Lipton, 1962; Spitz, 1945; Spitz & Wolf, 1946).

How does the cross-cultural literature support the consistent evidence that satisfaction of physical needs is not enough, that there must be steady interpersonal contact if the child is to become capable of developing positive and lasting affective responses to others? The fact is that even the lowest levels of infant care around the world do not approach the severe institutional deprivation reached in the West. No other group leaves babies without social contact for almost the full day. We would therefore be surprised, if the hypothesis is correct, to find whole societies of individuals behaving like the relatively affectless products of certain institutions. There are no such societies. It is doubtful that an entire group of affectively unresponsive individuals would be capable of the cooperation and reciprocity necessary to human social life. Even individual cases of affectlessness seem to be largely unique to the West, for the anthropological literature describes few, if any, individuals who behave affectlessly.

Cross-culturally, then, no society practices gross infant neglect.[2] In fact, almost all societies apparently gratify infants *beyond* a minimally adequate level and even indulge them. Barry (1969) points out, however, that in a few societies around the world the level of infant indulgence is relatively low, and the result seems to be an adult personality full of fearfulness and suspicion. Although too few of these societies exist for a statistical comparison, confirming examples for Barry's point can be found by a quick run-through of some of the groups with low scores on various ratings of infant care (Barry, Bacon, & Child, 1967; Barry & Paxson, 1971; Whiting & Child, 1953). Some of the societies rated as lowest on infant care variables include the Dobuans of Melanesia, who have been called paranoid because of their constant concern about theft (Benedict, 1934); the people of Taos Pueblo in New Mexico, who are notoriously difficult to work with, and who in recent years have not allowed anthropologists into the pueblo for even innocuous linguistic research;[3] the Jamaicans of Rocky Road and the Marquesans of Polynesia, who are said to have highly unusual

[2]It is difficult to discuss cross-cultural behavioral pathology because, for the past 50 years, anthropology has made a point of cultural relativity—that is, the equal validity or goodness of all ways of life (Herskovits, 1955). Today, popular writers can still speak of the "childlike" Trobrianders (Freund, 1965), and the case for relativism must therefore continue to be made. Nonetheless, some anthropologists have recently begun to attach a tentative label of "pathological" to certain phenomena (Barry, 1969; Rohner, 1970).

[3]This is not to deny that the pueblo attitude might be based on historical experience with whites.

patterns of nonsharing with others (Cohen, 1962); and the Aymara of the Andes, for whom the list of negative adjectives is so long that they have been referred to as the most unlikable people on earth (Pelto, 1967).

The period following infancy, that of early childhood, is theoretically less critical in the development of affective capacities. But the general effects of low indulgence during each period at least should be similar. A formal test of this hypothesis is possible because, unlike infancy, the early-childhood period is marked by a great variety of treatment as beginning gratifications are terminated, some societies weaning abruptly and wanting the child to behave as a miniature adult, some exposing the child to a slow and steady attrition of indulgence, and some alternating uncertainly between great expectations and an earlier latitude. A comprehensive study (Rohner, 1970; Rohner, in press; Rohner & Rohner, in press) has found a systematic set of affective relationships revolving around early-childhood care. Each society in a worldwide sample was assigned a score on a scale of child acceptance-rejection. Acceptance was indicated by warmth and affection shown the child, and was revealed in behaviors such as holding, comforting, and praising. Rejection was displayed in hostile, indifferent, and neglectful treatment. Societies that were scored as typically rejecting of children produced a familiar syndrome of adult personality characteristics—low emotional responsiveness, emotional instability, low self-evaluation, low generosity, and dependence. Some of these traits were already observable in childhood.

The rejection of children is apparently predictive of more than personality traits. In the above sample, as well as in several others (Lambert, Triandis, & Wolf, 1959; Spiro & D'Andrade, 1958; Whiting, 1959b), child rejection (or less indulgent infant care) is associated with a view of the supernatural world as malevolent. Something of the sort seems also to have occurred in the course of Western history: as Freud pointed out, the stern, punishing God of the Old Testament seemed to be a projection of the father in the patriarchal Hebrew family, and, in modern America, the Christian emphasis on Jesus Christ, friend, corresponds to the more nearly equalitarian relationship between father and child. The change in child training has been accompanied by a transformation in the perception of the supernatural world. As Erikson (1950) has phrased it, the inevitable infantile anxieties leave a lifelong residue of emotional immaturity which is given a consistent supernatural meaning. Or, to say it more pithily, man has created the gods in the image of his parents (Freud, 1916).

The Western-based finding on the need for infants and young children to form affectional ties with others seems supported in cross-cultural research. But because the amount of cross-cultural evidence is not great, it may be helpful to look at some of the data from a slightly different perspective. Only one society, the Alorese of the former Dutch East Indies, has received a score of very low infant satisfaction in all the cross-cultural ratings thus far compiled (Barry et al., 1967; Barry & Paxson, 1971; Whiting & Child, 1953) as well as a low score on the child acceptance-rejection scale referred to above (Rohner & Rohner, in press). So, by any definition, the Alorese child is rejected, and a detailed presentation of Alorese life and affective development should be of value.

The Alorese: A Case Study

In the Alorese division of labor, women are the principal food producers, being responsible for the cultivation and collection of vegetable foods (Du Bois, 1944). When a woman gives birth, she stops work in the fields, but begins again after only 10 to 14 days. The neonate is left behind in the village for about nine hours a day in the care of a sibling or an adult relative. Though the infant may receive premasticated food from the caretaker or may occasionally be breast-fed by an available adult female, the unsatisfactory nature of daytime feeding is evident from the frequency with which babies spew out the premasticated food and instead attempt to nurse at the breast of the father or an immature sibling. The infant is fed immediately when the mother returns from the fields in the afternoon, and for the rest of the evening it is nursed and fondled by her. But the comfort and care of the evening hardly suffice to overcome the infant's unassuaged hunger and frustration of the day. An adult's account of an incident from his childhood illustrates the point:

> Once mother and I were living in a field house near our gardens. She told me to carry Senmani [younger brother] while she worked. At noon he was hungry and wanted to nurse. I gave him food but he only vomited it. He cried and cried and wouldn't stop. I cried too. Finally I went and told mother to come and nurse him but she wouldn't. So I took Senmani, laid him down on a mat in the house and ran off to Folafeng. There from the ridge I shouted, "Mother, your child lies in the house. If you want to care for it, good. If you don't want to, that is also good. I am going to Atimelang to play."[4]

[4]From Du Bois, Cora, Attitudes toward food and hunger in Alor, In L. Spier, A. I. Hallowell, & S. Newman (Eds.), *Language, Culture, and Personality*. P. 274. Copyright 1941. This and all other quotations from the same source are reprinted by permission of the author.

The difficulties become even more serious when the infant begins to walk (sometime after 1 year of age). By the time he can get around alone, no one is responsible for feeding him and no one is greatly inconvenienced by his crying. Weaning at about this time adds to his problems, because he must now wait not simply for mother's return but for the preparation of the meal. From this point until he is 5 or 6—old enough to forage for himself—between seven A.M. and seven P.M. he eats only what older children are willing to cede to him when he begs. Figure 3-1 shows an Alorese child begging food. Teasing occurs; for example, the mother may show preference for some other child in order to stimulate jealousy in her baby. Also, adults constantly threaten to cut off children's ears or hands, and some children are greatly frightened by the accompanying brandishing of knives.

The apparent effects of this inconsistent and irregular care develop quickly and dramatically. Between the ages of 2 and 5, the child often has temper tantrums. The anthropologist Cora Du Bois (1944) was immediately made aware of them: "Rages are so consistent, so widespread, and of such long duration among young children that they were one of my first and most striking observations" (p. 51). The mother's departure for the fields is commonly the precipitator of a tantrum. Du Bois (1944) describes a 2-year-old who, over a nine-month period, had a violent rage every morning when his mother left: "He would begin by pursuing his mother; then as she outstripped him he would throw himself on the ground, roll back and forth, and often beat his head on the earth" (p. 51).

The child's rages are met with reactions just as unpredictable and inconsistent as other caretaking behavior: "One day a mother will ignore the child; the next she may be irritated and strike it; on still another occasion she may deceive it into thinking she is not deserting it, only to slip away when the child has been diverted; or on still other occasions, especially at night, the child may be threatened with the local bogy-man . . ." (Du Bois, 1941, p. 275).

Eventually, the ineffectual rages cease. Older children learn to obtain food on their own. Boys start to roam about in groups, often stealing food. Girls stay close to their mothers and begin to carry out domestic chores and agricultural work. In late adolescence, boys are ready for marriage and for the elaborate financial transactions that characterize adult-male activities.

The Alorese socialization system turns out an adult with the expected affective tendencies. The corroborating evidence is unusually convincing because Du Bois gathered materials from numerous sources and then solicited independent interpretations from several specialists. First, the ethnographic data reveal affective shallowness in

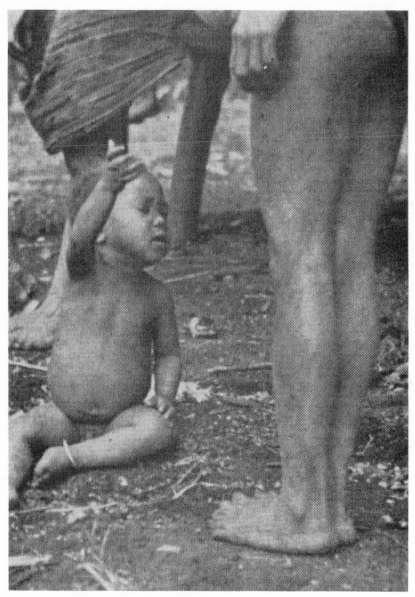

Figure 3-1.   Alorese child begging food. From Du Bois, C., *The People of Alor: A Social-Psychological Study of an East Indian Island*. The University of Minnesota Press, Minneapolis. © Copyright 1944, University of Minnesota. Reprinted by permission.

interpersonal relationships. Marriages are brittle; each adult is involved in an average of two divorces despite associated large financial penalties. Grieving for the dead is brief: "People will be concerned over the illness of a kinsman but, once he is dead, they go on to other things . . . . The expediency and realism in human relationships is basically a shallowness of positive affect" (Du Bois, 1944, p. 160). Suspicion and distrust are reflected in continual deception, lies, and chicanery. There is also a strong element of passivity, a tendency to give up as soon as problems arise. Even for minor illnesses, such as a headache or a cold, the suffering person will mope helplessly in the house, sure that he is going to die. A frightened individual reacts with a "freeze" response so characteristic of the Alorese that it is commented upon by Europeans who know the tribe only superficially.

Du Bois collected a series of autobiographical sketches, which included dream materials, and the analysis of them by a psychiatrist (Kardiner, 1945) is in close correspondence with inferences drawn from the ethnographic materials. One of the case histories concerns an adult male named Mangma, considered a normal man in Alorese culture. The analyst, without knowing the Alorese, noted that Mangma showed no evidence of having made any strong attachments to any person in his life. Furthermore, he was noted to display a profound distrust of others. A marked passivity is shown in his tendency to run away from problems. Incidents from his childhood are cited to show that there were early indications of his future character.

Du Bois also collected a set of Rorschach inkblot protocols, and these were given to a specialist who made a blind analysis. The questionable cross-cultural validity of projective tests has raised legitimate doubts about their use in non-Western societies (Lindzey, 1961), but in this instance the analysis gives remarkable confirmation to the other interpretations:

> The Alorese are suspicious and distrustful; they are so not only toward everything that is unknown and new to them, such as foreigners, for instance, but also among themselves. No one will trust another.
> They are indifferent and listless; they let things slide and get dilapidated, where we would feel the necessity of making repairs.
> There must be emotional outbursts and tempers, anger, and rage. . . .
> The Alorese must be lacking in individual personal contact, living beside one another but not with one another. . . . Either there are no friendships and relationships or there are none that are deeply rooted.[5]

[5]From Oberholzer, E. Rorschach's experiment and the Alorese. In Du Bois, Cora, *The People of Alor: A Social-Psychological Study of an East Indian Island*, pp. 596, 598, 599, 600. The University of Minnesota Press, Minneapolis. © Copyright by the University of Minnesota.

Finally, a set of children's drawings was subjected to blind analysis by another specialist, who spoke of their feelings of aloneness, of how they are apart from one another, and of how their relationships are poverty stricken.

The supernatural world of the Alorese also demonstrates the probable effects of the early rejection: "So slight is the tendency to idealize the parental imago that effigies are made in the most careless and slipshod manner, are used in the most perfunctory way, and are forthwith discarded. There is little emphasis on giving the spirits permanent housing or idealized form" (Kardiner, 1961, p. 190).

It has sometimes been suggested that the Alorese survive only because they are on an isolated island and that their precarious adjustment would collapse in the face of challenge from an external enemy (Barry, 1969). But this is pure conjecture. All we can say is that the Alorese have successfully met the minimal affective requirements for human social life, both today and in the past. To paraphrase one psychologist on a similar subject (N. Miller, 1959): any society that had not met such requirements would be descended from a long line of extinct ancestors.

Some Questions

For all the confirmation it gives, the Alorese study is only a single case. There is the additional problem that the argument is based on correlational data. Why should the tribulations of infancy be seen as determinant if all Alorese people experience a complete lifetime in a low-affect social environment? How can a causal factor be separated from simple cultural continuity? The answer is: it cannot. The Alorese data do support the findings from Western psychological research, but the support is circumstantial. So too for the other cross-cultural evidence. While it is true that the few societies failing to indulge infants appear to produce unusually distrustful adults and that the numerous societies that are neglectful of children in the postinfancy period also appear to produce adults with low capacities for positive affective relationships, none of the evidence directly relates to infantile deprivation and the ultimate stunting of affect. And finally, although no traditional society deprives infants of affective experiences as they are deprived in some Western institutions (nor does any society turn out adults who look like products of those institutions), this kind of evidence amounts only to a large set of negative instances. Therefore, the cross-cultural materials yield consistent, but neither powerful nor direct, support to hypotheses about the importance of early care for basic affective development.

A growing body of research in the West (reviewed in Ferguson, 1970) asks questions arising from the implication that early attachment is a part of normal development. Can some part of the neonate's behavior be interpreted as an active attempt to maintain contact with the mother and to solicit her attention (Schaffer & Emerson, 1964) and therefore be based on an inherited disposition and a normal sequence of perceptual-cognitive development? What happens when an infant who has developed a close attachment to its mother is then separated from her for a period of time? The resulting upset, or *separation anxiety*, is well documented, and the degree of upset (as measured by increased crying or cessation of normal behavior) is used as one measure of the strength of mother attachment (Littenberg, Tulkin, & Kagan, 1971; Schaffer, 1958). One careful study (Ainsworth, 1967) has shown that East African Baganda infants develop separation anxiety about four months earlier than American infants—at a mean age of 6 months versus 10 months. Indications of both separation anxiety and *stranger anxiety*, the distress displayed by an infant when confronted by a strange human face, appear somewhat earlier in Guatemalan Ladino infants than in American infants (Lester, Kotelchuck, Spelke, Sellers, & Klein, 1974). The display of both separation anxiety and stranger anxiety (in the absence of the mother) probably requires that the infant have the ability to formulate some representation of the mother or to remember her actions. Differential response to the stranger further involves a comparison of the stranger with the recollection of the absent mother—a task of some complexity (Schaffer, 1971). For both the Ugandan and Guatemalan infants, several environmental features are different from those found in samples of Western infants. Less frequent separations (from all people), closer living quarters, and larger numbers of siblings are all characteristic, but none of these features has been shown to be necessarily linked to an earlier display of distress during separation from the mother.

One issue concerning the mother's role has emerged from cross-cultural considerations—the question of whether multiple caretakers, as opposed to the mother alone, may produce in the child a "diffusion" of affect. Margaret Mead (1928) suggested 50 years ago that the Samoan adult tended to display only shallow emotional ties because the large number of caretakers in the extended family arrangement probably prevented formation of intensive affective capacities. The suggestion has since received several tantalizing but fragmentary pieces of support. Reanalysis of the above-mentioned data on the East African Baganda (Ainsworth, 1967) indicates that the more people there are in the house, the less attached to the mother is the infant. Intensity of affect, in other words, may vary inversely with the number of caretakers, as Mead has said in comparing the Samoan extended family with the typical American nuclear family. Again, in a study conducted with American infants, 1-year-olds were more emotionally dependent on their mothers and were involved in more emotional interaction with them when they had been reared exclusively by their mothers rather than by other females as well as their mothers (Caldwell, Hersher, Lipton, Richmond, Stern, Eddy, Drachman, & Rothman, 1963). Also fitting the Mead interpretation is the pattern reported for Israeli kibbutzim, in which children reared in communal nurseries subsequently form ties to their parents that are in some ways weaker than their peer attachments (Rabin, 1965). Whether the absolute intensity of their attachments is concomitantly weakened is still unclear, however. Similarly, the long-term consequences of the distribution of initial attachments are unknown. However, both Western and non-Western samples of infants yield a fairly large proportion of infants who form initial attachments with more than one person (Ainsworth, 1967; Schaffer & Emerson, 1964). As Schaffer (1971) has noted, initial single attachment is fairly rapidly supplemented by further attachments and, eventually, must be followed by a process of *detachment*—at least in the physical sense of separation from the object of the attachment. The physical signs of attachment may well be replaced, during this period of detachment, by internal responses to the representation of the object and, eventually, could form the substance of the capacity to experience and to express affect to selected others. Questions of this sort, involving the long-term effects of number, intensity, and duration of early attachments on affective capacities, should continue to be investigated in diverse cultural settings.

The major points in this chapter can be quickly summarized. Evidence both from lower animals and from Western studies of institutional deprivation prompts the following conclusion: the capacity for positive affective relations is a mammalian maturational phenomenon that fails to develop only under conditions of severe social deprivation in infancy. The cross-cultural materials uphold the conclusion that no society subjects infants to extreme social impoverishment and no society produces affectless adults. There are, however, societies with moderate social deprivation, either in infancy or in early childhood, and these do appear to produce adults with affective difficulties. If the primary conclusion is valid that early attachment occurs as part of the normal affective development, the many questions thereby raised can be partially answered through cross-cultural investigations. But, so far, non-Western materials have not been employed very extensively to this end.

Three Cultures

Ethnographic materials on the Ainu and Gusii are pertinent to issues raised in this chapter. The Ainu practice of suspending the infant in a cradle inside the hut all day and then ignoring his crying has prompted some investigators to score them as among the least indulgent of societies (Barry et al., 1967; Barry & Paxson, 1971). As discussed earlier, the few societies that are at such a low level of indulgence tend to produce adults with fearful and suspicious personalities. The Ainu appear to fit the pattern in that they are reported never to laugh and in that they exude an air of general depression (Batchelor, 1895; Landor, 1893). But the caution must be added that so free an interpretation of behavior from another culture is difficult to justify and may be little more than ethnocentric bias. At any rate, the solemnity with which the Ainu adult approaches life is not inconsistent with the extremely low indulgence granted him earlier as an infant.

The Gusii materials are relevant to the question of whether multiple caretakers contribute to diffusion of affect. In the Six Cultures Study carried out by the Whitings and their associates (Minturn & Lambert, 1964; Whiting, 1963; B. Whiting & Whiting, 1975) among societies in Africa, India, Mexico, Okinawa, the Philippines, and the United States, the African Gusii were one of the groups investigated. Among the six groups, it was the Gusii infants who were least frequently cared for by their mothers alone and who were most frequently cared for by their older siblings (Minturn & Lambert, 1964). Since the Gusii infant was most likely to experience multiple caretaking, the Gusii adult should have acquired the lowest level of affective intensity in the six societies. That this is true is suggested by the ethnographic evidence concerning the relative formality of interpersonal relationships, especially those within the nuclear family, and the capacity to ignore the emotional needs of others. The latter point is illustrated by the following quotation:

[A] child had been walking well for some time, and the mother wanted to have her weaned by the time she was 2 years old. On one occasion after the onset of weaning, we observed the child sitting on her mother's lap for 20 minutes, crying continuously and occasionally pulling at her mother's high-necked dress. Throughout the period of incessant crying the mother was looking at pictures we had brought and talking animatedly with a visiting neighbor. Only once did she pay any attention to the child's cries, shaking it briefly and then continuing her conversation as the child resumed crying. At one point, when the child's cries were loudest, the mother was laughing at a remark made by the other woman. Despite her almost unbelievable (to the observers) capacity for ignoring the bawling of the child being weaned, this woman was not less nurturant than other mothers in her treatment of her other children. Interestingly enough, she reported in an interview two months later that the child observed gave her no trouble during weaning.[6]

[6]From Nyansongo: A Gusii community in Kenya, by R. A. LeVine and B. B. LeVine, in B. B. Whiting (Ed.), *Six Cultures: Studies of Child Rearing,* pp. 150–151. Copyright © 1963 by John Wiley & Sons, Inc. Reprinted by permission of John Wiley & Sons, Inc.

Chapter Four

Language and Perception

Language

Language is, uniquely, a part of man's culture as well as the chief tool for transmitting culture to each succeeding generation. The emergence of a sophisticated communication system at a certain point in man's evolution must have allowed him both immediate advantage over other animals and a means by which the advantage could be continued, so the survival value of language was probably great. All contemporary human languages have a grammatical and semantic flexibility unknown in animal communication systems. Although bees, frogs, and monkeys communicate effectively with other members of their species, the variability of expression is limited: bees waggle about honey (von Frisch, 1967), frogs croak over sex (Marler & Hamilton, 1966), and rhesus monkeys bark, screech, and squeak about dominance or reactions to threat (Rowell & Hinde, 1962). The most recent of the language-teaching experiments with primates (Fouts, 1973; Gardner & Gardner, 1971; Gardner & Gardner, 1969; Premack, 1971; Rumbaugh, Gill, & von Glasersfeld, 1973) illustrate the chimpanzee's capacity for symbol learning without fully mastering the structure of the language, a mastery that is imperative if cultural complexities are to be transmitted. And the ability to use language creatively (that is, continually to produce new utterances) is beyond the chimpanzee and remains the distinctive property of man—at least so far.

Earlier observers often failed to credit non-Western man with language capacities much beyond those of the higher primates. A Jesuit missionary of the 18th century believed that the Paraguayan Indians were incapable of having evolved their own languages:

Truly admirable is their varied structure, of which no rational person can suppose these stupid savages to have been the architects and inventors. Led by this consideration, I have often affirmed that the variety and artful construction of languages should be reckoned amongst the other arguments to prove the existence of an eternal and omniscient God [Dobrizhoffer, 1822].

More common was the suggestion that some societies spoke only in sign language or by grunts and whistles (Wegner, 1928). These systems of communication always proved to be supplemental to language, as in the case of the Bolivian Siriono, whose whistle language is used to facilitate coordination among members of the same hunting party without frightening the prey (Holmberg, 1969). Humans use language in an effort to achieve technical, social, and conceptual competence, and additional forms of communication allow versatility of expression. Every human group possesses speech of sufficient complexity to meet the demands of its environment. An English-speaking person has a single word for rice, but a Hanunoo of the Philippines distinguishes 92 varieties (Brown, 1965). There is one English lexical category for snow, but Greenland Eskimo have words meaning "snow falling on the ground," "falling snow," "drifting snow," "a snowdrift," and so on (Williams, 1972). A reverse instance is the elaborate English lexicon denoting heavier-than-air flying machines, including *bomber, 707, biplane, SST,* and so on, but the single Up-Country Swahili word *ndege* means both "bird" and every kind of "airplane."

Besides lexical distinctions, languages also pose certain obligatory grammatical classifications, but these again do not appear to vary systematically on some scale of superiority of expression. In English we say "the stone falls"; Russians do not specify the object as definite or indefinite and are content with "stone falls"; Kwakiutl Indians must indicate whether the stone is visible to the speaker and whether it is nearest to the speaker, the listener, or a third party, yet they can make a statement that does not express the singular or plural number of the stone; and the Nootka Indian language produces a sentence that translates roughly as "it stones down" (Sapir, 1912). The designation of nouns as belonging to semantically arbitrary sex-gender classes is unusual around the world but occurs in languages as diverse as Arabic, French, Hottentot, Khasi (Assam), and Tunica (American Indian). In short, there is no evidence that any one language is superior to another.

The above paragraphs make the point that language is both species specific and species uniform (Dale, 1972). That is, only humans have language, all humans have it—down to the level of the severely mentally retarded (Lenneberg, 1967)—and all languages are communicatively equivalent. But the equivalence of languages goes deeper than mere nonsuperiority of some over others: numerous "universals" exist (Greenberg, 1966). In all languages a small stock of meaningless sounds is used in systematic ways to produce arbitrary but meaningful sound combinations, which are combined by rules to form a theoretically infinite number of sentences (Brown, 1965). There are always identifiable subjects and predicates, classes of nouns, pronouns, verbs, categories of persons, including an addresser (first person), an addressee (second person), and an impersonal (third person), and ways to ask questions, give commands, express negations and so on.

That there are language elements shared by all people and possessed *in toto* by no other animal suggests the possibility that *Homo sapiens* is endowed with a biological capacity for language (Chomsky, 1968; Lenneberg, 1967). Termed the *innateness hypothesis* (Dale, 1972), this concept has gained increasing favor in recent years. Children raised in isolation do not develop language until a speech model is provided (Davis, 1949), but the hypothesis of innateness does not hold that environmental experience is completely unnecessary. As with many animal behavior patterns that are conceived as inborn, language is thought to develop naturally and rapidly, given a normal environmental input. McNeill (1970) may be correct in proposing that maturation and learning are both necessary conditions. Further evidence on the question of language as an innate characteristic of man will be considered in the section on grammatical development.

Sound Development

Before infants are 6 months old, they vocalize little, and, after the age of a year or so, they begin to utter recognizable words. In between, they babble. Infants spontaneously produce almost all sounds of all languages while babbling, and later speech might be thought to emerge from this apparent "practice" period. But babbling and speech, though sometimes overlapping temporally, are discontinuous: (1) during the first year of life, the first consonant-like sounds are back-mouth (for example, k), and the first vowel-like sounds are front-mouth (for example, i as in *hit*), whereas with the appearance of words in the second year the earliest sounds to be formed are the front consonants (for example, p, t, and m) and the mid-to-back vowels (a as in *father*); (2) in the second year, the child now has difficulty in producing the back consonants and front vowels of the babble period (McNeill, 1970). Whether the prespeech sounds play any part at all in the emergence of language is unknown, but the relationship is at best indirect.[1]

The establishment of front consonants and mid-to-back vowels as the first phonemes, or linguistically significant sounds, extends beyond English. American children say *tut* before *cut*, Swedish children say *tata* before *kata*, and Japanese children say *ta* before *ka* (Jakobson, 1969). Baby talk used by adults to children also typically replaces back with front consonants—in English, *tum on* for *come on*—except in languages with strong emphasis on back consonants. To account for the similarities in first phoneme utterances across different language groups, Jakobson (1969; Jakobson & Halle, 1971) suggests a hypothesis based on sound contrasts. A maximal and therefore linguistically optimal contrast is afforded by the acoustic differences between the supposedly first-spoken consonant, *p*, and the supposedly first-spoken vowel, *a*. The *p* is formed at the front of the mouth, is unvoiced (produced without vocal tone), is a stop (air stream stopped and then released), and represents a minimum of acoustic energy, while the *a* is formed toward the back of the mouth, is fully voiced, and represents a maximum of acoustic energy. Further phonemic development is said to be a result of filling in the gap between the initial two phonemes; for example, the first-spoken consonant sounds should be followed by nasals, such as *m*. Jakobson's argument is supported, though not in all details, by the available evidence. In English the words *pa* and *ma* or (with reduplication) *papa* and *mama* are among the first acquired by children. The attachment of these early words to the parents is of particular interest because the mother and father are salient objects in the infant's environment. Since parents almost everywhere are socially important to their infants and are spatially close as well, if Jakobson is right, the words for mother and father in many languages ought to correspond to the *ma* and *pa* syndrome. A straightforward test of this hypothesis is difficult because of the enormous phonetic variety of kin terms, but Murdock (1959), working with data from hundreds of languages, has employed a set of simplifying operations to reduce the variety to a limited number of basic sound patterns. These have been used by Murdock to test a broadened form of the hypothesis. Instead of considering only the specific terms *pa* and *ma* as exemplifying a strong consonant-vowel contrast, we may take as supportive of Jakob-

---

[1]A measure of the child's language capability (amount of vocalization plus a speech quotient—hearing and speech items) at 6 months is related to language capability (language maturity and vocabulary) at 3 years for girls. The language measure at 6 months does not relate to boys' later vocabulary, comprehension, language maturity, or enunciation (Moore, 1967).

son's argument any similar type of contrast—that is, front-consonant/ back-vowel combinations and nasal-consonant/back-vowel combinations. Thus, acceptable consonants would be the front sounds such as *p, b, t, d,* as well as the nasals *m* and *n,* and acceptable vowels would be the mid-to-back sounds such as *a,ə,o,u.* The two contrasts, front-consonant/back-vowel and nasal-consonant/back-vowel, may be designated as *pa*-type and *ma*-type terms, respectively, and the other four possible combinations—front-consonant/front-vowel, back-consonant/front-vowel, back-consonant/back-vowel, and nasal-consonant/front-vowel (plus infrequent combinations like vowel-vowel)—would be regarded as failing to support the hypothesis.

Data classified in this way are shown in Table 4-1. Altogether, the *pa*-type and *ma*-type terms are used in 612 of 1072 cases, or 57% of the total, giving decisive validation to the hypothesis. Just as in English, however, the supposedly secondary *ma*-type terms, the nasals, are used more frequently for the primary caretaker, the mother, and the supposedly primary *pa*-type terms are used more frequently for the father. Why the reversal? Jakobson (1971) notes that infants emit a slight nasal murmur while sucking and says that the reversal may be due to this phonatory reaction to nursing and its later reproduction as an expression of discontent and impatient longing for the absent nurser. Whether the particular explanation given here is correct or not, the broad form of the hypothesis is upheld, and the generalization can be made that some nursery sounds "overstep the limits of the nurseries, enter into the general usage of the adult society, and build a specific infantile layer in standard vocabulary" (Jakobson, 1971, p. 213).

The exceptional cases in Table 4-1 raise intriguing possibilities. Perhaps in societies in which *ma* and *pa* words are not applied to the parents, the nuclear family is of less than central impor-

Table 4-1. Parental kin terms and sound classes*

	Parental Kin Terms			
Sound Classes	*Denoting Mother*		*Denoting Father*	
Pa-type	48	(9%)	296	(55%)
Ma-type	204	(38%)	64	(12%)
All others	279	(53%)	181	(33%)
Totals	531	(100%)	541	(100%)

*Adapted from Cross-language parallels in parental kin terms, by G. P. Murdock, *Anthropological Linguistics,* 1959, *1*(9), 4. Copyright 1959 by Indiana University. Reprinted by permission.

tance. Perhaps where the *ma* word is applied to the father rather than the mother, the relationship between father and children is particularly intimate. But this is pure speculation; the research remains to be done.

The discussion has proceeded as if phonemes from different languages were comparable entities, which is true only in a rough way. Because the English phoneme /t/ and French phoneme /t/ fit similarly into the phonological structures of their languages and share certain features, such as being stops, being unvoiced, and apical (produced by the apex of the tongue), we treat them as the same. But the English /t/ is also alveolar (the tip of the tongue is brought to the alveolar ridge behind the upper teeth) and, in some positions, aspirated (breath escapes with audible friction, as in *ten*), while the French /t/ is dental (the tip of the tongue is brought to the teeth) and unaspirated. So phonemic comparability is dependent on the overall degree of matching of subphonemic characteristics such as those mentioned above. These characteristics, called *distinctive features*, can be defined in both articulatory and acoustic terms. They are only about 15 in number, but they are apparently used universally to generate the various phonemes used in the languages of the world (Jakobson, Fant, & Halle, 1963). Both their universality and their small number are probably a consequence of the anatomical structure and the perceptual capacities of human beings.

According to Jakobson, there is an identity between the child's order of acquisition of phonemes and the distribution of phonemes among the world's languages. Children acquire front consonants before back consonants; correspondingly, all languages have front consonants, some have both front and back consonants, but none have only back consonants. Further, if a language possesses a phoneme that is rare in the world, the children who speak that language tend to acquire the sound very late in their phonemic development. The phoneme /θ/, as in the initial sound of *thing*, is unusual around the world and is a late acquisition for English-speaking children. The production of a rare phoneme generally requires more numerous and more subtle articulatory distinctions than are necessary for a common phoneme, and the apparent result of the greater "effort" needed is the emergence of an identical order for both distribution and acquisition. As McNeill (1970) puts it, "It is as if, when children must push farther and farther from the universal core of language, fewer and fewer languages force them to do so" (p. 1135).

There has been no research on the question of why some languages force children well beyond the universal core, or, to put it another way, why some languages have large phoneme inventories. English, with 45 phonemes, is midway between the extremes of about

15 phonemes for some Polynesian languages and more than 75 phonemes for some languages in the Caucasus region. Another related cross-cultural problem is syllabification. *Beg* is a syllable in English, and *geb*, a different combination of the same phonemes, could be but is not a syllable, while the other combinations, *ebg, egb, bge,* and *gbe,* could never be syllables according to the rules of English phonology. Though any combination might theoretically be used to form a syllable, some are allowable within a given language, others are not. As in the example above, clusters of consonants (such as *bg* or *gb*) are found less frequently on a cross-cultural basis than are sequences such as consonant-vowel (as *be* or *ge*) or vowel-consonant (as *eb* or *eg*). Likewise, an infant's first-spoken syllables are simple consonant-vowel or vowel-consonant combinations (and occasionally vowel-vowel), never consonant clusters. This is not to say that some conceivable combinations are impossible for the speaker to produce, but rather that, for phonemic sequences as well as individual phonemes, there may be levels of articulatory difficulty that produce an identical order for world distribution and the child's acquisition. Jakobson's point about optimal contrasts is pertinent here. Optimally contrasting sound combinations may occur more frequently across different languages. If so, the higher rate of occurrence may be due to the distinctiveness afforded the listener and the added efficiency of oral communication. There is only impressionistic evidence available at this point, but the hypothesis could be put to systematic test.

Whatever the potential level of difficulty of particular items, all the sounds of a language are mastered by its speakers well before adulthood. Slavic delights like the Russian *vzglyad* ("view") and the Serbo-Croatian *zhvrk* ("spur tip") are not a problem for native speakers, and in English we regularly produce sequences that out of context we might have judged unpronounceable, such as the /ksθs/ at the end of *sixths*. Only limited studies of sound development have been undertaken, but the evidence available indicates that, as Jakobson proposed, the child begins with a few primitive distinctions and then divides and redivides these through successive learning of new contrasts. Introduction of a new contrast may frequently be the occasion for reorganization of the system rather than simply a single change. In one study, a child who had used voiced and voiceless consonants without contrasting them began immediately, once the distinction was learned, to apply the feature to numerous sound classes (Velten, 1943). It was as if the child had intuited a principle and then put it to use in a systematic way. Little work at this level of detail has been carried out for non-Western languages.

The consequence of learning a single linguistic system of sound categories and contrasts is that we become perceptually attuned only to those acoustic distinctions made in our own language and simultaneously less sensitive to those of another language, especially after our early teen years. The contrast between *s* and *z* is significant in many words in English, and the speaker has no trouble in distinguishing them, but the Spanish speaker has not had to learn a comparable distinction and often in pronouncing English will have problems with pairs like /rais/ *rice* and /raiz/ *rise*. In the same way, the English speaker in learning Hindi may not be able to hear the differences among four contrasting voiceless stops, all quite distinctive but all sounding like *t* to his untutored ear.

Grammatical Development

Until the last decade or so, the study of language development was a humdrum matter of measuring deviation from adult language and counting vocabulary size, on the basic premise that the child was merely speaking a garbled version of the adult tongue while slowly increasing his knowledge and eliminating errors (Dale, 1972). Now, however, hypotheses about the acquisition of language have changed dramatically, and new excitement has been sparked in the entire field. Evidently the child's language is not just a perturbation of adult patterns but is instead a coherent, lawful system—in fact, a series of systems regularly following one another. Cross-culturally, the earlier approach meant that there were few interesting questions to pursue, but the recent movement has generated a whole series of non-Western studies of language learning in children. The total number of cases is still small and the conclusions therefore tentative, but the most important result of these studies has been the discovery that children everywhere seem to go through the same early stages despite the great diversity of the languages to which they are exposed.

Around the age of 11 to 12 months, the infant utters his first recognizable word. For a period of approximately six months to a year thereafter, he adds numerous one-word utterances but does not combine them. The words are generally nouns identifying objects, animals, or people seen every day (Slobin, 1972) and might serve a nominative, or naming, function. But another view is that they are predicative; that is, they serve as comments on the situation in which the child finds himself and therefore correspond to full sentences conceptually (McNeill, 1970). In the first case, *mama* would mean only that the child had learned a name for the mother and said it when she appeared. In the second case, *mama* might mean "Here comes mama," "Mama, stay!" or "I want mama."[2] If the second is true, the child's comprehension clearly is outstripping his language performance—an effect commonly found throughout linguistic development (Slobin, 1973).

Between the ages of about 18 and 24 months, the infant begins a two-word stage. Even within this restricted format the child can convey many fundamental ideas as his vocabulary grows. One English-speaking child enlarged his cumulative number of different two-word utterances in successive months as follows: 14, 24, 54, 89, 350, 1400, 2500+ (Braine, 1963). Basic grammatical devices like intonation and inflection are also used, so the child is now producing rudimentary sentences (Slobin, 1971, 1972). The following examples of such sentences are taken from English, German, Russian, Finnish, Turkish, Samoan, and Luo (East Africa):

> IDENTIFICATION: *See doggie.*
> LOCATION: *Book there.*
> REPETITION: *More milk.*
> NONEXISTENCE: *Allgone thing.*
> NEGATION: *Not wolf.*
> QUESTION: *Where ball?*
> POSSESSION: *My candy.*
> ATTRIBUTION: *Big car.*
> AGENT–ACTION: *Mama walk.*
> AGENT–OBJECT: *Mama book* (meaning, "Mama read book").
> ACTION–LOCATION: *Sit chair.*
> ACTION–DIRECT OBJECT: *Hit you.*
> ACTION–INDIRECT OBJECT: *Give papa.*
> ACTION–INSTRUMENT: *Cut knife.*[3]

Apparently any sentence at this stage conveys one of two types of meanings, regardless of the language a child is acquiring: an *operations-of-reference* meaning—namely, statements of the presence, recurrence, or nonexistence of an item—or a *relation-type* meaning—namely, statements of a predicational sort (Brown, 1973). The first six statements in the above list are examples of operations-

[2]One study (Menyuk & Bernholz, 1969) indicates that through intonation a child can probably use a single word to express at least three different intentions: declaration, question, and emphasis.

[3]From Children and language: They learn the same way all around the world, by D.I. Slobin, *Psychology Today,* 1972, 6(2), 73. Reprinted by permission from *Psychology Today* Magazine, July 1972. Copyright © Ziff Davis Publishing Company.

of-reference, and the remaining statements are examples of relation-types. In addition to the small set of meaning-types, striking correspondence of terms has turned up among languages. In English, the word *there* is common, and terms with much the same meaning are found in German *(da)*, Russian *(tam)*, Finnish *(tuossa)*, and Samoan *(lea)* (Slobin, 1971). Slobin (1970) says that "If you ignore word order, and read through transcriptions of two-word utterances in the various languages we have studied, the utterances read like direct translations of one another" (p. 177).

Although abstract semantic functions like predication, negation, and modification appear near the very beginning of language, the two-word stage does not include certain highly sophisticated concepts—for instance, hypothetical events, causality, number, and the past and the future (Brown, 1973). Both this limited range of semantic complexity and the two-word stage itself are probably based on limitations in information processing and perception and thus may be produced by universal constraints on children's linguistic performance (Slobin, 1973). Brown (1973) argues, in fact, that the first sentences express and extend the kind of intelligence called *sensorimotor,* which Piaget sees as developing out of the infant's commerce with people and objects. But whatever the child's limitations, by the age of 2 he is capable of acquiring much of the particular native language to which he is exposed.

Three-word utterances have regularly emerged after the two-word stage in all the languages studied thus far (Slobin, 1972). The third word usually fills in a gap that was implicit in the earlier two-word sentences or expands the thought. Up to this point the child could say *mama read, read book,* and *mama book* without being able to put all three words together, but now he can do so: *mama read book.* Gradually the sentences expand; grammatical operations become more complex. In English the child learns correctly to invert the subject and auxiliary in a yes-no question like "Can he ride in a truck?" but cannot do this while at the same time asking a question with a "wh" word *(what, who, why,* and so on). Such a sentence comes out as "What he can ride in?" (Slobin, 1971). Before long, he has mastered the simultaneous handling of these transformations. Slobin's data (1972) indicate that the basic grammatical operations are acquired by the time the child is about 4 years old.

It may prove possible eventually to find a set of *operating principles,* or "self-instructions," used by children to organize and store language. One example of an operating principle is the tendency for children to "attend to the ends of words when scanning linguistic input in a search for cues to meaning" (Slobin, 1973, p. 191). The self-instruction would be: "pay attention to the ends of words." Evidence for the principle comes from the fact that locative markers (particles expressing location in space) are acquired earlier in development if they are suffixes than if they are prefixes or prepositions, and from the fact that articles are acquired earlier if they are attached as noun suffixes. The evidence is consistent with observations like the fact that the first negative element acquired in a French child's speech is *pas*—the final part of the separated negative *ne . . . pas* (Slobin, 1973).

The preceding discussion should make clear that the order of acquisition of grammatical features is determined not only by their semantic or cognitive complexity but also by their formal linguistic complexity (C. Chomsky, 1969; Slobin, 1973). The English-speaking child, for example, must deal with irregularities of the past tense in many common verbs, such as *went, sat, brought*. The result is a strong tendency to apply the standard past-tense form in all cases, and the "over-regularization" typically leads to words like *goed*, *sitted*, and even *broughted*. In Russian, a noun must be assigned to one of six case endings depending on its function in the sentence. Because the endings also differ according to gender and number, the inflectional system for nouns is complex, and Russian children go through a series of over-generalizations. They first use perhaps only feminine endings with the accusative (direct object) case, then only masculine endings, until finally the appropriate inflections are sorted out by the age of 7 or 8. In Egyptian Arabic, the complexity of plural markings is so great that even 15-year-olds err in assigning plurals to familiar nouns (Slobin, 1973). But whatever difficulties are posed by a given language, the basic grammatical operations are always grasped early. Further, the errors committed by children do not interfere with their ability to communicate central meaning to adults and to one another. This ability is, indeed, already present when the first of the one-word utterances is voiced by the young child.

The learning-theory variables of imitation, practice, and reinforcement do not fare well when applied to the facts of language development. Children are unlikely to be imitating adults when they say *allgone sticky* after their hands are washed or *allgone outside* after the door is closed (Braine, 1963). Even when asked to repeat adult statements, they produce their own versions: *he's going out* becomes *he go out* (Brown & Bellugi, 1964). Regarding the question of practice, Lenneberg (1962) reported the case of a boy who was unable to produce normal speech but who demonstrated full understanding of English through his ability to carry out instructions, to answer questions by pointing, and so on. Reinforcement for correct utterances would seem important in shaping the child's language to the level of adult competence, but again the evidence does not support such a view. The longitudinal observation of Brown and his associates indicated that:

> Most commonly . . . the grounds on which an utterance was approved or disapproved . . . were not strictly linguistic at all. When Eve expressed the opinion that her mother was a girl by saying *He a girl*, her mother answered *That's right*. The child's utterance was ungrammatical, but her mother did not respond to that fact; instead, she responded to the truth of the proposition the child intended to express. In general, the parents fitted propositions to the child's utterances . . . and then approved or not according to the correspondence between proposition and reality. Thus, *Her curl my hair* was approved because the mother was, in fact, curling Eve's hair. However, Sarah's grammatically impeccable *There's the animal farmhouse* was disapproved because the building was a lighthouse, and Adam's *Walt Disney comes on on Tuesday* was disapproved because Walt Disney came on on some other day. It seems, then, to be truth value rather than syntactic well-formedness that chiefly governs explicit verbal reinforcement by parents—which renders mildly paradoxical the fact that the usual product of such a training schedule is an adult whose speech is highly grammatical but not notably truthful.[4]

Besides these problems, learning theory seems unable to account for certain early linguistic capabilities (Rebelsky, Starr, & Luria, 1967). The extremely rapid acquisition of grammatical operations means among other things that a child can understand complex utterances in which the connection between parts is remote. Consider this sentence: *The people who called and wanted to rent your house when you go away next year are from California* (Miller & Chomsky, 1963). Comprehension requires that the connection between the second word, *people,* and the seventeenth word, *are,* be understood. Suppose that sentences were learned as strings of grammatical categories. Miller and Chomsky (1963) have pointed out that, if an average of four grammatical categories can occur at any point in a sentence (a conservative estimate), then detection of the relation between *people* and *are* would imply the learning of at least 4^{15}, or 10^9, grammatical transitions during a childhood that has lasted only 10^8 seconds. But no theory proposes that the child can learn ten transitions per second. However, the connection between *people* and *are* could be understood if one has grasped the idea of *embedding*—the nesting of one component inside another like itself (McNeill, 1970). A formulation of this sort seems well within the capacity of those who have been engaged in the crea-

[4]Brown, R., Cazden, C., and Bellugi-Klima, U. The child's grammar from I to III, pp. 70-71, in *Minnesota Symposium on Child Psychology,* Vol. 2, edited by John P. Hill. University of Minnesota Press, Minneapolis. © Copyright 1969 by the University of Minnesota. Reprinted by permission.

tion, refinement, and discarding of rule systems at all stages of their grammatical development.

Both the existence of apparent universals in language development and evidence that even young children master some of the abstract features of language offer further support to the hypothesis of linguistic innateness in man. Whether innateness is taken to mean something as specific as preprogrammed neurological mechanisms that specifically facilitate language or, rather, a more general cognitive capacity to process language and form internal structures, it is clear that traditional learning theory is insufficient as the sole explanation for complex acquisition. A hypothesis joining the innate capacity with environmental stimulation and/or reinforcement may eventually allow parsimonious explanation. But the total data base is still small, and many important questions have yet to be asked, let alone answered, in this field.

Environmental Effects on Language Skill

Language acquisition may follow a universal *sequence* of emergence, but children's *rates* of development differ markedly. Many factors are associated with advancement or lag in language development, including aspects of the visual environment and quality of interpersonal relationships. Most highly correlated with this pace, however, are frequency, variety, and richness in the language environment of the child. The child raised in a bilingual household, for example, learns to speak later than the child who is exposed to only one language. Laterborn children speak later than firstborns, presumably because the parents distribute their speech output among more listeners after the first child. The institutionalized child, who has one-fifth to one-ninth less speech directed at him than the child in a home environment, vocalizes less frequently in the babbling stage (Rheingold, 1960, 1961), is less developed linguistically at the age of 5 (Dennis & Najarian, 1957), and continues to have speech difficulties after leaving the institution (Dennis, 1960). At 1½ years of age, the U.S. child of middle-class parents already shows speech sound superiority over the child of working-class parents (Irwin, 1948). There was even an increase in the length of sentences uttered by 3- to 8-year-olds between the 1930s and 1957, due perhaps to the linguistic stimulation provided by radio and television (Kagan & Havemann, 1972). Both responsiveness to children's utterances and direct language training are effective in promoting development. In a training experiment, Russian babies between 9 and 18 months of age learned new words by experiencing objects and repetition of the objects' names (cited in Mussen, Conger, & Kagan, 1969). Thirteen-month-old American children, provided with 18 months of the more general experience of being read to by their mothers for 15 to 20 minutes a day, were compared with a group of infants not provided with the reading experience. By the age of 17 months, the infants who had the reading experience were vocalizing more (higher phoneme frequency) than the other group. The group exposed to reading continued, through 30 months of age, to excel in speech-sound production when compared with the control group.

Most of the above findings refer to U.S. data, but the sparse evidence available gives the impression that in many non-Western societies the children receive little direct verbal stimulation and develop concomitantly poor verbal skills, at least in the early years. Slobin (1972) reports that in all the non-Western groups for which he has data (except the Maya) children receive little verbal input from adults, and the emergence of the two-word stage occurs typically at the age of 2. In contrast, the Western child is typically inundated with speech from the mother and is surrounded by a highly verbal society, and he usually begins the two-word stage at about 18 months (Braine, 1963; El'konin, 1973; Guillaume, 1973; Klima & Bellugi-Klima, 1971). Similarly, among the children of one of these non-Western groups, the Luo of Kenya, negative commands do not appear until near the age of 3 (Blount, 1972), whereas Russian (Slobin, 1971) and American children (Albright & Albright, 1971; Brown, Cazden, & Bellugi-Klima, 1969) begin uttering such commands closer to the age of 2. Whether the apparent differences in stimulation and in developmental rates continue at later ages is unknown, but systematic work along these lines might be profitable.

The flexible use of language is unique to man, and man's languages have communicative equivalence. Cross-cultural similarities in the words for mother and father are probably due to association between the infant's first human contacts—his parents—and his primitive articulatory capacities. Grammatical similarities among infants and young children in widely differing language groups lend credence to the hypothesis that all humans share an innate ability to learn language. The rate of language learning appears to be affected by environmental variation. Most notably, responsiveness to the child's utterances, direct language training, and the stimulation value of other elements in the child's immediate language environment appear to promote rapid development.

Three Cultures

The Ainu, Trobrianders, and Gusii are not part of the small group of societies for which intensive studies of language development have been carried out, so little can be added here except a few scraps of information. If Jakobson's (1969) hypothesis about the use of *ma*- and *pa*-type terms for the parents is applied to the three societies, we find only partial support: the Ainu do not fit the scheme; the Trobrianders use a *pa*-type term for father, but their word for mother combines a nasal (*n*) with a front consonant (*i*) instead of a back one; the Gusii use *pa*-type terms—that is, a front consonant with a back vowel—for both parents (father = *tata,* mother = *baba*). The simplified language often adopted by adults to communicate with children employs front rather than back consonants beyond a chance level. Such consonants are reported for the Gusii in the two baby-talk words *titi* (used to train infants to get into position for being carried on the back) and *ta, ta* (used to encourage the infant to walk) (LeVine & LeVine, 1963). Finally, among both Ainu and Trobrianders, the term for mother is reported to be the first word learned by the infant.

Perception

Experience plays some part in perceptual development. Animals raised in restricted environments cannot make normal discriminations (Riesen, 1961). Human beings who have been blind from infancy but who have had their sight restored surgically need training to identify specific shapes (Senden, 1932). However, children in all societies are provided with sufficient environmental stimulation that perceptual systems universally develop without severe deficits of this sort. Further, given the essential anatomical and physiological unity of the human species and the overwhelming number of common experiences with the physical world shared by all persons, a strong case can be made that physically normal adults everywhere have the same fundamental perceptual competencies—for example, *object constancy, depth perception, intersensory integration* (coordination of information from several sensory sources). Anthropological data give little reason to doubt the validity of such a conclusion, and the occasional piece of evidence to the contrary can probably be explained without resorting to questions of radical differences in perception. When a forest Pygmy first ventures onto an open plain and identifies distant buffalo as insects (Turnbull, 1962), it seems safer to say that his lack of experience with buffalo at large distances has created an error of scale than to say that he lacks the ability to recognize familiar objects under varied conditions. This vivid example of misperception overshadows our knowledge that Pygmies perceive with accuracy in their home environment.

But less central perceptual aptitudes sometimes differ strikingly among cultures. The discussion of this research will be brief, however, because even the most reliable findings tend to be obscured by ambiguity of interpretation. A detailed review of the literature is available elsewhere (Lloyd, 1972).

The work on spatial perception by Witkin and others (Witkin & Berry, in press) has important cognitive implications and is considered in Chapter Five.

Color

In English we have 11 basic color terms, while the Jalé of Highland New Guinea have only two terms, which are roughly translated as "dark" and "light," or black and white. All other languages fall somewhere within this range (Berlin & Kay, 1969). The difference between our 11 color names and the Jalé's two terms appears trivial when we consider that normal individuals can discriminate several million *just-noticeable differences* on a color cube (Brown, 1958). The size of the color lexicon would thus seem dependent on cultural, not perceptual, factors, and such an association has been found: the more complex the culture, the larger the number of color terms (Berlin & Kay, 1969; Hays, Margolis, Naroll, & Perkins, 1972). Collapsed color-naming systems appear near the equator in tropical societies that, like the Jalé, are technologically simple and have no need for elaborate color lexicons. But an entirely different explanation focuses on the fact that heavy ocular pigmentation is characteristic of tropical populations, and that individuals with a high degree of ocular pigmentation are somewhat insensitive to short-wavelength (blue) colors. The explanation concludes that collapsed color-naming systems appear near the equator by reason of actual perceptual differences among human groups (Bornstein, 1973). For now, the two contrasting hypotheses remain unresolved.

Perceptual implications are also present in other features of color systems. Informants from diverse cultures agree closely about the examples that best represent any shared basic color terms (Heider, 1972); for instance, "red" is placed at nearly the same location on a color wheel by all individuals. But the informants disagree about the boundaries between two colors (sometimes necessarily, since different cultures often have different numbers of terms), and, if given repeated tests, they fail individually to establish stable boundaries for themselves (Berlin & Kay, 1969). So people agree, whatever their culture, on the *focal point,* or best example, of a red and disagree on the boundary between red and orange. The boundary problem once gave rise to the idea that the spectrum is divided up without regard to psychological or physiological considerations—that is, without any natural divisions (Ray, 1953). But the cross-cultural consensus on focal points, together with the small upper limit of 11 basic terms, indicates that color terminology may reflect the operation of elementary perceptual processes. If the "core meanings" of colors are universally the same, then the focal areas of the color space must be more salient than the areas near the boundaries between colors; if they are, they ought to attract attention more readily than nonfocal areas. Developmental support for this idea comes from a finding that 3-year-old American children, when asked to "show me a color" from an array, choose focal over nonfocal examples well beyond chance (Heider, 1971).

The 11 basic terms are tied up with another regularity. They are subject to certain distributional restraints, which emerge as follows: (1) if a language has only a two-color classification, the terms will be for black and white (or dark and light); (2) if there are three terms, the colors will be black, white, and red; (3) if there are four terms, the colors will be black, white, red, and either green or yellow (the latter two colors are equally likely to appear as the fourth term); (4) if there are five terms, the colors will be black, white, red, green, *and* yellow; and so on. In other words, if you know the number of basic terms in a language, you can tell what colors they will be (Berlin & Kay, 1969).[5] The full sequence looks like this:

$$\begin{bmatrix} \text{white} \\ \text{black} \end{bmatrix} \rightarrow \text{red} \rightarrow \begin{bmatrix} \text{green} \\ \text{yellow} \end{bmatrix} \rightarrow \text{blue} \longrightarrow \text{brown} \rightarrow \begin{bmatrix} \text{gray} \\ \text{pink} \\ \text{orange} \\ \text{purple} \end{bmatrix}$$

The colors gray, pink, orange, and purple are lumped together since all four appear when a language goes beyond seven color terms.

Why might the presence of a brown imply the presence of a red but not vice versa? Evidently because red is even more salient than brown. We recall from the language section that in the worldwide

[5]Subsequent research (Berlin & Berlin, 1975) has indicated that the priority of emergence among green, yellow, and blue varies considerably from one language to another.

distribution of phonemes, back consonants are universal and front consonants occur only in some languages; likewise, in phonological development, back consonants are learned before front ones. If we construct the same formal argument for the emergence of color names, we would predict that a child will learn black, white, and red before he learns green and yellow, blue, brown, and so forth. To find out, however, it would not do to wait for the child to begin uttering color terms, since he uses mostly nouns and verbs (and seldom adjectives, which color terms are) in the one and two-word stages, which occur long after he presumably can distinguish among the colors. A color-discrimination test given to infants might get at the problem.

Visual Illusions

Illusion susceptibility varies greatly from one society to another. No fully satisfactory explanation for cross-cultural differences is available (Lloyd, 1972), but a case will be made here for the strongest hypothesis to date. Some of the problems with this hypothesis will then be enumerated.

An optical illusion marks an instance in which the individual's ordinary visual-inference habits prove to be unreliable. The individual is misled by the presentation of familiar cues in new material, leading him to draw inappropriate conclusions. According to one view, visual cues are misjudged due to an illusion's ecological unrepresentativeness (Segall, Campbell, & Herskovits, 1966). Common characteristics of objects in an environment are recognized from many different perspectives, indicating that the same visual inference is drawn from at least several retinal images.

What typical ecological factors can be identified that would lead Western individuals to make incorrect visual inferences about the well-known Müller-Lyer illusion (Figure 4-1)? In the Western world, the physical environment is replete with rectangular objects, which on the retina are projected as obtuse and acute angles but which the individual learns to interpret as right angles extended into space. When an individual from the Western or *carpentered* world is shown the two Müller-Lyer figures, he evidently perceives them as representations of three-dimensional rectangular objects extended into space. Given this interpretation, the right-hand stimulus in Figure 4-1 appears to be the front edge of a box-like object, while the left-hand stimulus appears to be a back edge and thus farther away in perspective and apparently longer. Individuals in traditional societies, who live in less carpentered

Figure 4-1.   Müller-Lyer illusion.

environments than Westerners, have proved to be much more immune to the illusion (Segall et al., 1966).

With the horizontal-vertical illusion (Figure 4-2), Westerners display only medium susceptibility, and the Arunta Aborigines in Australia are more susceptible than any group yet reported (Dawson, Young, & Choi, 1973; Segall et al., 1966). The Arunta live in flat, open desert. An individual habituated to this vista would have typically seen before him great stretches of distance that, on the retina, would be projected as foreshortened planes but that he would learn to interpret as lengthier planes extending away into space. Shown the horizontal-vertical illusion, such a person should perceive the vertical line as representing a plane extending along his line of vision and should therefore perceive it as longer than the horizontal line. Both Westerners and traditional peoples who are without vast open spaces like those of the Australian desert have been less susceptible to the illusion than the Arunta.

The ecological hypothesis sounds convincing in the above examples, but it has been applied to two extreme environmental cases. A medium degree of carpenteredness should yield a medium level of susceptibility to the Müller-Lyer, and a low degree of carpenteredness should yield a low level; but it does not work that way. The same is true of the horizontal-vertical illusion; only the strongest cases seem to fit the hypothesis in a precise way (Jahoda, 1966; Segall et al., 1966). The point has also been made that persons with the ability to make three-dimensional inferences (height, breadth, depth) from two-dimensional representations (pictures) might be more likely to be susceptible to the illusions (Jahoda, 1966; Mundy-Castle & Nelson, 1962). Depiction of depth in pictures depends, in part, upon varied angles (including those angles in the Müller-Lyer illusion). Since those environments rated as medium in carpenteredness tend to be medium in acculturation, residents would have variable experience and expertise

Figure 4-2.   Horizontal-vertical illusion.

in interpretation of pictures. The relationship between illusion-susceptibility and degree of carpenteredness thus might be weakened by the varying degree of expertise in picture interpretation. Finally, as with color-naming systems, a physiological hypothesis has been advanced for illusion effectiveness. Some evidence indicates that degree of retinal pigmentation may affect contour detectability and thus susceptibility to illusion (Berry, 1971; Jahoda, 1971).[6]

Pictorial Depth Perception

In Western pictorial representations, several conventions are customarily employed to depict three-dimensionality. The conventions used to convey depth or distance in two dimensions include: (1) *superimposition* of close objects over distant objects, (2) representation of close objects as larger in *size* than distant objects, (3) *position* on the page to designate the distance of an object's base, and (4) the upward convergence of vertically oriented lines to provide *linear perspective*. Although these conventions faithfully reflect our retinal imagery, a three-dimensional "reading" of pictures is neither innate nor automatic. Extensive testing in traditional groups has revealed that increased experience with the perception of objects, such as occurs naturally with increasing age, does not necessarily improve the ability to interpret the depiction of objects. (A comprehensive review of the research can be found in Duncan, Gourlay, & Hudson, 1973.) Greater accuracy of interpretation does occur under certain sociocultural conditions (Deregowski, 1968a, 1969; Hudson, 1962, 1967; Kilbride, Robbins, & Freeman, 1968; Mundy-Castle, 1966). Illiterate South African mine workers, for example, were unable to make three-dimensional interpretations at all, but primary school children were better at the task (Hudson, 1960). Increased years of schooling do increase the accuracy of interpretation (Kilbride & Robbins, 1968; Omari & MacGinitie, 1974). In Zambia, male domestic servants who were exposed to pictorial depth representation in the homes where they worked were nonetheless unable to make many three-dimensional interpretations (Deregowski, 1968b), and the conclusion may be drawn that passive experience alone has insufficient impact. But, as would be expected, direct training in three-dimensional perception in a Sierra Leone adult sample produced significant improvement (Dawson, 1967a).

The problem experienced by subjects unfamiliar with pictorial material appears to be a difficulty in making the transition from object

---

[6]Recent research (Bolton, Michelson, Wilde, & Bolton, in press) in which the design allowed a critical test of the ecological hypothesis and the physiological hypothesis yielded fairly strong support for the former.

to depiction rather than any perceptual difficulty with the pictures themselves. Zambian adult female subjects were able to match a picture from a displayed array with a standard picture and to match a model from a displayed array with a standard model. A high rate of error occurred, however, when attempts were made to match pictures with the objects themselves or objects with pictures of the objects (Deregowski, 1971). The positive role of repeated exposure and of direct training in the interpretation of pictorial material is clear; some other types of training, such as learning to read and write in school, may also facilitate the transition from depth and distance perception of real objects to interpretation of the conventions used to depict depth and distance in pictures. Finally, the current cross-cultural work has been conducted primarily in Africa with a relatively small set of stimulus materials, and conclusions about differences in interpretation of pictorial representations, as well as about the factors influencing the differences, require an extension of the sample to other non-Western groups (R. Miller, 1973).

On present evidence it appears that fundamental panhuman perceptual skills emerge given ordinary environmental stimulation and that all societies typically offer adequate stimulation. However, less central perceptual phenomena seem to be susceptible to change as a result of environmental circumstances.

The cultural differences in perception documented in the preceding paragraphs have been difficult to trace developmentally because of several confounding variables. With illusions, for example, increasing age connotes greater experience with the environment and therefore presumably greater susceptibility to appropriate visual illusions; yet increasing age is also associated with overall improvement in perceptual abilities and should therefore lead to *lowered* susceptibility (Piaget, 1969; Witkin, Goodenough, & Karp, 1967). A second problem is that studies using a wide age range of subjects have no way to control for the broad educational and acculturative influences to which the younger members of a sample have been exposed in traditional societies during recent years, and, again, perceptual abilities may be affected. In addition to these problems, there is almost no material from traditional groups on development of the basic perceptual abilities in the first two years of life. Thus we know much more about cultural differences in perception than we do about the development of these differences.

Chapter Five

Cognition

Peoples with simple technologies often appear to possess simple minds. The seminomadic Bolivian Siriono, one of the few tribes in the world without knowledge of firemaking, have a number system that translates as *one, two, three, many*. A Siriono hunter, when asked a question about the number of animals he encountered in the forest, will, if the number is below four, "hold up the appropriate number of fingers to his nose and say the number; if it is above three he may hold up a confused number of fingers and just say 'many'; if it is very great he may demonstrate his toes as well" (Holmberg, 1969, p. 121). Similarly, the Siriono make few distinctions concerning time. Any day beyond tomorrow is referred to as the "brother of tomorrow." Broad, indefinite classifications like the number and time systems of the Siriono have occasioned the opinion that the cognitive capacities of individuals in simple societies are no greater than those of animals or mental retardates.

Yet language, religion, social rules, and economic knowledge have been the property of every human group. Instances of the special complexities of Siriono culture include the preferred form of marriage between a man and his mother's brother's daughter (and prohibition against marriage with the father's sister's daughter), the marking and following of temporary hunting trails in different locales, and the skill shown by cooperating hunters who communicate with their specialized language of whistles and who imitate perfectly the calls of birds, monkeys, tapirs, and peccaries. Unlike the cognitively less capable animals, human beings everywhere both participate in and pass on to the next generation a rich and intricate culture.

The children in all societies are neophytes. Even comparisons of young children from societies having elaborated technologies with adults from societies having simple technologies would show the adults strongly leading on most facets of intelligence. However, to say merely that adults and children always differ cognitively, whatever the complexity of the culture to which they belong, is only a beginning. There are questions to be asked about the pace, sequence, and final outcome of cognitive development. And most of the studies in this field are very recent.

Birth to Two Years

Human infants have little adaptive capacity and must depend on older persons in the society for their survival. At birth and through the first month, the infant's learning is quite limited. Until the infant is approximately 1 month of age, he cannot learn and maintain performance of even very simple conditioned responses. On the other hand, neonates have a number of reflexive responses; they can use their major senses—two hours after birth they can follow a moving light with their eyes—and they begin immediately to interact with their environment, quickly gaining in ability to process complex inputs and to make more efficient responses. Throughout the first year there is a clear growth in adaptive capacity, with more complex inputs and more efficient responses occurring with rapidity. By the age of 2, children have become creatures of their culture: they can make meaningful utterances, initiate interaction, and display complicated likes and dislikes.

Through the use of developmental tests, it is possible to chart roughly the growth of capacities, skills, and adaptive behavior. The average Western child can reach for a dangling string at approximately 3 months of age, look for a fallen object at 6 months, build a tower of two cubes at 14 months, and demonstrate understanding of two prepositional concepts such as *on* or *in* at 28 months (Bayley, 1969). The child's increasing mastery is evident in these examples, but so too is the growing importance of culture. Comprehension of a preposition like *in* may be influenced by both linguistic structure and usage factors (Chapter Four). However, in an infant's early months, the problem of culture raises few difficulties, and infant testing in the first year of life probably gives us as close to culture-free findings as we are likely to get.

What is performance like in other societies? Although the testing in non-Western societies has not been extensive enough to develop within-culture normative data, some 50 studies have been carried out (see Werner, 1972), with Western norms employed to evaluate the results. The results are clear-cut: infants from Europe and the United States usually fall well below non-Western infants in psychomotor development. Thus, since developmental tests have been standardized around a mean of 100, almost all non-Western groups have an average above 100.

The documentation of accelerated infant psychomotor development in non-Western societies has come most consistently from studies conducted in Africa. Samples from at least seven sub-Saharan nations have demonstrated a distinct pattern of advancement. (For an opposing viewpoint, see Warren, 1972.) Ugandan infants examined at birth showed levels of motor development corresponding to the Euro-American norms for infants a month old or more (for instance, strong control of head and trunk, and absence of primitive reflex activity such as grasping). In the first six months, mean motor scores for the Ugandan infants were above 130, and their adaptive and sound-development scores were above 120.[1] Infants from Latin America and India were also advanced, but not so strongly, and their scores tended to fall between the African and Euro-American norms. Within non-Western ethnic groups, the degree of acceleration is found to be negatively correlated with less permissive infant-care patterns (sleeping alone and having less access to the mother's breast), Westernization, and urbanization, though some superiority to Western norms is still maintained.

Consistent ethnic differences at birth might seem to point to a genetic origin for the early pattern of development, but several prenatal influences may be operative. The mother's nutritional intake, an obvious environmental difference, is presumably more adequate in Western societies and so would create the reverse effect—more advanced development for Western infants. Aside from this nutrition puzzle, at least two other environmental factors might have some bearing on the developmental level: the mother's physical activity and her feeling of stress during pregnancy. The physical-activity level is almost certainly higher among traditional women than among women in Euro-American communities. Physical exertion could affect both the mother's health and, indirectly, *in utero* development. It is possible that the fetal oxygen supply could be a mediating variable with direct consequences for development, but no reported research supports this speculation. The infant's activity level, which could be affected by the mother's own level of activity or by her health, has a known positive relationship to the infant's responsiveness to the environment (Escalona, 1968; Osofsky & Danzger, 1974). The second environmental factor—degree

[1]Extensive testing indicates differences between white infants and black infants on the motor scale but not on the mental scale (Bayley, 1969).

of stress experienced by the mother during pregnancy—might be influential in Western communities because of the difficulties and uncertainties surrounding child rearing and family life in complex societies. Either developmental level at birth or responsiveness immediately after birth can be negatively affected by stressful situations during pregnancy. Disturbances in the mother's hormonal balance are speculated to be the physical agent involved (Montagu, 1962). Prenatal factors, including nutrition, physical activity of the mother, and stress, deserve closer examination before environmental differences are abandoned as contributors to the observed neonatal acceleration of non-Western infants.

The environmental factors that slow down the advanced psychomotor development of non-Western infants all seem to be restrictive or even stimulus-depriving (Werner, 1972). But Western infants, compared with those in traditional societies, appear to be subject to even more of these restrictive experiences—being carried less frequently, being more scheduled, and being alone more of the time. Within the West itself, Dutch infants are given less stimulation than American infants during the first months of life (Rebelsky, 1967), and the Dutch 3-month and 6-month developmental quotients are at 70 and 79, respectively (Rebelsky, 1972). (Stimulation increases as Dutch children grow older, and by the age of 24 months they have reached the Western mean of 100.) Perhaps the lower Western scores can be seen as due to an attenuated version of what happens in institutional deprivation (Dennis, 1960; Dennis & Najarian, 1957; Kohen-Raz, 1967, 1968), which is associated with significant psychomotor retardation. This is not to imply that Western infants are truly deprived, but it may be accurate to say that they receive less constant contact with people than do non-Westerners and that, developmentally, they fall at the "low normal" end of the scale. Early developmental backwardness, even when severe, does not appear to be irreversible (Dennis & Najarian, 1957; Skeels, 1966), however, unless extreme social and physical deprivation continues past infancy.

The high developmental test scores of infants in traditional societies soon decline (Werner, 1972). Between the infant's first and second years, a downward trend begins, and, after age 2, the mean scores have fallen below those of Western children. Although the causes of the decline are not entirely clear, numerous factors have been proposed. Almost all involve the idea of *discontinuity* between near-optimal early developmental conditions and later changes so contrastive that they are traumatic for the infant. For example: if the infant is fed only breast milk, then after the first year, the mother no longer has an adequate amount; if a replacement feeding is introduced, there

may be a nutrition problem (under present-day conditions of acculturation); if sudden weaning occurs, the infant will probably be expected to
be more independent, but often there is little encouragement or direct
instruction along these lines; if a sibling is born, the attention formerly
given the child is now transferred to the newborn, so the level of
stimulation may suddenly be reduced. It is ironic that Ruth Benedict
(1938), the anthropologist who lucidly pointed to the possibly deleterious effects of discontinuities in child rearing, was concerned to show
how most traditional societies maintained a line of continuity in child
care that was largely absent in the Western world. In these examples,
however, continuity is noticeably absent.

Support for the discontinuity hypothesis comes from a pair of
non-Western groups in which infants are relatively unstimulated socially and physically throughout their early life (Werner, 1972). Among
both the Japanese and the Zinacanteco (Mexico), infants are not accelerated in development in the early months—thus being highly unusual
among non-Western groups—and do not suffer a decline during the
second year. Also, among upper-middle-class urban sections of various ethnic groups, the typically small first-year acceleration is not
followed by a second-year decline, and development instead proceeds
at a pace comparable to that of Western infants. In these cases, both
level of stimulation and resulting psychomotor development show essential continuity.

Discontinuous socialization, though a highly plausible hypothesis, may not really have as much to do with drops in developmental scores as the nature of the tests and the testing situation. The
early acceleration may allow such a high proportion of items passed
that a ceiling effect is achieved (there are too few items of difficulty to
test the level adequately). There is also a gradual shift from motor to
mental items on the tests, which were created and "normed" for
Western infants and which become increasingly culture-bound and
therefore more difficult for non-Westerners beyond the age of 1 year.
And, finally, the older infants may be wary of the experimenter and the
demands of the testing situation. But supposing the second-year fall-off
mirrors some actual decline in relative capabilities, then the pattern of
infant development in most traditional societies may be summarized as
follows: either favorable prenatal conditions or a high level of early
stimulation apparently results in first-year psychomotor developmental
precocity, which, in the second year, erodes and dissolves as the
stimulation level is reduced, as the social expectations change, and as
the nutritional situation deteriorates. The upshot is a developmental
quotient on Western-based tests somewhat below the norm for Western 2-year-olds. In contrast, among Western groups and in moderniz-

ing sectors of traditional societies, infants may experience different prenatal conditions or may receive a lower level of early stimulation that remains more or less stable throughout the infancy period and that appears to eventuate in a steady and unfluctuating development.

In the West, infant tests do not correlate well with later IQ performance (Bayley, 1955), but the question of correlation cannot even be asked for traditional societies, in which the testing of infants and the testing of children have been almost completely independent enterprises. The need for longitudinal research in the traditional world is nowhere more apparent than in the sphere of cognitive development.

Childhood and Adulthood

Important changes occur in the treatment and behavior of the child when he is approximately 2 years old. Typically, both comprehension and use of language expand rapidly (Chapter Four), and behavior is much more under linguistic control. The child is usually weaned and is walking; he is seldom given the same degree of supervision as in earlier months. But little is known cross-culturally about the implications of these changes (or subsequent changes up to about school age) for cognitive development.

Most of the cross-cultural work has centered on the differences between the early and later school-age child. In these age groups in the West, growth in cognitive competency has been measured by numerous assessment devices, including the standard IQ test, but severe cultural limitations have prevented non-Western application of all but a few of these. Even among the tests that have been used frequently, the methodological problems have been many. Among the most common types of difficulties encountered are: (1) the subject's unfamiliarity with testing materials, as when Porteus (1931) asked Australian Aborigines to trace mazes (Figure 5-1), and (2) cultural inappropriateness of the test demands, as when the Aborigines were given tests scored on speed and did poorly because, as Porteus (1931) put it, "The aborigine in his natural state has all the time there is and probably has never heard the injunction to hurry in his life" (p. 308). Because of all the built-in disadvantages of this kind, it might be expected that non-Western children would score relatively poorly and would fail to show the characteristic Western improvements from one age level to the next. This is generally, though not always, the case, and a long list of such low performances could be compiled (for examples, see Berry & Dasen, 1974; Dasen, 1972a).

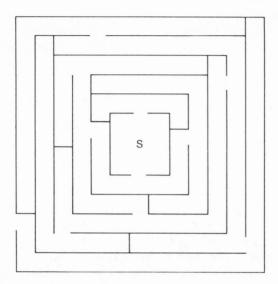

Figure 5-1. Item from Porteus Maze Test. Year XII. From *Porteus Maze Test: Fifty Years' Application,* by S. D. Porteus. Pacific Books, 1965. Copyright 1933 by S. D. Porteus. Reprinted by permission of the Estate of Stanley D. Porteus.

The three types of cognitive tests with sufficient frequency and diversity of use to allow comparative statements are Piagetian conservation problems,[2] classification modes, and attainment of concepts.

The typical Piagetian *conservation* problem effectively demonstrates a change in level of understanding between the younger and older child in the West. An average 5-year-old does not understand that changing the shape of a liquid or a solid leaves the quantity unaffected, but a 7-year-old does possess this understanding and can show it. If two identical beakers are filled to the same level with water, and then the water from one beaker is poured into a longer, thinner beaker, thus causing the level to be higher in the longer beaker, the 5-year-old will say that the higher level means that there is more water in the longer beaker, whereas the 7-year-old not only can say that the amount remains unchanged but can also demonstrate attention to two stimulus dimensions concurrently ("longer but thinner") and the

---

[2]The piecemeal character of cross-cultural research allows little possibility of evaluating Piaget's theory of cognitive development (1950) on the basis of non-Western findings—with the recent exception of a systematic attempt to validate in three cultures the upper three of the four Piagetian hierarchical stages (Feldman, Lee, McLean, Pillemer, & Murray, 1974). A few reviews (for example, Dasen, 1972a; Lloyd, 1972), however, have drawn together the literature and attempted interpretive summaries.

reversibility of the operation ("if it is poured back into the other beaker it will be the same"). The 7-year-old is said to have attained conservation. The change is reliable and well documented and in Piaget's scheme is representative of the shift from *perceptual* to *conceptual* thinking.

In Senegal, Greenfield (1966) administered this same task to several Wolof samples, among them a group of unschooled rural children. Although about a quarter of the children had attained conservation by the age of 7, performance soon leveled off, and approximately half the sample had not reached conservation by ages 11 to 13.

With respect to *classification modes,* a Western child of 6 to 8 years usually makes groupings in terms of perceptible and concrete characteristics such as color and form. For instance, a peach and a potato may be grouped together because they are both round. As the child grows older he begins to employ abstract concepts using formal or functional criteria: peach, potato, meat, milk, air, and water may be grouped together because they are necessary to maintain life. Contrastingly, in a rural Mexican village, the classifying done by 12- to 13-year-olds remained at the same concrete level as that of the 6- to 8-year-old children (Maccoby & Modiano, 1966).

Concept attainment reaches increasingly complex levels as the Western child matures. Canadian children of 6 years were able to construct a diagonal by placing checkers in slots on a board (as a demonstration of acquisition of the concept of diagonality), whereas 4-year-olds made errors at the task. The children could recognize a diagonal at an earlier age than they could construct one. In East Africa, only a quarter of 6- and 7-year-olds from two traditional societies, the Kipsigis and the Logoli, could construct the diagonal, and the percentage of successful constructions rose to only 70% for 13-year-olds (Olson, 1970). Figure 5-2 shows three typical attempts.

The differences in performance between Western and non-Western peoples tend to persist into adulthood. The period of formal thought, the final stage in the Piagetian scheme, was not found in a sample of 14- to 16-year-old subjects in New Guinea (Dasen, 1972a). In a learning experiment, Ganda (Uganda) adults learned to sort by color, but those who had had less than four years of schooling failed to learn to sort by function (Evans & Segall, 1969). The Australian Aborigines studied by Porteus (1931) performed on the maze test at a level comparable to an IQ performance of 80.

Given the disadvantages under which traditional peoples operate in taking Western tests, one could adopt the position that performance is almost bound to be depressed and that comparisons are therefore meaningless. However, under certain conditions the quality of

Figure 5-2. A model diagonal and typical errors of reproduction made by Kenyan children.

performance is improved, and it is worth considering the nature of these modifying factors. Schooling, for example, typically brings results closer to Western norms, but only rarely does the non-Western performance equal that of Western children. For example: (1) in the Wolof investigation, even schooled children did not all exhibit conservation until ages 11 to 13; (2) in the Mexican rural village, the sample of children who used concrete modes of classification were all schoolgoers; and (3) the construction of diagonals in East Africa reached its peak among children who had gone to school for three or more years, but the success rate was still only around 80%.

Unsurprisingly, several groups have done well under conditions of urban life. Although the effects of urban cultural stimulation in non-Western societies usually are overridden by disruptive acculturation, the relatively old cities of Ibadan and Hong Kong are more stable. Yoruba children from the indigenous Nigerian city of Ibadan achieved conservation as early as Western children and made comparable Stanford-Binet IQ scores (Lloyd, 1971). Chinese children in Hong Kong, without schooling, mastered some conservation tasks at the same age as Western children (Goodnow, 1962). Similarly, the surpassing of Euro-American mathematics norms by Japanese schoolchildren (Husén, 1967) may be accounted for in part by Japan's extremely rapid modernization without drastic sociocultural disruption (also see Maccoby & Modiano, 1966). As an example of the obverse, only 20% of a sample of adults in rural Sardinia achieved conservation of volume (Peluffo, 1967)—a somewhat more difficult task than conservation of liquid, but one that nevertheless can be accomplished by Euro-Americans in most samples by the ages of 12 to 15 (Elkind, 1961; Piaget & Inhelder, 1941). Westerners of Sardinia, not exposed to urban life, are performing like members of a traditional society.

The use of familiar materials often effects sharp changes (Cole, Gay, Glick, & Sharp, 1971; Gay & Cole, 1967; Kagan, 1972; Okonji, 1971), but not in all cases (Greenfield, 1966; Lloyd, 1971). Probably the most telling example is a study of conservation tasks carried out with 6- to 9-year-old Mexican school children from pottery-making and nonpottery-making families (Price-Williams, Gordon, & Ramirez, 1969). Experience in the manipulation of clay should have given the children from pottery-making families an advantage in the conservation of substances, specifically in the conservation of clay. Two sets of findings emerged: (1) in a *town* where the tests were administered, the potters' children performed significantly better than the nonpotters' children on the conservation of substance (clay)—just as expected—but not on tests for conservation of liquid, weight, volume, or number; (2) in a *village* where the same tests were given, the potters' children were superior on all five conservation tasks. In the rural village setting, the experience with clay evidently gave the potters' children a large-scale advantage over others; that is, experience with one substance apparently generalized to experience with other substances and operations. But in the town, where overall experiences may have been more varied and complex, the daily exposure to the properties of clay was associated with superior conservation in that particular medium only.

Gains in performance can be expected under conditions like those discussed above. But there are two cases in which traditional individuals have virtually matched Western standards without the usual urban-modern facilitators (both samples were in fact nonliterate). The studies are especially valuable because the reasons for strong performance can be tentatively identified. The first case involves the Tiv of central Nigeria (Price-Williams, 1969). The number of Tiv children going to school was much smaller than the number of nonliterates, and the investigator deliberately chose a sample of nonschoolgoers between the ages of 5 and 8. Several conservation tasks were administered. The youngest groups were largely unsuccessful, but the second oldest group, children between 7 and 7½ years old, got about half the problems right, and the oldest nine children, who were between 7½ and 8, solved all the problems without difficulty. These last nine made only a single error among them when given seven tasks each. The successful children demonstrated their understanding by giving explanations in terms of the operations: "The experimenter had taken the glass and poured the earth into two other glasses—it must be the same"(Price-Williams, 1969, p. 207). It has been said that the child who has attained conservation sees a necessity in the correct answer and that, when he says the amounts are the same, there is an implicit "naturally" in his intonation (Brown, 1965). Price-Williams' (1969) description of the conserving Tiv children when asked for an explanation also conveys this attitude: "A great majority of them appeared as if the question demanded of them was one that only a European would ask" (p. 207).

But the most remarkable thing about the Tiv in this experiment was their intrusion into the testing situation. Instead of simply answering the questions as requested, they supported their conserving responses by spontaneously reversing the sequence of operations—picking up the containers and pouring the earth back into the original glasses to show that the quantity was the same. An active approach of this kind is known sometimes to improve performance on conservation tasks (Greenfield, 1966; Sonstroem, 1966), but the Tiv children were behaving in this fashion after having already given their conserving responses. They also were behaving this way without being told or encouraged to do so. The explanation may be simply that Price-Williams had achieved excellent *rapport* with his sample and that they felt relaxed enough with him to take such liberties, but a different line of evidence indicates that the Tiv were acting more or less normally—for them. If so, their unusual conservation performance and their active participation in the experiment might be meaningfully related.

The Tiv were one of 110 societies whose ethnographic reports were scored for child training in compliance and assertiveness (Barry, Bacon, & Child, 1967; Barry, Child, & Bacon, 1959). In this world sample, sub-Saharan Africa stands out because the emphasis on compliance is very marked and almost universal there (Doob, 1965; Munroe, Munroe, & LeVine, 1972). Observers have repeatedly remarked on the pervasive training in obedience and the strongly inculcated respect for authority (Fox, 1967; Gay & Cole, 1967; Klingelhofer, 1971; LeVine, 1963; B. Whiting & Whiting, 1971). The authority emphasis carries over from the home into the school setting, and the resulting unquestioning attitude has often been proposed as a block against understanding in school. The whole syndrome is illustrated in the experience of the Gays in Liberia:

> In one case a teacher in a nearby school told a child that insects have eight legs. This child (who worked in the Gay household) one day happened to bring an insect to Mrs. Gay. They discussed the fact that it had six legs, contrary to the teacher's remark. The child, with Mrs. Gay's encouragement, took the insect to school to show the teacher. The child was beaten for his efforts—and insects continued to have "eight legs." From the teacher's point of view, the important thing to learn was a set of words and respect for authority (Gay & Cole, 1967, p. 33).

Against the African background of emphasis on compliance training, the Tiv are unique. Their pressures toward compliance *(vis-à-vis* assertiveness) in socialization are lower than those for any other

African society. (The cross-cultural ratings are for males only; ratings for females are not available for the Tiv.) The correspondence between the push toward assertiveness in child training and the bold and accurate performance in the experiment is therefore probably more than coincidental. And, as adults, the Tiv are said to be extremely practical and of an independent turn of mind. The first European to be killed by a Tiv had been asked whether it was really true that all Europeans were immortal. When he said yes, it was true, the questioner took out an arrow, shot him on the spot, and said to those present: "I didn't really believe it" (Bohannan, 1965, p. 516). The common thread among the attributes of the Tiv is an unusual independence and assertiveness, with apparent effects in the cognitive sphere. Of course, the link between independence in behavior and cognitive functioning is weak and needs much more investigation. It is, however, a promising path to pursue.

Thus far cognitive activity has been discussed as if intelligence were a unitary variable and all measures could be treated as tapping identical processes. This approach has been due not to a theoretical stance on the issue but to a simple paucity of materials. Seldom are there multiple measures available to allow careful discrimination among types of cognitive processes. However, the second case of strong performance by a traditional people does allow a sorting of measures, which results in some useful distinctions.

There are many Eskimo groups, but all of them thus far tested share an impressive *spatial ability* (Berry, 1966; MacArthur, 1967; Vernon, 1969). Facility in spatial analysis means sorting out the components of the environment, separating an element from its context, and locating oneself accurately in relation to environmental features.

When a simple figure is hidden within a complex figure, many individuals have difficulty in finding it. A set of complicated designs of this sort (Figure 5-3), called the Embedded Figures Test (Witkin,

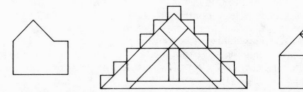

Figure 5-3. Items from the Embedded Figures Test. The simple figure on the left is located in each of the other two figures. From Individual differences in ease of perception of embedded figures, by H. A. Witkin, *Journal of Personality*, 1950, *19*, 4. Reprinted by permission.

Oltman, Raskin, & Karp, 1971), has been administered to various samples. Adults do better than children, males better than females, and Westerners better than non-Westerners—except the Eskimo.[3] A sample of 91 mostly nonliterate, adult Baffin Island Eskimo (70 with no schooling, 21 with an average of less than a half-grade) performed as well on the Embedded Figures Test as a Scottish sample with a mean education of ten years. They also performed unusually well on other spatial tests (Berry, 1966). High spatial test ability is not surprising for a people who have been noted to have "a remarkable memory for the details of their territory" and a proverbial accuracy in observing and mentally recording "the contours of the terrain" (Briggs, 1970, p. 34). Not only are the Eskimo able to find their way during hunts and nomadic moves and remember the many places where they may have cached food and supplies within a large territory, but they also demonstrate outstanding map-reading and map-making abilities (Briggs, 1970).

The Eskimo are not, however, some sort of non-Western intellectual superstars, since they do less well than other Amerindians on mental imagery tests and less well than Jamaicans on certain verbal tests (Vernon, 1969). The spatial development seems to be primarily a response to demands of the environment—demands not made in other areas of intellectual functioning. Traditionally hunters of seal, caribou, and fox, the Eskimo must range widely over a bleak environment to make their livelihood. In the long winter, land and sea merge into whiteness, while in the few weeks of summer the land takes on a uniform gray-brown tone from moss and lichen. The Eskimo inhabit a world of little visual stimulation (see Figure 5-4), and so it is probably necessary for survival that they learn spatial awareness—that is, knowledge about their "present location in relation to objects around them" (Berry, 1966, p. 212).

Eskimo individuals ought to develop spatial ability (and they do), but Berry (1966) carries the survival theory a step further. If the environmental situation makes specific psychological developments necessary, facilitating institutional adjustments should arise. Child-rearing practices, for example, might be expected to encourage the

[3]Witkin and his associates (Witkin, 1967; Witkin & Berry, in press; Witkin, Dyk, Faterson, Goodenough, & Karp, 1962; Witkin, Lewis, Hertzman, Machover, Meissner, & Wapner, 1954) have generated a large body of research on cognitive styles— "characteristic self-consistent modes of functioning found pervasively throughout an individual's cognitive, that is, perceptual and intellectual, activities" (Witkin, 1967, p. 234). The two major styles of cognitive functioning, labeled *field independence* (or *psychological differentiation*) and *field dependence*, have proved to be operative concepts in the cross-cultural setting (Berry, 1966; Dawson, 1967a, 1967b; Wober, 1966, 1967). The Eskimo, with their highly developed spatial ability, offer an unusual example of a strongly field-independent non-Western people.

Figure 5-4. Bleak environment inhabited by the Eskimo. Courtesy of the Flaherty Study Center, School of Theology at Claremont, California.

emergence of strong spatial ability. Accounts of child training from standard ethnographies and from adult recall are in agreement that the Eskimo grant a great deal of freedom to children and yet make the few rules clear and consistent. The Eskimo do *not* vacillate in early discipline or impose the highly restrictive rules which, in the West, sharply limit the development of good performance on the Embedded Figures

Test (Witkin et al., 1962). And in language, the Eskimo possess a set of sophisticated geometrical-spatial terms as well as an intricate system of obligatory "localizers" that aid in the location of objects in space. The ease of communication about space is thereby enhanced.

For the Eskimo, as for the Tiv, the antecedent and outcome variables are not clearly tied together, and many other factors might be responsible for the relationships discovered. Eskimo spatial ability may be directly a product of child rearing, or perhaps of the linguistic localizers and geometrical-spatial terms, and not a response to environmental imperatives. But the demands of the environment carry at least a logical priority and would seem to offer the most likely starting place for further research.[4]

A common and obvious principle is operating in the studies described in this section: convergence in learning environments produces convergence in cognitive skills. When traditional societies have long urban histories or when they begin to send their children to school or to modernize, their cognitive skills change in the direction of Western norms. When an African society, unlike its neighbors but like urban-industrial Western groups (Peterson & Migliorino, 1967), allows or trains its children to be assertive, the performance on cognitive tasks nearly rivals that of Westerners. When a society in the Arctic is confronted with a near-featureless environment and must necessarily breed spatial awareness, the performance on spatial tests reaches approximately Western levels. With findings like these before us, the question is not whether traditional peoples are capable of attaining Western levels but rather what can be learned from the performances that more typically occur. What factors in the Western environment and in the traditional environment produce the cognitive skills we usually see? The next section takes up this question.

Intellective Differences: Western and Traditional Societies

Traditional peoples, children, and mental patients used to be classed together because their thought modes were said to be similar, while peoples of the modern world were assigned to a separate and superior class (Lévy-Bruhl, 1966; Werner, 1948). We have seen in the above section that this categorical distinction is inappropriate because

[4]Berry (1974) has offered a similar analysis of Australian Aborigine spatial scores, which are higher than those of most traditional peoples, though not as high as those of the Eskimo.

(1) some Western groups (as in Sardinia) fail to demonstrate superior cognitive skills, and (2) samples from some traditional societies perform at a level comparable to those of Western samples. Further, no matter what the performance level, it is clear that "all culture groups thus far studied have demonstrated the capacity to remember, generalize, form concepts, operate with abstractions, and reason logically" (Scribner & Cole, 1973, p. 553). Yet, in a great number of cases there is still a difference—a quantitative instead of qualitative difference—and it needs explaining.

We may begin by considering modal tendencies in the overall learning environments of Western and traditional societies. In Western culture, systematization and structure are highly salient features, and the child is taught early in terms of this organization both at home and shortly thereafter in school. Labels, categories, terminologies, and classifications abound. Settlement patterns, transportation systems, business operations, technology—all physical aspects of the culture— are suffused with consciously imposed structure. Temporal organization is present too, as time is divided and scheduled and treated as a scarce resource. Even in sports and games, the emphasis on quantitative evaluation of performance is pervasive. Before long, the child has internalized a view of the world as a system and has begun to impose structure on problems he faces. Rule-seeking is a powerful problem-solving device in the Western world and, because of its success, eventually becomes a more or less automatic strategy. The tendency of children to engage in rule-seeking behavior increases as they get older (Neimark, Slotnick, & Ulrich, 1971). After five or six years of education, children exhibit significant semantic clustering of materials on the first trial in a recall task (Cole, Frankel, & Sharp, 1971). By high school age, the typical American student will mnemonically arrive at his own subjective organization even when materials are designed to avoid obvious semantic connections (Tulving, 1968). Cole et al. (1971) found that American schoolchildren would so persistently look for a particular unstated rule in problem solving that, even when conditions of the problem made taxonomic classification impossible, they would violate instructions in order to maintain such classification and thereby, of course, fail to solve the problem. In further experiments, Americans learned random classes of depicted objects very slowly because, rather than simply using memory to recall correct instances, they went to great lengths to discover a rule where there was none, in the meantime neglecting to learn the particular items themselves. But these failures are unusual, and rule-seeking behavior is more frequently successful and therefore rewarded.

As the child grows older, not only does he more often and more ably exhibit rule-seeking behavior, but the educational system supplies him with tools of greater power. Formal systems of symbols like mathematics and logic are applicable to any set of empirical materials and can even generate internal problems (for example, algebraic equations) that can be solved within the system itself. Additionally, the maturing individual now can apply his thinking to *possible* as well as *real* situations, and at this point the complex structure of theory building and hypothesis testing—that is, scientific thinking—becomes available to him (Inhelder & Piaget, 1958).

The situation in traditional societies is quite different. The child typically confronts a much less structured sociocultural environment, and also one that is less continually conceptualized and presented as such by the transmitters of the culture. Therefore, when the individual does learn an abstract concept or mode of classification, it is peculiar to that usage and is not easily generalizable to other contexts. The intensive work of Cole, Gay, and their associates (Cole et al., 1971; Cole & Scribner, 1974; Gay & Cole, 1967) on the Kpelle of Liberia makes this point clearly. The Kpelle have a pair of measurement units called the arm-span, used to measure things like rope or a bridge, and the hand-span, used to measure short objects such as cutlasses and hoe handles. When a group of Kpelle adults was asked to apply the hand-span unit to estimate 6- to 18-foot distances, for which the arm-span unit would have been culturally more appropriate, they made average errors of 40 to 90%, indicating that the different units of length were not interchangeable for them. American adults made much smaller errors on the same task because, according to self-reports, they translated the hand-span units into more familiar inches and feet.

There is in Kpelle thinking—and probably in traditional thought generally—a quality of *embeddedness* that makes cross-contextual applications difficult. Learned in one context, a concept or rule can be applied easily only in that context. The Kpelle showed greatly improved recall of items in a memory task when the items were placed in traditional-style folk stories. The stories provided the structure that ordinarily served to organize remembering, and the structure of recall matched the structure of the stories. But in other free-recall tasks for which no structure was provided, the Kpelle subjects who were nonliterate or in elementary school did not improve with practice and, significantly, did not create their own organizational structure. By high school, despite little home practice and a history of rote memorization techniques in school, Kpelle students would routinely impose a structure that enabled them to store and retrieve information. But difficulties arose when subjects were asked to learn new and arbitrary concepts. Nonliterate adults at times used approaches to problem solving that actually hindered their efforts. Often, even after individuals chose the correct response, therefore showing they had "attained" the concept, they could not verbalize the reasons for their choices. A request for a description of the concept was frequently disturbing to the subjects; they were able only to describe the particular stimulus in front of them and were unable to state a rule.

Certain linguistic characteristics help to reinforce context-bound thinking. Classification systems usually reflect the particular concerns of the culture but do not extend beyond these concerns. Rice is the staple food of the Kpelle and is of ceremonial importance as well. There are many terms for rice measurement that fit into a complex and internally coherent system, and Kpelle adults have been shown to be greatly superior to American adults in estimating measures of rice. But the system does not extend to other items; the Kpelle did not show general superiority in other measurement estimates. Thus the complex systems of concepts coded into linguistic form tend to be closely related to the sociocultural environment in which they are used and do not independently act to overcome the embeddedness of traditional thinking. In addition, the style of language used in child rearing typically works to support context-bound thought. Explicit verbal instruction is rarely given, so the child in traditional society learns by observation and subsequent imitation (Cazden & John, 1971; Fortes, 1970; Gay & Cole, 1967; Mead, 1964). This mode of learning binds both the content and the process to the context. Literacy would help to break this tight bond by promoting the noncontextual use of language. Schooling itself would give the child practice in using language outside a context in which his linguistic reference is supported by the structure of the situation (Bruner, 1966).

Inhelder and Piaget (1958) predicted that the highest level in the Piagetian scheme, that of formal operations, might not be reached by any individuals in some societies, and the cross-cultural data confirm the prediction. Insofar as the level of formal thought is dependent on generalized problem-solving skill, which is in turn built on the ability to dissociate the operations performed from the content of the problem—the very process that is so difficult for the context-bound individual—the Piagetian model and the present analysis are in agreement. But formal operations seems to be not so much a qualitatively different level of thought as a systematic application of the tools of mathematics, logic, and experimental method. When individuals do apply formal operational thought, it is usually under the specialized problem-solving conditions found in scientific, technological, or scholastic settings, and even then as many as half the subjects in American schoolgoing and adult samples do not successfully employ formal thought under standard test procedures (Elkind, 1961; Tomlinson-Keasey, 1972). A still smaller proportion of Western individuals think this way under ordinary conditions of life. This being so, and given that traditional peoples do not think in formal operational terms, it is probably inaccurate to propose that a relatively recent Western "invention" be treated as a discrete stage of thinking.[5] Perhaps we can say, however, that formal thought represents a heightening of the universal ability to use abstract concepts and that it reflects a highly polished skill at transferring conceptual abilities to all manner of situations.

What ultimately accounts for the contextual thought of traditional peoples? Probably it exists basically because of its survival value. In stable societies, context-bound thought is part of the adaptive fit between the individual and his total physical and sociocultural environments. Categories and processes of thought operate with what is immediately relevant—as culturally defined—and this is seldom knowledge for its own sake. A generalized orientation toward problem solving, the basis of which is the isolation of elements and systematic exploration of all possible solutions, is unlikely to arise. Rather, specific problems arise, and they are answered in terms of particularistic solutions. Even when these solutions happen to be highly abstract, they are not generalized to other situations in which they are unneeded.

In Western societies, by contrast, intellectual functioning operates to produce more and more flexible and general schemata. These too are adaptive, but in a different kind of world—one in which, since the Renaissance and especially since the beginning of the industrial age, rapid change has created a myriad of problems necessitating the evolution of new systems of thought. Problems were too many to be solved uniquely, and their very number meant that similarities among them had to be perceived and general solutions proposed if effective answers were to be found. All this became more likely to occur because the system fed upon itself, with the answers improving the standard of living and allowing specialization, which in turn produced indi-

---

[5]The same objection would seem to hold for any cognitive-developmental typology that at the highest level depends on a divorce between content and the operations performed. In Kohlberg's (1970) scheme of three levels of moral development, the third, or *postconventional,* level emerges when there is a major thrust toward "autonomous moral principles that have validity and application apart from the authority of the group of persons that hold them " (p. 110). The postconventional level is more or less dominant by age 16 in the U.S. samples Kohlberg (1969b) has tested, but among isolated villagers of the same age in Yucatan and Turkey and among Black Carib 16-year-olds of both town and village in British Honduras (Gorsuch & Barnes, 1973), the postconventional level is almost nowhere to be seen. One would expect to find few individuals in traditional societies who could solve moral problems independently of context.

viduals who had the time to focus and produce still more answers—and concomitant problems. For example, new machines were created first in response to problems of economics and war, but eventually the quest for structure became a goal in itself. And modern science and associated knowledge-building specialties were beneficiaries. It was only natural that the needs of the larger sociocultural system would generate methods of child training that would produce individuals cognitively capable of assimilating and competently entering this distinctive system, and indeed universal education in formal settings was a response to these needs.

The oft-discussed "difference-versus-deficit" issue centers around the question of whether Western and non-Western (or ethnic Western) intellectual divergences are due simply to separate but equal processes or rather to a fundamental inequality. The evidence indicates that in the process of development the typical child in a traditional society does not acquire the same wide range of applicability of abstract concepts as does the Western child. As long as each individual remains within his own society, his mode of approach is adequate and the difference is just that—a difference. However, when the traditional society is impinged upon by the processes of change, the smaller proportion of situations in which the traditionally reared individual can apply his abstracting ability means that the difference becomes, effectively, a deficit. It would not matter in traditional society if adults found learning to sort materials in several ways to be a highly difficult task, because such conditions would seldom, if ever, arise. But in the modern setting, the failure could be maladaptive. At one African university recently, the first-year science students, who were chosen from the elite of the nation's high school students (who themselves represented the top 10% of the grade school students), failed the first-year mathematics course at a 75 % rate. The great majority of these students had come from traditional backgrounds, and their poor performance was a reflection of the sharply cumulative nature of rule-seeking skills. Given comparatively little early practice in application of abstract concepts in broader and more numerous contexts, they were almost certain to have later difficulties in using the most powerful conceptual tools.

Intelligence, Race, and Genetics

The discussion to this point has assumed that experiential factors are responsible for group differences on tests of cognitive functioning. But since many individual talents and skills, including cognitive abilities, run in families and thus seem to be largely inherited (Erlenmeyer-Kimling & Jarvik, 1963), why should group abilities not be regarded in the same way? If two racial groups consistently differ, the difference might be due more to genetic than to environmental variables.

The genetic argument is an old one, but ideological and social considerations have rendered dispassionate examination of it quite difficult. The most comprehensive recent statement of the position has been made by Jensen (1969a, 1969b, 1973), an educational psychologist. Jensen's full statement cannot be elaborated here, but the elements most pertinent to cross-cultural materials can be briefly presented. First, in his view, IQ tests can be accepted as a universally valid measure of intelligence in Western society. Second, IQ scores are argued to be more the product of a stable factor like genetic inheritance than of the numerous and varied environmental conditions to which we are exposed, because, among other reasons, IQ scores are themselves stable—that is, relatively unchanging over time for individuals. Third, a genetic factor is proposed to explain the continuing existence, over 50 years of testing, of a 15-point average difference between Caucasoid and Negroid IQ scores. (The difference reduces to 11 points when gross socioeconomic factors are controlled.)

Although Jensen does take the position that the IQ test has applicability and validity everywhere, he also concedes that the scores of ethnic groups would be depressed by several factors. For example, 8 to 10 points are attributable to unfamiliarity with the test situation and another 5 to the effects of poor environment. Deutsch (1969) points out that when these are added together, Jensen seems to have destroyed his own argument. Nonetheless, the second and third points in the discussion should be considered.

IQ is indeed highly stable most of the time, as Jensen argues, but large changes do occur under certain conditions, and it is critical to Jensen's position that he readily explain them. He distinguishes between extreme environmental deprivation, which he agrees is capable of depressing intellectual development, and ordinary cultural disadvantagement, which he believes to be sufficiently stimulating and varied to allow the genotypic value of the IQ to emerge. By deprivation Jensen means strong early sensorimotor restrictions and social isolation. In contrast, typically disadvantaged children, he argues, are not subject to deprivation, and tests indicate that their early developmental level is normal. Further, the slight initial gain in IQ that they usually show after a few months of school attendance is counteracted in a sizable percentage of children by a gradual decline in IQ throughout the subsequent years of schooling. As they mature, their IQs are gravitating toward their hereditarily determined values. Environment therefore is said to act primarily as a threshold, and everybody gets beyond sub-threshold deprivation except some institutional cases and occasional children who have been reared abnormally.

One well-known study fails completely to fit this neat formulation. In 1930, over 3000 Tennessee mountain children between the ages of 6 and 16 were given IQ tests, and their overall mean was only 82. During the next 10 years, the introduction of federal and state programs resulted in great improvements in economic conditions, health-care standards, and educational opportunities. When children of the same age range were tested again in 1940, the average IQ had risen 10 points to 92 (Wheeler, 1970). This result seems to indicate a large and permanent rise, in a nondeprived group (Jensen's definition), under the control of environmental changes, but Jensen focuses on a different aspect of the findings—a downward gravitation from younger to older. In 1930 the 6-year-olds had attained a mean of 95, but older children showed decreasing IQs, and the 16-year-olds scored an average of only 74. The same trend appeared in 1940, with the drop going from 103 at age 6 to 80 at age 16. Jensen argues that the IQs in both cases were falling because the whites in the Tennessee mountains were a "below-average group," by which he presumably means genetically inferior. (The hills of Tennessee in the pre-World-War-II era harbored a Caucasoid population that was probably as close to pure Anglo-Saxon stock as we would be likely to find anywhere in the United States, but here it is curiously being labeled as hereditarily subnormal.)

By what reasoning does Jensen conclude that the 1940 6-year-olds who attained a mean IQ of 103 were "below average"? The position is untenable since he has himself insisted on the validity of IQ scores in the measurement of intelligence. But he attempts to maintain the argument by looking instead at the overall pattern of declining scores. Geneticists have pointed out, however, that the effects of environment rather than of heredity should become progressively patent with increasing age, and that a decline in IQ would seem to be evidence *against* genetic determinism (Cavalli-Sforza & Bodmer, 1971).

Data have shown that another, even more impressive, increase in IQ seems to have taken place among males from throughout the United States. When American soldiers in World War II were administered the same intelligence test that had been given to World War I soldiers, they scored a full 15 points higher (Tuddenham, 1948). The rise applied to both blacks and whites. According to Jensen, this large an increase should occur only under removal of extreme environmental deprivation, but he has already argued that natural environments are not deprivational.

The first two elements in Jensen's argument are weak, but the concluding point, that the difference between Caucasoids and Negroids is probably of genetic origin, could be valid if the IQ discrepancy held up under strong environmental variations. Jensen (1969b) and Eysenck (1971) have cited a study disclosing that Australian Aborigines with ⅛ to ¼ Caucasoid ancestry were superior to pure Aborigines on several Piagetian conservation tasks (de Lemos, 1969). The finding seems to corroborate the idea of white mental superiority, but no such conclusion can be drawn if the following points are considered: (1) a reanalysis of the data brings the original findings into severe question (Vetta, 1972); (2) an attempt at replication, using Aborigines with even greater proportions of Caucasoid ancestry than in the original study, failed to produce any findings (Dasen, 1972b); (3) Aborigine children adopted at an early age by Australian white families were cognitively advanced over all groups in the original study and were almost identical to middle-class European children (Dasen, 1972b); (4) recent testing of Aborigine schoolchildren on the Porteus Mazes yielded a mean of 109 (David, 1967). The original finding does not seem very reliable.

In individuals of mixed racial parentage, it should not matter to the genetic hypothesis which parent is Negroid and which Caucasoid. But in a sample of hybrids with one white and one black parent, children with white mothers had higher IQs than those with black mothers (Willerman, Naylor, & Myrianthopoulos, 1970). Since the mother is more involved than the father with the socialization of the child, the evidence points toward early experience, not genetics, as the critical influence on intelligence. Similarly, among 4-year-old black, white, and hybrid children who had been reared identically in residential nurseries of high quality, IQ scores were slightly above 100 and did not differ by race (Tizard, 1974).

Other environmental variations also strongly influence scores. The typical IQ difference between urban and rural children is 10 points (Anastasi, 1958)—that is, a full ⅔ as much as the Caucasoid-Negroid discrepancy. The amenities of city life are surely sufficient to account for the urban-rural difference that has appeared in many countries (Chopra, 1968), though genetically oriented theorists undoubtedly could posit a selective-migration hypothesis (that is, the "better elements" regularly leave the farms for the city). However, a genetic hypothesis could not handle the intellectual sex difference among the East Indian Alorese (Chapter Three), in which, on the Porteus Mazes, the men scored 30 points higher than the women and were so close to

Western norms that Porteus confessed he was surprised at the high level of their performance. Du Bois (1944) cogently noted that the constant financial transactions of the Alorese males might be responsible for their superior abilities.

Under poor environmental conditions, Caucasoids can perform abominably. A group of English children who grew up on canal boats and attended school only 5% of the time attained a mean IQ of 70 (Gordon, 1970). In Appalachia, of 20 physically disabled miners, 17 could not calculate 8 times 9 or subtract 9 from 23 (Inkeles, 1966). If these are seen as "below-average" Caucasoids, the same could not be said of the Caucasoid Gypsies of England, who are not at the bottom of the system but, by choice, outside it and who certainly get all the freedom to interact and to "run about out-of-doors" that Jensen feels is enough to produce normal intellectual development. Yet their IQ level is 75. More to the point than their genetic inheritance are their seminomadic existence and their poverty (Gordon, 1970). And finally, what is to be said of the Irish, whose IQ level falls 15 points below that of the English—just as the IQ level of blacks falls 15 points below that of whites in the United States? Eysenck (1971) has sidestepped the problem by assuming that the more intelligent Irish have emigrated. But, as Willerman (1973) has pointed out, for that conjecture to be valid, the top 62% of the Irish population in the last generation would have had to leave for other parts—a brain drain of legendary proportions and of mythical unlikelihood.

Under improved environmental conditions, Negroes do show better performance. In Ontario Province, Canada, where discrimination is not so harsh as in the United States, rural Negro students attained a mean IQ score of 93. Although blacks and whites attended the same schools, social equality had still not been achieved. The attendance of the blacks was less regular, and there were socioeconomic differences between the groups (Tanser, 1939).

As important as socioeconomic factors are, they are not the whole story. Lower-class black mothers in the United States use a response style, termed "relational-contextual," that is characterized by three elements: relatively little reflection, little attention to detail, and *little evaluation of alternatives* (Hess & Shipman, 1965). The last characteristic parallels very suggestively the problem-solving approach used in traditional societies. The style implies a kind of particularism in which communication tends to take place along concrete personal lines (Bernstein, 1971). Four-year-old children of these mothers also used much the same types of response, suggesting that they had already learned the pattern. Further, a relative paucity of verbal interaction meant that the children would not easily develop the verbal facility typical of the middle-class child. An extreme form of this kind of training was seen in a rural Louisiana community in which speaking by children was automatically labeled "bad" (the less said the better) and resulted in a 28-month-old child's uttering a total of four different words in four months of frequent taping by an ethnographer (Ward, 1971). In dramatic contrast, an upper-middle-class child of comparable age uttered more than 400 words in one taping (Brown & Frazer, 1963). But again, as with non-Western children, it must not be supposed that abstract or complex thought is lacking. Labov (1969) has shown that young blacks who would be assessed as linguistically impoverished and academically unpromising can enter conversations in a way that demonstrates their linguistic competence and their ability to use clever arguments.

Sometimes, however, the socialization practices that produce these cognitive styles are themselves subjected to the scrutiny of the genetic hypothesis. If parents are turning out children who may have abstracting abilities but who can apply them only in a limited range of situations, it may be partly because the parents are genetically capable of only limited socialization techniques. Jensen (1969a) asks if a parent's genotype does not to some extent affect the environment of his or her children. The implication is that genetically superior parents will inevitably adopt optimal socialization practices and will create the best possible environments. And since Caucasoids are thought to be genetically superior to Negroes as a group, they will make better environments. But how can we thus account for the many environmental fluctuations in the West—the torpor of the Dark Ages sandwiched between the Classical Period and the Renaissance, the march of the Renaissance from southern to northern Europe, the cultural rise and fall of peoples like the early-colonial Dutch and Spanish? Were not some of these environments rich, then deprived, then rich again, all within a single gene pool?

A genetic argument ought to be based on genetic data, and these Jensen has not supplied. His attempts to show the weaknesses in environmental explanations have been faulted at a number of points. Furthermore, although race and learning ability may someday prove to be biologically linked, it is well to remember that dominant groups commonly and easily arrive at the conclusion that they are superior because they were made that way. The Romans felt the Germanic peoples to be incapable of higher civilization. And Cicero said, "Do not obtain your slaves from the Britons, for the Britons are so stupid and so dull that they are not fit to be slaves" (Hoebel, 1949, p. 92). The 19th century, dominated by Britannia, would have seen fit to take issue with Cicero.

Early infant test scores indicate accelerated developmental levels for non-Western infants. The accelerated development appears to be as attributable to environmental factors as to genetic factors, until a more exhaustive analysis of the influence of prenatal events is pursued. After 2 years of age, non-Western infants begin to lose the developmental advantage: a severe and rapid decline from near-optimal early conditions may be a possible explanation. Little is known about cognitive development in traditional society from the end of infancy to the age of 5 or 6. But for older children, Western test results obtained from non-Western groups show less capable performances in the tested areas of conservation, classification modes, and concept attainment. Tests with adults give much the same results. Typically, urbanization and schooling improve performance on these tasks, as do particular environmental features and child-rearing variations that encourage assertive behavior. Better performances also often result from modification of tasks to approximate the real experience of children in societies tested. Context-bound thought appears to be adaptive for traditional societies and is encouraged by communication style, expectations, and task demands. In cognition, as in other features of development, genetic transmission undoubtedly plays a role, but it appears unlikely that it can explain the ethnic differences obtained throughout the world.

Three Cultures

When reading about traditional societies, we sometimes are apt to confuse culturally held beliefs with individual cognitive processes. The Trobrianders believe that two sons will resemble their father, but they also believe that the brothers cannot resemble each other. The ethnographer Malinowski (1929) once was struck by the resemblance between one of his friends and a newly arrived apparent stranger, and when he inquired and found that the stranger was actually his friend's elder brother, he said: "Ah, truly! I asked about you because your face is alike—alike to that of Moradeda" (p. 205). His statement was greeted by such a hush that he was startled. The stranger turned and left, and part of the company that was present soon dispersed after averting their faces in a half-offended, half-embarrassed manner. Malinowski had committed a breach of custom. Because the Trobrianders believe that brothers cannot be physically similar to one another, are they incapable of following a logical argument? If we say that a son, A, resembles his father, F, we are saying that a large proportion of the characteristics used to describe A are also used to describe F. If we further say that son B resembles the same father, F, we are saying that a large proportion of the characteristics used to describe B are used to describe F. Consequently, son A and son B will almost certainly share some characteristics if many Trobriander families are considered. We are therefore entitled to conclude that son A and son B will at least sometimes resemble each other. But the Trobrianders argue that they do not and they cannot. Malinowski (1929) contends, however, that the Trobrianders are only behaving as we often do under the pressure of maintaining our values:

> A Trobriander is simply irritated and insulted if striking instances [of brother resemblance] are pointed out to him, in exactly the same way as, in our own society, we irritate our next-door neighbour by bringing before him a glaring truth which contradicts some cherished opinion, political, religious, or moral . . . [p. 206].

We recall from Chapter One that the Trobrianders also believe no connection exists between sexual intercourse and pregnancy. One writer (Freund, 1965) has called this an instance of exceptional dull-wittedness. But consider Trobriander reasoning on this subject. They cited to Malinowski an old, unmarried woman, almost an idiot, who in youth had been notorious for her hideousness, repulsive face, and deformed body. The Trobrianders argued the impossibility of anyone's being her lover—and then pointed out the fact that she had had a child.

The belief about pregnancy happens to be empirically at variance with Western scientific knowledge, but the members of the culture applied rigorous logic in order to defend it. In the case of their refusal to acknowledge physiognomic similarity between brothers, there was indeed a lapse of logic. But the problem must be seen in terms of a culturally sensitive belief that was passionately defended and not as a general weakness in reasoning ability. We can see a comparable lack of logical consistency in the Christian doctrine of the trinity, in which somehow the one Godhead is also three persons—Father, Son, and Holy Ghost. We might conclude that individual Christians are incapable of following the argument: 3 is greater than 1; therefore, 3 does not equal 1. In both instances, however, the cultural premise fails to tell us about the level of reasoning at which individuals usually operate.

Neither the Ainu nor the Trobrianders nor the Gusii have special environmental features, such as were described for the Eskimo, that would necessitate hyperdevelopment of some particular aspect of cognitive functioning. As far as the other suggested indigenous factor of importance is concerned—the training of children in general *assertiveness* (as was typical of the Nigerian Tiv)—both the Ainu and the Gusii strongly emphasize *compliance* in their socialization practices (Barry, Bacon, & Child, 1967; LeVine & LeVine, 1963) and therefore do not differ from most traditional groups on this dimension. The Trobrianders, however, display socialization pressures for assertiveness that more or less equal those of the Tiv (the ratings for the Trobrianders are incomplete and thus not fully interpretable) (Barry et al., 1967). But because no program of testing the cognitive-developmental skills of traditional Trobrianders has been carried out, there is no way to discover whether their level of functioning is particularly high.

In none of the three tribal societies is there any specialized educational institution, and the development of cognitive skills therefore takes place largely in informal, everyday settings, without explicit instruction. Trobriander children have great freedom and spend much of their time together in play, forming what Malinowski calls the "children's republic." The child nonetheless works with his parents and is taught to garden properly. As a boy grows older he comes under the influence of his maternal uncle, who teaches him arts, crafts, and magic and passes traditions on to him. A girl enjoys a period of personal freedom at the beginning of puberty and then, in later adolescence, takes on domestic duties at home. What the Trobriander child is directly taught seems to be mostly technical skills, the major exception being the traditions—the tribal laws and prohibitions, and the myths and legends of the clan—that a boy learns from his mother's brother. Only in this latter area, wherein memory skills are emphasized, do the Trobrianders orient the young (and only males at that) toward a heightening of cognitive-developmental attainments. For the Ainu, it is much the same except that there is less early freedom; both boys and girls are instructed in economic duties and by age 5 or 6 are introduced to a kind of on-the-job training in their respective sex-role tasks. Again, memory skills are heightened as children are taught traditions and are told folk stories and cautionary tales, and the most capable grandson is chosen to assimilate the ancestral history. Gusii children are the most restricted of all and are inducted into economic activities as soon as their capacities allow. As they grow older, they participate ever more fully in the subsistence pattern. At initiation, both sexes engage in rituals, and boys undergo hazing and are exposed to secrets associated with their rites. The initiation experience thus represents a formal teaching situation, but it lasts only about a month and even for boys is concerned only with the ingraining of specific moral lessons about respect and avoidance rules. For girls, the rites have a sexual theme and do not involve any direct instruction. So for the Gusii, as well as for the Ainu and the Trobrianders, there is little in the way of a conscious effort to stimulate cognitive development.

The situation in the three traditional societies can be contrasted with the Western system, in which a child spends upward of 20% of his waking time between the ages of 6 and 18 in school. A good part of Western schooling emphasizes the three Rs, and the resulting facility in verbal and quantitative expression yields, in the long run, an individual who has acquired the requisite tools for developing a generalized problem-solving orientation. Prior to beginning school, the Western child has already been exposed to a highly systematized world, which he must apprehend if he is to thrive. In recent years, of course, the incursion of the modern world into traditional societies has brought the schoolroom with it, and the Trobrianders, Gusii, and Ainu now attend school regularly. For example, only 3% of the children in a Gusii community of 208 people attended school in 1956 (LeVine & LeVine, 1963), but by 1970 the figure had risen to almost 90%. As traditional societies adopt educational systems that are essentially like those found elsewhere, we may expect that the educated products of those systems will grow increasingly alike and that the cognitive skills of different groups will show more and more convergence. For instance, toward the end of the 19th century the Ainu resisted the first attempts of the Japanese government to educate them, and parents often "kidnapped" their children from boarding schools (Hilger, 1971). But eventually they came to accept formal education. By the 1930s, when the Porteus Mazes were administered to a sample of Ainu, compulsory universal education was in effect, and the schoolgoers attained a mean score of 103 (Porteus, 1937). Contrastingly, a sample of Ainu adults, some of whom probably had not been educated or had been only minimally exposed to formal education (this information was not supplied in the report), attained a mean score of only 92. Although comparable data are not available for the Trobrianders and the Gusii, a similar convergence can be expected.

The educational difficulties experienced by members of minority groups in the United States make it apparent that the foregoing presentation is vastly oversimplified, that—as noted in the body of the chapter—cognitive convergence does not follow automatically with the appearance of classrooms and teachers, and that many other sociocultural factors will influence the outcomes. The purpose of this section was to delineate general trends, not to specify the precise route that cognitive change will take.

Chapter Six

Dependence, Aggression, and Sex

All mammals conspicuously display dependence, aggression, and sex, but only sexuality can confidently be said to have an innate basis. Dependence and aggression arise unavoidably in the course of mammalian social life, and they may or may not have a genetic component. Dependence is a necessary part of early life because the newborn's survival is contingent upon nurturance from an older member of the species. As for aggression, no fully harmonious society exists, and, among the various outcomes of discord, some aggressive behavior can always be found. In human societies each of the three behavior systems appears early, each is rewarded at least part of the time, and each is subjected to a careful cultural channeling that specifies under what circumstances and with whom one can be dependent, aggressive, or sexy.

For Western children there are detailed investigations of dependence, aggression, and sex[1] (reviewed in Zigler & Child, 1969). But for the non-Western world very few individual-level data exist on these behavior systems. What are available instead are studies using the cross-cultural method (see the Introduction), in which indirect measures of personality have been employed. Nevertheless, we can ask whether the overall thrust of work using this method leads to the same general conclusions as the Western findings.

The discussion will not dwell on the levels of dependent, aggressive, and sexual behavior that are produced in the West on the one hand and in traditional societies on the other. For all three types of behavior, American children, at least, appear to fall within the range exhibited by children of traditional societies around the world (Whiting & Child, 1953), and comparison on this basis does not seem profitable.

[1] Data on sex are obtained largely from retrospective accounts in adulthood.

Dependence

Reliance on others for help or for nurturance, though decreasing rapidly after infancy, persists throughout the entire period of the child's socialization. This reliance, taken together with the social learning necessary for normal development of affect, language, and cognition, suggests that a dependence motive cannot be either avoided or easily extinguished. The Western research literature on children generally shows, then, not only that reinforcement and overprotection increase the number of dependent responses but that deprivation (withdrawal of nurturance or the absence of adult social reinforcement) also leads to greater dependence (Zigler & Child, 1969). It is possible to reduce dependent behavior through active punishment, but punishment evidently serves only to arouse anxiety and thus inhibit overt dependency responses without diminishing dependent tendencies.

How do the major cross-cultural findings on dependence fit the Western literature? The strongest and most consistent relationships stem from the severity of training imposed on the young child as he is required to give up his initial infant dependence tendencies. Since most of the training consists of techniques of punishment (Whiting & Child, 1953), the findings relate to the point made above for the West—that punishment inhibits overt dependence but probably increases anxiety and leaves dependent tendencies undiminished. Societies with severe socialization of dependence frequently attribute illness to the work of powerful supernatural beings (through soul loss, whereby the soul leaves the body to commune with spirits, or spirit possession, when a spirit enters the body). In either soul loss or spirit possession, the welfare of the patient depends on a powerful "other." Early severe socialization of dependence is also present in societies in which sick adults are *not* permitted to be dependent on others during therapy (Whiting & Child, 1953). The latter custom is instructive. Serious illness often induces regression to a childlike level of dependence (eating, elimination, or simple tasks can all become major problems), and it is the very societies with severe dependence socialization that do not let sick adults indulge in this sort of regression. Their therapeutic practices involve isolating the patient from others or removing him from his home. Thus childhood punishment for dependence is associated in adulthood both with apparent dependence anxiety and with avoidance of the opportunity to exhibit childlike dependent behavior. A sign that strong dependent tendencies still lurk among adults in such societies is the fact that their religious systems emphasize obedience to the gods and the performance of propitiatory ritual (Spiro & D'Andrade, 1958), which may be interpreted as fantasy gratification of dependence wishes. But how convincing are these associations? It sounds believable that if the children in a society are punished for dependence they will as adults evolve customs consistent with and expressive of their dependence concerns. Yet the jump is great from that statement to the proposition: *severe dependence socialization leads to therapy practices that isolate the patient from other people*. The many assumptions in a proposition like this are admittedly too numerous and too little supported (Danziger, 1971), but a general congruence does seem to emerge between Western and cross-cultural research concerning early punishment for dependence and the development of later anxiety as a result. At the same time, the cross-cultural literature does not resolve the question of whether positive reinforcement and deprivation strengthen dependence responses, as the Western research tends to show.

Aggression

Two general points can be made about aggressive behavior and its genesis. First, the odds are good that some of the variance in aggression is attributable to biophysical factors, including innate ones. For example, the ease of eliciting aggression varies among breeds of dogs, and appropriate electrical stimulation of the brain in many infrahuman species produces aggressive responses like hissing and growling when enemies are present (Zigler & Child, 1969). Western children who are highly active also are consistently more aggressive than low-activity children (Patterson, Littman, & Bricker, 1967), and, cross-culturally, boys in the Six Cultures Study engage in aggressive behavior more often than girls (B. Whiting & Edwards, 1973)—both trends indicating possible biophysical determinants. In a sample of Peruvian Qolla, who manifest extremely high rates of homicide and violence despite explicit cultural condemnation of aggression, the incidence of low blood-glucose levels (hypoglycemia) was beyond 50%. These low levels marked the most aggressive individuals in the community (Bolton, 1973). The precise mechanisms involved in mediating between glucose levels and aggressiveness are not known at this time, but again biophysical variables need to be taken into account.

The second point is that the classical frustration-aggression hypothesis has turned out to be a highly oversimplified version of a complex relationship, which perhaps ought now to be understood as "a statement of how people become aroused or activated for *potential* aggressive activities. . ." (Geen, 1972, p. 21) (emphasis added). In other words aggression frequently follows frustration but sometimes does not, and the external conditions become all important in determining whether aggression occurs.

Positive reinforcement and permissive conditions clearly increase overt aggressive behavior both under experimental conditions and in natural settings. Western studies of family life indicate that parents who encourage aggression have children who aggress (Bandura & Walters, 1959, 1963). The anthropological literature abounds with societies that value and reward aggression and produce highly aggressive adults (for example, Chagnon, 1968).

Aggressiveness also regularly results from punitive socialization, according to Western research. Punitiveness toward children can take the form of hostile treatment or physical punishment for aggression or shouting and verbal threats, but for each the outcome is more rather than less aggression (Zigler & Child, 1969). (Highly permissive child rearing, as opposed to restrictive child rearing, also yields aggressive behavior but not when combined with warmth.) The strongest cross-cultural findings for aggression, as with dependence, are based on this same broad factor—effects of punishment. Societies with severe socialization for aggression have the following adult customs: a belief that aggressive behavior is a cause of illness; a belief that one's self is a cause of illness; a strong fear of others, as expressed in fears of the ghosts of the dead and the belief that sorcerers commonly cause illness (Whiting, 1959b; Whiting & Child, 1953); and a high intensity of aggression in folktales (Wright, 1954). All this seems to have a different emphasis from that of Western findings. For the cross-cultural data, these customs sound more like anxiety about aggression than actual aggressive behavior. And it happens that this severe socialization for aggression occurs in societies with extended-family households—that is, households with large numbers of individuals living under one roof (Table 6-1) (Whiting, 1959a). This suggests that "the expression of aggression cannot be tolerated in circumstances where so many people are living in such crowded quarters" (Harrington & Whiting, 1972, p. 481). This is sometimes called chronic cabin fever.

A discrepancy has arisen. Taken as a whole, the cross-cultural findings imply that aggression must be controlled under conditions of high density, that control is achieved by punishing aggression as it appears in children, and that the long-range effects of punishment are high anxiety about aggression—and, inferentially, low aggressivity in actual behavior. But the Western findings, on the other hand, indicate that a punitive upbringing leads to high, not low, aggression. The issue has been clarified by the recently completed analysis of behavioral

Table 6-1.   Household types and severity of socialization for aggression*

Household Types	Socialization Aggression Severity	
	Societies above the Median	Societies below the Median
Extended	Hopi Jivaro Lepcha Maori Papago Samoans Tenino Yakut Zuni	 Ontong-Javanese
All Others: Nuclear, Mother- child, Polygynous, Miscellaneous	Ainu Alorese Arapesh Ashanti Azande Chamorro Chiricahua Dahomeans Dobuans Kiwai Kutenai Omaha Paiute Palaung Rwala Slave Tanala Taos Teton Western Apache	Abipone Andamanese Baiga Balinese Chagga Chenchu Comanche Dusun Ifugao Kurtatchi Lakher Lamba Lesu Manus Marquesans Marshallese Masai Murngin Navaho Pukapukans Siriono Thonga Tikopia Tiv Trobrianders Wogeo Yagua Yungar

Nine of ten societies (90%) with extended households are severe in their training of child aggression, whereas only 20 of 48 societies (42%) with other household types are severe in socialization of aggression. The finding is unlikely to have occurred by chance ($p < .01$, Fisher exact test).

*The household typology and coding are taken from Murdock (1957b). Extended households include the small extended ("lineal") and minimal extended ("stem") as well as large extended categories of Murdock. The scores on socialization of aggression are taken from Whiting and Child (1953).

observations from the Six Cultures Study,[2] one of the very few non-Western sources of quantified individual-level data on aggression (B. Whiting & Whiting, 1975). The primary domestic unit in three of the societies was the extended family and in the other three the nuclear family. Children from the extended-family societies displayed *more* aggression, not less. The finding runs counter to expectations generated by previous cross-cultural work. Given the further fact that mothers of aggressive children expressed highly negative attitudes toward aggression, it is apparent that the Western link between punitive training and child aggressivity is upheld in the Six Cultures Study. It is also apparent that the earlier cross-cultural findings need reexamination. The extended family not only treats aggression harshly but also breeds aggression. Is this because, as first assumed, high density cannot easily tolerate aggression and punishes it on appearance, but the high density is stressful and produces aggression anyway? Or is it because high density cannot tolerate aggression and punishes it, and then the punishment produces aggression? Or is it perhaps because the density first produces the aggression, and the punishment is a reaction to it? In the last case the causal sequence would be reversed, and some of the Western research would then need reinterpretation as well (see also Hart, 1957). The answer is not forthcoming with present knowledge, but the discrepancy between Western and cross-cultural findings is overcome.

Sex

Human sexual behavior is marked by several unusual features. Although "unlearned," sex differs from hunger and other primary drives in that it is not necessary to the survival of the individual. The difference may be basic enough to bring sex under the control of somewhat distinct behavioral laws (Beach, 1956). Certainly the role of experience is immense, allowing as it does great modification in the forms of expression and satisfaction of the drive (Ford & Beach, 1951). Sexual arousal, for instance, is often caused by symbolic stimuli far removed from the immediate and the physical (Zigler & Child, 1969). As an example of cultural variation in expression, the Yapese position for intercourse is said to be so strange by our standards (see Three Cultures section) that probably not even the most experimentally

[2]The study involved ethnographic coverage of socialization (B. Whiting, 1963), mother interviews (Minturn & Lambert, 1964), and systematic behavioral observations of children aged 3 to 11 (B. Whiting & Whiting, 1975). The findings in the Six Cultures Study are a complex mix of both cultural comparisons and individual differences, which for lack of space cannot be considered separately in this discussion.

minded American couple has ever hit upon it (Murdock, 1957a). Related to this variability are the vast numbers and types of rules and inhibitory controls surrounding sex. They include restrictions on the woman during menstruation, limits on sexual activity outside the marriage relationship, sexual modesty in clothing and speech, and a preference for privacy (Stephens, 1972). Some of these restrictions are observed almost everywhere. Given the variety of expression and the great influence of experience, it is not surprising that certain nonsexual variables have an indirect but powerful effect on sex. For example, there are class differences in sexual behavior in the United States, and socially mobile American males adopt sex patterns appropriate to their new status prior to the actual class change (Kinsey, Pomeroy, & Martin, 1948). Additionally, a finding from primate research suggests a link between an early relationship with the mother and later development of normal sexual behavior. Deprivation of the macaque infant's early dependence on the mother resulted in either abnormal sexual behavior (for example, inappropriate mating attempts) or lack of participation in sexual activity (Harlow, 1962).

Moral strictures in the West prevent direct inquiry into childhood sexuality and sex training. Most studies have therefore relied on less-than-satisfactory *recall* methods of inquiry. The limited evidence available supports the role of direct positive reinforcement in sexual activity (aside from the reinforcing value of sex itself) and the inhibiting and anxiety-producing effects of parents' sexual anxiety (Zigler & Child, 1969). Cross-culturally, as with dependence and aggression, most of the findings involve the effects of severity of training, but there is one almost startling relationship concerning positive reinforcement. The assumption usually made about obscenity and sexual humor is that they signify guilt over tabooed impulses and resentment at sexual restrictions, but a cross-cultural survey suggests just the opposite (Stephens, 1972). The tribes that are sexually most free—exhibiting little modesty and few taboos—are enormously preoccupied with sex, constantly talking about it, making jokes about it, and finding it intrinsically funny. The Lepchas of Sikkim are a case in point: "For the Lepchas . . . sexual activity is practically divorced from emotion; it is a pleasant and amusing experience, and as much a necessity as food and drink; and like food and drink it does not matter from whom you receive it, as long as you get it" (Gorer, 1938, p. 170). The mere mention of sex is said to be funny. "I found this continual harping on the humorous aspects of sexual physiology puzzling, since most Lepchas have a full and adequate sex life, and face sex extremely simply, without guilt or secrecy" (Gorer, 1938, p. 262).

Severe sex training, consisting primarily of punishment for sexual activity, is related cross-culturally to numerous adult customs that could be seen as manifestations of sex anxiety: therapeutic practices that include abstention from intercourse (Whiting & Child, 1953); restrictions and concerns over sexual matters, including prohibitions on premarital intercourse, lengthy sex taboos during pregnancy, and the use of love magic (Ayres, 1967; Shirley & Romney, 1962; Stephens, 1962); homosexuality (Minturn, Grosse, & Haider, 1969); and the belief that sorcerers commonly cause illness (Whiting & Child, 1953). This last finding is interpretable in Freudian terms as indicative of paranoid, and hence sexual, anxiety but complicated by the fact that sorcery-caused illness is associated with severe aggression training (preceding section) as well as severe sex training (Whiting, 1959b). The thread of consistency between Western and cross-cultural research on sex socialization and adult sexual patterns is a positive sign, but the overall Western findings are too few to supply a base of confidence.

The existence of the familial incest taboo in all human societies inevitably raises questions about innateness, but anthropologists have assumed the taboo to be culturally determined. In several major theories of society the taboo is considered the key to understanding culture. Freud (1913) held that culture began when ancient men atoned for an act of patricide by renouncing forever the women of the group. Lévi-Strauss (1969) argued that man became a cultural animal when he initiated reciprocal exchange of women, the most valuable resource. The exchange provides a compelling reason for cooperation among neighboring groups and makes the incest taboo, in this reasoning, a by-product of balanced trade.

Might the incest taboo be a response to the deleterious effects of inbreeding? Until recently, this suggestion could be considered unlikely because successful inbreeding is possible for some animal strains and because a significant proportion of human societies practice without apparent penalty a mild form of inbreeding in the custom of first-cousin marriage. Recent research on very close inbreeding, however, does lend some support to the interpretation of the taboo as being universal because inbreeding is dangerous to species survival. Close intrafamilial breeding has now been shown to produce a marked increase in lethal effects and abnormalities due to homozygosity of defective genes. The most dramatic findings come from a comparison of 161 Czechoslovakian children of incestuous unions with 95 children born of the same women but of nonincestuous unions (Seemanova, 1971). The half-siblings of the incestuous offspring formed a control group. In the nonincest group, there were five early deaths and four physical abnormalities, whereas the children of incestuous unions suffered 15 deaths and a 40% incidence of abnormalities, including severe mental retardation, dwarfism, and heart and brain deformities. Thus a sound biological basis exists for the incest taboo. The means by which the taboo is continued—genetic or cultural—is, however, not known.

But what role is played by the observed inclination of unrelated individuals not to mate when brought up together? In the kibbutzim of Israel, children raised in the same nursery have no sexual interest among themselves and do not marry one another—despite the absence of prohibitions (Spiro, 1958; Talmon, 1964). When Chinese parents arrange a marriage for a son, if the future daughter-in-law is brought as a young girl to be raised at home with the son, the probability greatly increases that the relationship will be marked by adultery (for both husband and wife), relatively few children, and attempts by both the son and his bride-to-be to break the marriage commitment prior to the consummation (Wolf, 1966, 1970). The kibbutz and Chinese cases may reflect the operation of a biological tendency to develop sexual inhibition given extended and close contact during the period of sexual immaturity (Burton, 1973). This hypothetical inhibition would presumably also affect the sexually mature who are in contact with immature individuals, as among the rhesus monkeys that avoid mother-son copulation (Sade, 1968). Due to the existence of the family in almost all societies, this "revulsion" would be mutually developed in the parent-child and sibling-sibling relationships rather than between nonrelatives and, in the normal case, would suffice to prevent intrafamilial breeding. The aversion can be viewed as an evolved adaptive mechanism, and the incest taboo is then interpretable as a safety device, or a rule imposed to help shore up inhibitory tendencies that are strong but hardly inviolable. The interpretation set forth here, based on Burton (1973), differs sharply from most others but represents an attempt to integrate three lines of empirical observation—the universal taboo against intrafamilial breeding, the biological effects of such breeding, and the aversion to sexual union created by long and close childhood association.

Freud was convinced that the intimacy of the early parent-child relationship, particularly that of mother and son, led not to aversion but to strong incestuous wishes that were later repressed. Under conditions of intensive and prolonged contact it may be that the inhibitory tendencies are overcome.[3] Were this so, the incest taboo, despite its strength, might be insufficient of itself to prevent sexual relations between parent and child. A provocative piece of cross-cultural evidence supporting this idea is that in many societies with extended households or nuclear households the male children are allowed to stay at home until marriage, but, in societies with mother-child households—the mother and her children living together, and the father sleeping and eating elsewhere—the male children are always required to leave the maternal house by the age of puberty (Stephens, 1962). The long years of mother-son intimacy are evidently countered with an institutional arrangement that separates the two physically before the son reaches sexual maturity. If the general point is valid that conditions of extreme closeness between parent and child can cause potential problems for the smooth functioning of incest regulations, then consideration should be given to another widespread practice that may contribute to mother-son intimacy—the long *postpartum sex taboo*. This taboo, an intercourse prohibition observed by a woman after giving birth, often lasts for a year or longer. During this period of sexual privation for a mother, her husband usually has access to a second wife, a situation likely to result in lowered emotional attachment between the parents. The mother, meanwhile, suckles the infant throughout the duration of the taboo, and, under the circumstances, the possibilities for a seductively close relationship between them would seem great. Infants exposed to a long postpartum taboo might be likely to develop an erotically tinged, or *Oedipal*, attachment to the mother. Any such desire, unfulfillable and clashing as it must with the incest taboo, could ultimately give way to castration fears. The presence of a long postpartum sex taboo is linked with several customs that can reasonably be argued as reflecting castration anxiety—for example, strong menstrual taboos (Stephens, 1962). A woman bleeding from the genitals is displaying a vivid example of what appears to be a genital injury, and societies with men who might be prone to fear such injuries isolate their women by placing them in special huts, avoid contamination by forbidding them to cook, and so on.

In addition to the long postpartum sex taboo, extensive menstrual taboos are also associated with other possible sources of castration anxiety. One of these other variables, early sex training, points up the difficulty in adopting recondite Freudian concepts. Why

[3]The argument may seem self-contradictory. If close contact produces sexual aversion, how can even closer contact produce a sexual attraction? Some data from animal behavior show how this could work. Several animal species (mostly primates but also the Canada goose) follow the human pattern of a long period of mother-infant intimacy together with subsequent avoidance of copulation between mother and male offspring. The degree of contact is biologically programmed not to exceed certain limits, and it decreases rapidly as the animal attains independence of its mother. However, mother-son copulation can occur under unusual circumstances. If a wild gander and a domesticated goose are bred, the offspring attains sexual maturity while still at the mother-following stage, and a young male bird will thus mate with his mother (Tanner, 1961). Among human beings, the degree of contact (being culturally specified and subject to great variability) in some societies might exceed the limits within which the aversion would naturally form. The relationship between parent-child intimacy and aversion, in other words, may be curvilinear: either too much contact or too little, and aversion will fail to develop.

not make the parsimonious assumption that the menstrual taboos are a product of severe sexual socialization and represent not so much castration fears as general sexual anxiety? Undoubtedly the latter interpretation is simpler. The hypothesis that punishment for sex leads to anxiety about sex is consistent with relationships found in dependence and aggression research as reported earlier, and with the limited amount of research on sex. There is, moreover, nothing in the Western research literature demonstrating a connection between castration anxiety and early mother-son intimacy, though the usefulness of the concept of castration anxiety seems established (Zigler & Child, 1969). But a characteristic of the cross-cultural relationship that suggests its believability is the peculiar appropriateness of the customs used as measures. Mother-child households and long postpartum sex taboos appear to be prime generators of erotic attachment between mother and son, and menstrual taboos, if interpreted as individual phobias, transparently reflect concern about genital hurt. Freud, who thought that both the early sexual fixation on the mother and the later castration anxiety growing out of it were inevitable, may have perceived a relationship that crops up only occasionally in Western societies but that seems to recur frequently in the traditional world.

When the mother and her son are in close and prolonged contact—to the general exclusion of the father—another process besides Oedipal fixation and its resolution seems to be strongly affected: the son's acquisition of appropriately sex-typed behavior. Chapter Seven takes up this issue.

Both in Western and in traditional societies, dependence, aggression, and sex are all, when positively reinforced, somewhat subject to response-strengthening effects and, when punished, subject to anxiety-producing but not necessarily response-weakening effects. Sexual behavior shows some anomalous aspects that conceivably are due to its unusual status as a biological drive (the satisfaction of which is not necessary to the survival of the individual) or perhaps that are due to the psychological implications of the universal ban on incest.

For many other personality variables (for example, nurturance, approval, power, and affiliation), cross-cultural investigations are too few to allow meaningful comparisons with findings made in the West. For still others the relationships are either weak or inconsistent.

In Western research, both orality and anality show clustering of the traits suggested by the concepts of the oral and anal characters (Zigler & Child, 1969). In cross-cultural research, orality but not anality is related to hypothesized antecedents (Whiting & Child, 1953); however, in Western studies, neither has any regular association with early-childhood experiences.

Three Cultures

Severe socialization of dependence, as we saw earlier, is related cross-culturally to two types of customs. First, adult illness is explained as sometimes due to symbolic expressions of dependence, and, second, sick adults are prevented from expressing dependence during illness by being removed from home or by being isolated from others. For the first relationship, the Ainu, Trobrianders, and Gusii all are above the median on severity of dependence socialization,[4] and all three should therefore explain adult illnesses in terms of symbolic expressions of dependence. Both the Ainu and the Gusii conform to prediction, but the Trobrianders do not explain illness in this fashion, and thus they represent a negative case (LeVine & LeVine, 1963; Whiting & Child, 1953). The second relationship involves a more serious problem: all three societies, given their severe socialization of child dependence, should observe a custom of patient isolation or removal from home during illness, but none of the three actually does so (LeVine & LeVine, 1963; Whiting & Child, 1953). The failure of the finding to pan out in any of these three societies illustrates the probabilistic character of behavioral-science relationships—that is, the fact that a significant association may not hold up for particular cases.

For aggression, severe socialization is related cross-culturally to numerous adult customs. We shall briefly discuss one—aggressive explanations of illness. Both the Ainu and the Gusii are above the median on severity of aggression socialization, but only the Gusii explain illness as being sometimes due to aggression (LeVine & LeVine, 1963; Whiting & Child, 1953). The Trobrianders, who are below the median, do not attribute illness to the expression of aggression (Whiting & Child, 1953). Thus, two of the three cases are consistent with the general finding.

[4]The "median" refers to placement above or below the halfway point among the 75 societies in the Whiting and Child (1953) study. Scores are available from that study for the Ainu and Trobrianders. For the Gusii, informal assignment has been based on the standard ethnography (LeVine & LeVine, 1963).

The cross-cultural data seemed at first to indicate that punitive socialization leads to anxiety about aggression but not to actual aggressive behavior, a result at variance with Western findings. The Six Cultures Study, however, included observations of children's behavior and found that the societies with extended-family domestic units, which probably cannot easily tolerate aggressive behavior, produced children with more instead of less aggression, despite (or perhaps because of) the fact that mothers of aggressive children expressed highly negative attitudes toward aggression. The finding, in other words, supports the Western results. The Gusii, as one of the three societies we are examining here as well as one of those in the Six Cultures Study, demonstrate this relationship. Gusii children engaged in both "assaulting" and "reprimanding" behavior more frequently than children in any of the other five societies. Their level of "assaulting" was one-third higher than that of the next society and three times higher than that of the bottom group (B. Whiting & Whiting, 1975). Further, the Gusii mothers, compared with mothers in the other five societies, more frequently indicated in interviews that they were likely to respond punitively to their children's anger (Minturn & Lambert, 1964). A typical attitude is shown in the statement of a 5-year-old's mother:

> I can only cane him if I find him becoming angry and hitting me. If he is near I would get hold of him and cane him, but if he runs away I would refuse him food for a couple of days more and he will learn himself what he has done wrong [Minturn & Lambert, 1964, p. 332].

We noted that the third behavior system, sex, is marked by great variety in forms of expression and satisfaction. The Trobrianders offer an excellent example, their standard position for intercourse being similar to that of the Yapese, whose own position is supposedly outside the range of American sexual experimentation (Murdock, 1957a). In the Trobriander version, the woman lies on her back with her legs spread and raised and her knees flexed. The man squats in front of her, his hands resting on the ground, and moves toward her or pulls her toward him by taking hold of her legs. Insertion takes place when the sexual organs are close. The woman's legs embrace the man's arms and rest on his elbows (Malinowski, 1929).

Another instance of variety is the Ainu practice of biting in sexual foreplay. A traveler describes his amorous encounter with an Ainu girl:

> Loving and biting went together with her. She could not do the one without doing the other. As we sat on a stone in the semi-darkness she began by gently biting my fingers, without hurting me, as affectionate

dogs often do to their masters; she then bit my arm, then my shoulder, and when she had worked herself up into a passion she put her arms round my neck and bit my cheeks [Landor, 1893, p. 141].

The Trobrianders provide an example of the restrictions and inhibitory controls surrounding sex in all societies. Although Trobriander children begin sexual activity as early as 4 or 5, and the topic of sex is not banned in conversation, a preference for sexual privacy holds for them no less than for other peoples: "Public display of the sexual act or of erotic approaches is almost completely absent from tribal life. Lack of care in avoiding publicity, curiosity and any attempt to spy on other people's love-making are regarded as unseemly and contemptible" (Malinowski, 1929, p. 454).

Tribes that are sexually most free in their behavior have, surprisingly, turned out to be preoccupied with sex on the verbal level. Data on this question are not available for the Ainu, but the Trobrianders and Gusii give confirming evidence. Stephens (1972) rates the Trobrianders as just a shade below the sexually most permissive societies in his sample. (Trobriander brothers and sisters do, however, observe a sharp social and sexual avoidance.) Correspondingly, sexual elements are found in Trobriander conversation, in joking and swearing, in games and sports, and in folktales. Numerous string figures or cat's cradles made by the Trobrianders are openly sexual and have bawdy sayings connected with them. In contrast, the Gusii are quite restrictive sexually, especially in childhood sexuality, and they display a like degree of verbal control concerning sex. Individuals of adjacent generations, particularly parents and children, experience *ensoni*, or sexual shame, in interactions that might be construed as sexual. Rules governing adjacent-generation behavior include prohibition on shaking hands with one another (a customary Gusii greeting pattern) or bathing in one another's presence. In addition, joking insults (usually obscene for the Gusii) and discussion of sexual matters are avoided. "The maintenance of properly restrained behavior causing embarrassment to no one is facilitated by the use of an elaborate euphemistic vocabulary for sex and bodily functions in discussion between adjacent generation persons" (LeVine & LeVine, 1963, p. 51). Even animal sexuality provokes embarrassment: "An informant expressed the mortification experienced by the crowd at a magical ceremony when two chickens happened to copulate, by saying, 'It was shameful; [clan] "fathers" and "daughters" were there' " (LeVine & LeVine, 1963, p. 51). These rules, however, fail to apply to clansmen who are not of adjacent generations (for example, an individual and his grandfather), so that the Gusii cannot be said to reach an extreme in sexual verbal modesty.

But it is of interest that the Gusii restrictiveness seems to be tied up with a very high frequency of rape (LeVine, 1959) and also with ritualized outbursts of obscenity like that of the adult women during female initiation.

Abstention from intercourse as a therapeutic practice was interpreted earlier as one indicator of sexual anxiety stemming from severe early sex training. None of the three societies practices sexual abstention therapeutically, and all three should therefore be below the median on severity of sexual socialization. Although the Ainu and Trobrianders fall below the median, the Gusii, as we have seen, strongly discourage sexual behavior in children: "The sex play of children elicits even greater disapproval than fighting from Nyansongan [Gusii] parents. More than three fourths of the mothers questioned said that they would cane their 3-year-old children on discovery of masturbation and older children on discovery of heterosexual play" (LeVine & LeVine, 1963, p. 177). Thus two of the three cases support the general cross-cultural relationship.

The extensive menstrual taboos observed in many societies do not occur among the Ainu, Trobrianders, or Gusii. The Gusii, in fact, believe that conception can take place only while the female is menstruating, and intercourse, accordingly, takes place at this time. Extensive taboos have been interpreted earlier as possibly reflecting castration anxiety resulting from Oedipal fixation on the mother, and the long postpartum sex taboo has been identified as a possible contributor to such mother fixation. Without strong menstrual taboos, the three societies should not observe long postpartum sexual abstention. But the Trobrianders do prohibit intercourse for almost two years. Again, two of the three cases support the general cross-cultural finding.

Chapter Seven

Sex Role

Among the lower animals, sex differences tend to serve only a reproductive function. But as the phylogenetic scale is ascended, two potent evolutionary tendencies emerge. Increasingly one finds a larger differentiation between the sexes: structurally, sexual dimorphism is manifested in the greater size and strength of males and in the appearance of secondary sex characteristics; behaviorally, males become more active and dominant and females become more passive (Rosenberg & Sutton-Smith, 1972). At the same time, the sex-related behavior of higher animals is less determined by innate factors and comes more under the control of experience. In very complex ways, both these tendencies are at work in human beings.

The Universality of Sex Differences

Although strong sex-differentiated behavior does not appear among all mammals, man's primate relatives display marked sex differences. Adult male baboons, for example, form a dominance hierarchy in which females take no part (DeVore, 1965). Moreover, baboons display a linking of sexual and social behavior found frequently among the higher animals, in that a male's opportunities to copulate with estrous females are closely related to his position in the dominance hierarchy. Caretaking is a female activity, and even immature, juvenile females are greatly attracted to infants and attempt to handle them frequently. Preadolescent female rhesus monkeys direct significantly more positive and fewer hostile social behaviors toward infants than do immature males (Chamove, Harlow, & Mitchell, 1967). Immature males of several primate species venture farther from the mother than do females. When rhesus monkeys are deprived of the opportunity to learn sex-appropriate behavior by being raised in isolation, males still exhibit more threatening behavior and less withdrawal and passivity than females (Harlow, 1965). The injection of the male hormone into a subordinate male chimpanzee resulted in his revolting against and overthrowing another male that had previously been dominant over him (Clark & Birch, 1945). The existence in the highest animal order of salient sex differences with strong hereditary elements is pertinent to an understanding of sex-role behavior in man. The human parallels to the animal evidence are compelling.

In all known human societies adult males differ from adult females in both primary and secondary sex characteristics. Males have, on the average, higher oxygen-carrying capacity in the blood (Tanner, 1961), a higher muscle-fat ratio, more body hair, a more massive skeleton, and greater height (D'Andrade, 1966). (These differences hold only within populations, not between, and refer to mean scores and not individuals.) Behaviorally there are also modal sex differences in every society—sometimes strong, sometimes weak, but always present. At the adult level the division of labor is always different for the two sexes. Ultimate military and political authority always resides in a body of males (though occasionally a female may occupy the single highest political position, as in modern India and Israel). For children, sex differences are reported for all 45 societies on which full ratings are available concerning six classes of behavior— nurturance, responsibility, obedience, self-reliance, achievement, and independence (Barry, Bacon, & Child, 1967).[1] Differences between males and females appear extremely early in life. Male neonates are larger, have more muscle development, have higher basal metabolism rates, have a higher pain threshold, and are more vigorously active (Rosenberg & Sutton-Smith, 1972). Female neonates react more positively to comforting than males (Moss, 1967). By 14 weeks of age, girls may be conditioned through the use of auditory reinforcers, and boys may be conditioned through the use of visual reinforcers, but not vice versa (Watson, 1969). And, by the age of 4 months, girls attend longer than boys to facelike masks; apparently, by this age, girls are more interested in faces or face-like configurations (Kagan, 1970).

[1]The ratings referred to in the 45 societies apply to child *behavior*. Other ratings in the same study apply to child *training*, and these show a similar outcome, with sex differences in socialization reported for 34 of 35 societies on which full ratings are available. (The Yagua of South America are the sole exception.) It is possible to argue, of course, that the ubiquitous training for sex differences has produced the behavioral differences, but this argument begs the question.

Besides these apparently universal differences, there are other behaviors that in most societies are attached to females and in a few societies to both sexes equally but in no society are attached to males alone. For example, in social behavior, the wife is culturally required to show deference to the husband in three of every four societies, but in no case does the husband display ritualistic acknowledgment of the wife's power (Stephens, 1963). In socialization, responsibility falls either exclusively to females or to both sexes but not to males alone. The behavior of children also yields regularities of this type, with female children never displaying more self-reliance or independence than male children, though in 15-20% of societies the two sexes display self-reliance and independence approximately equally (Barry et al., 1967). At the most general level, distinctions between roles for fathers and mothers characterize, also, the differences between all males and all females. In the great majority of societies, the father role is more instrumental, or goal oriented, and the mother role more expressive, or oriented toward the maintenance of integrative, harmonious relationships. Sometimes the mother and father roles are equally instrumental or expressive, but not in a single case among 56 societies were the roles fully reversed (Zelditch, 1955). The instrumental-expressive distinction is found in typical form in the United States despite recent efforts by reform groups to abolish or at least minimize sex-role differences.

Numerous other behaviors are largely associated with one sex; these behaviors show only infrequent reversals across cultures. In the division of labor, cooking is carried out primarily by females in well over 90% of societies. The manufacture of musical instruments is almost entirely a male occupation. Sexual initiative is largely reserved to men. Sexual modesty is primarily a female trait: men and women may both expose the pubic region, or males may be nude while females wear clothing, but females very seldom go nude where males cover the genitals (Ford & Beach, 1951; Stephens, 1972). In social organization, polygamy is allowed to males in three-quarters of all societies, whereas females are permitted to have more than one husband in fewer than 1% of all societies. Fantasy productions, such as drawings and designs, and projective preferences suggest that males typically are represented by, and make, projecting angular designs and females more open, rounded designs (Kohlberg, 1966; Whiting, n.d.), a difference often interpreted to be the result of body imagery. In the Six Cultures Study (B. Whiting & Edwards, 1973), boys engaged in physical aggression more frequently than girls.

The strength and persistence of sex differences are seen in the poignant story of an Israeli kibbutz:

When the vattikim [original settlers] first settled on the land, there
was no sexual division of labor. Women, like men, worked in the
fields and drove tractors; men, like women, worked in the kitchen and
in the laundry. Men and women, it was assumed, were equal and
could perform their jobs equally well. It was soon discovered, however, that men and women were not equal. For obvious biological
reasons, women could not undertake many of the physical tasks of
which men were capable; tractor driving, harvesting, and other heavy
labor proved too difficult for them. Moreover, women were compel-
led at times to take temporary leave from that physical labor of which
they were capable. A pregnant woman, for example, could not work
too long, even in the vegetable garden, and a nursing mother had to
work near the Infants House in order to be able to feed her child.
Hence, as the kibbutz grew older and the birth rate increased, more
and more women were forced to leave the "productive" branches of
the economy and enter its "service" branches. But as they left the
"productive" branches, it was necessary that their places be filled,
and they were filled by men. The result was that the women found
themselves in the same jobs from which they were supposed to have
been emancipated—cooking, cleaning, laundering, teaching, caring
for children, etc. . . .

What has been substituted for the traditional routine of housekeeping . . . is more housekeeping—and a restricted and narrow kind of
housekeeping at that. Instead of cooking and sewing and baking and
cleaning and laundering and caring for children, the woman in Kiryat
Yedidim cooks *or* sews *or* launders *or* takes care of children for eight
hours a day. She has become a specialist in one aspect of housekeeping. But this new housekeeping is more boring and less rewarding
than the traditional type. . . . It is small wonder, then, given this
combination of low prestige, difficult working conditions, and
monotony, that the chavera [female member of the kibbutz] has found
little happiness in her economic activities.[2]

That inherited tendencies help to produce widespread regularities in sex roles is indicated by a convincing clinical study. Five
patients who were anatomically normal males and who had been raised
as boys showed childhood interest only in female activities. At adolescence they developed female secondary sex characteristics, thus confirming their earlier behavioral preferences. A sixth patient, a female,
showed the reverse pattern and, at adolescence, developed male secondary sex characteristics (Baker & Stoller, 1967). These results,
powerful though they seem, must be viewed against equally strong
clinical findings (reviewed below) that demonstrate the complementary
effect of initial sex-role assignment and socialization.

[2]From *Kibbutz: Venture in Utopia*, by M. E. Spiro, pp. 224–225; 228–229.
Copyright 1956 by the President and Fellows of Harvard College. Reprinted by permission of the publisher, Harvard University Press.

Human sex differences faithfully reflect evolutionary trends, but their underlying causes might not be primarily attributable to the direct operation of genetic or hormonal factors. Many aspects of sex specialization may instead be a result of simple physical differences or of generalization to activities anticipatory to such differences (D'Andrade, 1966). The strongest training for sex differences occurs in societies in which subsistence requires the superior strength of males, as in the hunting of large animals or in the growing of grain rather than root crops (Barry et al., 1957). Thus the association of males with subsistence activities requiring strenuous and mobile behavior could be due to their size, strength, and speed. As to women, their contribution to subsistence seems to depend on the demands of child care (J. Brown, 1970). When subsistence tasks do not require rapt attention and do not oblige participants to be far from home—activities that would tend to interfere with child care—then women are important contributors. Child rearing itself, which is a major responsibility of women in all societies, may be universally associated with females due to generalization from biological motherhood and breast feeding of the neonate. D'Andrade (1966) points to the probable interaction between inborn predispositions and cultural outcomes:

> Some of the [sex] differences on various response measures will be innately determined rather than learned. . . . These differences compound into complex causal chains, resulting in sets of institutional structures that "act back" on the conditions that created them in the first place, sometimes amplifying the original conditions, sometimes elaborating them in a variety of ways [p. 202].

The evidence strongly favors an interpretation of sex differences as partly determined by hereditary factors. To adopt a wholly environmentalist position would be to argue that human behavior patterns and those of other animals are basically different despite both shared evolutionary ancestry and present behavioral similarities. This situation is unlikely. Yet specific sex-role behaviors are a matter of learning as well, and this evidence is considered below.

Plasticity in Sex-Role Behavior

We know from experience that variability in sex-role behavior is a common occurrence. Most people in a society adopt most of the behaviors defined as appropriate to their biological sex, but the exceptions are many. The multidimensional nature of sex roles is evident from the acceptance of varying patterns of behavior as *masculine* or *feminine*. Two males might differ considerably in attitudes, interests and mode of interaction, and yet both be considered masculine. Just as the society allows a fairly wide range of behavior in each sex-role category, within-individual adherence to sex-appropriate behavior is also flexible. An American male may display typically masculine fantasies and choose an engineering career but exhibit a feminine speech pattern, or he might have a high preference for verbal subjects in school, dress in full conformity with the "jock" image, and exhibit female-like behaviors such as examining his fingernails with his palm facing down instead of up and carrying books tucked against his chest. The diverse response patterns between and within individuals give ample testimony to the influence of experience and learning on sex-role behavior. Clinical materials reinforce this conclusion. In more than 100 cases of contradiction between the sex of rearing and one or more of five biological sex variables—chromosomal, gonadal, and hormonal sex, internal accessory organs, and external genital appearance—the crucial factors in determining sex-role behavior were the sex assigned at birth and subsequent socialization (Hampson & Hampson, 1961). The results not so much contradict the previously reported clinical finding on the importance of biological factors in behavior (Baker & Stoller, 1967) as indicate the complementary strength of social-psychological factors.

Of course, sex roles are themselves highly variable, by age and by social class among other ways. The stringency of expectations also differs, so that females in the United States can violate sex-role norms with fewer explicit sanctions than can males. Across societies, even the number of sex roles is subject to variation, with many groups having institutionalized roles for transvestites, celibates, and virgins. American culture at this time provides no established mode of total escape from biological sex categories, but for many Amerindian groups an escape into a standardized cross-sex role is available to boys and, in some groups, to girls as well. The roles vary from simple cross-dressing to nearly full participation as an opposite-sex member of the society. Among the Mohave, marriage to a man, mock menstruation, and imitation of birth are all included in the shaman (curer) role for males (Devereaux, 1937). The Papago, with a transvestite role available, provide a unique choice procedure for young males who appear to have feminine tendencies. The boy is placed in a small enclosure with both basketry materials and a bow and arrows. The enclosure is set on fire. The boy remains a male if he emerges from the burning enclosure with the bow and arrows; if he emerges with the basketry materials, he is classified as a transvestite (Underhill, 1939).

Language, dress, posture, gesture—innumerable sociocultural categories—may be chosen as a point of departure for sex distinctions. And when they are so chosen, specific items of behavior vary in an apparently arbitrary way. The most extreme and dramatic anthropological case of sex-role variation is illustrated by Margaret Mead's research on three New Guinea tribes, among whom all the logical contrasts to American sex typing are discovered:

> We have now considered in detail the approved personalities of each sex among three primitive peoples. We found the Arapesh—both men and women—displaying a personality that, out of our historically limited preoccupations, we would call maternal in its parental aspects, and feminine in its sexual aspects. We found men, as well as women, trained to be co-operative, unaggressive, responsive to the needs and demands of others. We found no idea that sex was a powerful driving force either for men or for women. In marked contrast to these attitudes, we found among the Mundugumor that both men and women developed as ruthless, aggressive, positively sexed individuals, with the maternal cherishing aspects of personality at a minimum. Both men and women approximated to a personality type that we in our culture would find only in an undisciplined and very violent male. Neither the Arapesh nor the Mundugumor profit by a contrast between the sexes; the Arapesh ideal is the mild, responsive man married to the mild, responsive woman; the Mundugumor ideal is the violent aggressive man married to the violent aggressive woman. In the third tribe, the Tchambuli, we found a genuine reversal of the sex-attitudes of our own culture, with the woman the dominant, impersonal, managing partner, the man the less responsible and the emotionally dependent person. These three situations suggest, then, a very definite conclusion. If those temperamental attitudes which we have traditionally regarded as feminine—such as passivity, responsiveness, and a willingness to cherish children—can so easily be set up as the masculine pattern in one tribe, and in another be outlawed for the majority of women as well as for the majority of men, we no longer have any basis for regarding such aspects of behavior as sex-linked.
>
> We are forced to conclude that human nature is almost unbelievably malleable, responding accurately and contrastingly to contrasting cultural conditions. . . . Standardized personality differences between the sexes are of this order, cultural creations to which each generation, male and female, is trained to conform.[3]

The three tribes, taken together with Western culture, display all the possible major combinations of sex and temperament. It might be tempting to conclude, with Mead, that human nature is indeed almost unbelievably malleable, but the situation is not so simple. There

---

[3]Reprinted by permission of William Morrow & Company, Inc. from *Sex and Temperament in Three Primitive Societies*, pp. 279-281. Morrow paperback ed. Copyright © 1935, 1950, 1963 by Margaret Mead.

is a sexual division of labor in each of the three societies. The warriors in all three groups are males, and the "emotionally dependent" Tchambuli men were headhunters until the colonial administration forced them to abandon the practice prior to Mead's arrival. The husbands in all three tribes practice polygamy, but in none can the wife take more than a single spouse. Although Arapesh husbands share the rearing of children, socialization is not the primary responsibility of the men in any of the three groups. Moreover, a methodological question arises because an independent observer (Fortune, 1939) of the Arapesh expresses doubt that they have the same temperamental expectations for both sexes and cites their proverb: "Men's hearts are different; women's hearts are different." He also points out that there is a class of "women males," or effeminate men, who have definite functions and are given a special subordinate place at feasts. A social category of this kind would hardly be expected in a society in which the sexes are thought to possess the same idealized temperament.

To summarize, plasticity in sex roles seems to run one way only. Societies can and often do elaborate sex differences almost endlessly, but they never manage to eliminate them. There are always some irreducible distinctions, even beyond the several pancultural behaviors named in the preceding section. If the male and female roles can be reliably distinguished in any society, a person can always be placed on a continuum of relative masculinity-femininity for his or her own group. Although sex-role behavior is complex—and the problem is complicated by the possibility of defensive behavior, such as compensatory masculinity—measurement of a number of response modes should yield a pattern of consistency and enable overall assessment of an individual. Moreover, an important advantage accrues to the study of any aspect of behavior organized stably enough to appear regularly and recognizably everywhere, and that is the likelihood that findings made in one society will have some applicability to other societies. Research into sex-role development has been able to operate with this likelihood in its favor.

Sex and Sex Typing

Psychological research on the development of sex typing has been marked by a great variety of theoretical and methodological approaches, and the number of background factors shown to be influential is quite large (Barry et al., 1957; Maccoby, 1966; Mischel, 1970; Mussen, 1969; J. Roberts & Sutton-Smith, 1962). Almost all theoretical positions, however, whether they specify the effective developmental or socializing mechanism to be identification, imitation, or the use of rewards and punishment, assume the critical importance of a same-sex adult in the development of sex-appropriate behavior. (Kohlberg, 1969a, takes a contrary position.) The empirical findings support this assumption, at least for males. In contrast to those from intact homes, young boys who have spent part of their early years without a father frequently display one or more of the following characteristics: feminine sex-role preferences, feminine self-concepts, feminine game preferences, high dependence, low assertiveness, few activities involving physical contact, low physical aggression, high verbal aggression (Bach, 1946; Biller, 1968b, 1969; D'Andrade, 1973; Hetherington, 1966; Sears, 1951). (A few studies have failed to find differences of this sort [Barclay & Cusumano, 1967; Greenstein, 1966]). As they grow older, father-absent boys continue to exhibit some feminine characteristics but also may begin to manifest exaggeratedly masculine behavior such as physical aggression (Hoffman, 1971; Lynn & Sawrey, 1959; McCord, McCord, & Thurber, 1962; Siegman, 1966) and to contribute a more than proportionate share to delinquent samples (Glueck & Glueck, 1950; Gregory, 1965). Assertiveness and aggression are the most distinctive elements of the male role and may, therefore, be fiercely exhibited in an attempt to cover up or deny an underlying femininity. An emphasis on *machismo*, or an appearance of manliness at all costs, in Latin cultures is the most widely publicized example of the syndrome, which may be explained as defensive, or compensatory, masculinity (Garibay Patron, 1969). The show of behavior in the defensive syndrome ultimately goes beyond the normal male role to a point near caricature (Hetherington & Deur, 1972). To complicate matters, strong feminine sex typing without apparent defensive masculinity has also been found among father-absent adolescent boys (Carlsmith, 1973; Harrington, 1970). The findings do not in any way deny the influence of all family members on one another (Sutton-Smith, Roberts, & Rosenberg, 1964), but the evidence indicates that the father has the single most intensive impact on the development of masculinity in his sons (Biller, 1968a; Santrock, 1970; Wohlford, Santrock, Berger, & Liberman, 1971).

In several Caribbean groups, early father absence is associated with feminine sex-typed behavior for males (Burton, 1972; Cutter, 1964; Rodgers & Long, 1968). Beyond this, and pertinent to the relationship between father absence and defensive masculinity, in a sample of 48 societies there was more personal crime and theft in societies with a high frequency of father absence (Bacon, Child, & Barry, 1963). Similar findings have been made for adult aggression (B. Whiting, 1965) and for emphasis on glory in warfare (Whiting, 1969).

From studies conducted in the United States, it appears that the mother's attitudes and behavior can modify appreciably the son's path of development in a father-absent home. As distinguished from mothers in father-present homes, mothers in homes where the father was absent engaged in a higher rate of interaction with their sons, including offering their sons support more frequently. These behaviors of the mother were, in turn, strongly related to the degree of femininity in semantic ratings made by the boys (Longabaugh, 1973). On the other hand, mothers who are positive about the absent father (Bach, 1946), who behave in a competent fashion in the dual mother-father role (Hilgard, Neuman, & Fisk, 1960), and who make sex-appropriate demands on their sons (Biller, 1969) appear to erase or reduce many of the typical characteristics of father-absent boys. In two polygynous African societies in which adult males are often not found as regular household members, investigation (Ember, 1973; Nerlove, 1969) indicates that preadolescent males who are assigned feminine tasks display female modes of interaction, such as prosocial dominance (true of girls in the Six Cultures Study) and closeness to other children, and also fewer masculine behaviors, such as aggression. Each of these studies supports the importance of sex-appropriate demands as a factor in the development of sex-appropriate behavior.

The above findings refer to individuals. But also a general institutional response appears to evolve in societies with either widespread father absence or similar conditions under which the availability of the father or other adult males to young boys is relatively low. *Low male salience*, the collective term for these conditions, is manifested in circumstances such as father absence itself, mother-infant sleeping arrangements (the father sleeps elsewhere), the mother-child household (the father stays elsewhere), and postmarital matrilocal residence (the adult males come from elsewhere). If in the first few years of life a boy is exposed to low male salience, and then, still in childhood, he enters a society in which maleness is emphasized, any tendency to behave with feminine sex-typed behavior becomes highly inappropriate. Such societies, with low male salience in infancy followed by strong sex differentiation and male social dominance, practice male initiation ceremonies that include circumcision (Burton & Whiting. 1961; Harrington, 1968; Whiting, 1962). The rites can be interpreted as an attempt to expunge unacceptably feminine tendencies in young males.[4] The interpretation is bolstered by the symbolic appropriateness of the genital operation (Figure 7-1).

What if the boy experiences low male salience and the society does not structurally emphasize maleness? In societies of this kind, and particularly under conditions of low salience in both infancy and later childhood (as in mother-infant sleeping arrangements and matrilocal residence), initiation-circumcision ceremonies do not occur. The tendency toward feminine behavior therefore should remain very strong and should carry through into adulthood. Biological factors make it impossible for the male to carry his feminine orientation to the logical conclusion—giving birth to a child. And, as we have seen, the adult sex roles are different in all societies. The dilemma for males in these societies is clear: an inclination, presumably, toward behavior that is nowhere allowed as a general course. The solution seems to have taken the form of a disguised imitation of the female role, in the institution of couvade (Chapter One). Sometimes called "male childbed," the couvade consists of taboos and restrictions observed by the father around the time of his child's birth—taboos that are of the same genre as those observed by the mother. In intensive observances, the father abstains completely from his usual activities, just as, in the great majority of societies, the mother recuperates after the birth. Given the

[4]Several complex problems are raised in the above discussion of initiation ceremonies and require at least brief notice. First, the long postpartum sex taboo (see Chapter Six) is clearly still another indicator of low male salience, but it is excluded from the list for a technical reason. The postpartum taboo is a strong antecedent of only one of the two institutional responses discussed below—male initiation-circumcision ceremonies but not the couvade—because the particular institutional response exhibited by a society depends on a secondary factor of degree of male salience in later childhood as well as upon the initial degree of salience in infancy, and it happens that the long postpartum taboo (an infancy indicator of low male salience) is highly correlated with the secondary factor that leads only to male initiation-circumcision ceremonies. Since the other institutional response is negatively related to this secondary factor, it is also negatively related to the postpartum sex taboo. Therefore, on the basis of the artifactual character of the differential relation of the postpartum taboo to the two institutions, the role of the taboo is not further discussed in this chapter. Second, the findings for initiation-circumcision ceremonies have been interpreted by Whiting and his associates as supporting a specific hypothesis about sex identity, conflict, and the operation of status envy and resource control in the process of identification. Because the findings fit not only that hypothesis but several others concerning the mechanisms involved in sex-role development, the present discussion remains at a generalized level and introduces as few constructs as possible. Third, only those initiation ceremonies that include circumcision are argued to be interpretable in terms of sex-typing concepts. Other types of initiation ceremonies may have different functions (for example, Granzberg, 1972, 1973a). Fourth, a longstanding debate in anthropology centers on the question of whether individual psychological dispositions can explain sociocultural, or institutional-level phenomena (Durkheim, 1938; Homans & Schneider, 1955; Needham, 1962; Whiting & Child, 1953; Young, 1965). The remainder of the chapter presents affirmative evidence on this question, but no pretense is made that the larger issue is resolved.

Figure 7-1.   Gusii circumcision. Courtesy of Robert A. LeVine.

interpretation offered, it is not surprising that the cultural rationale for the couvade is usually in terms of the health of the infant (Munroe, Munroe, & Whiting, 1973).

The complementary distribution of the couvade and initiation-circumcision ceremonies is meaningful theoretically (Burton &

Whiting, 1961; Harrington & Whiting, 1972). The rites often include painful hazing, seclusion from women, and tests of endurance and manliness. The symbolic associations of these actions and the often protracted and difficult character of the ceremonies may indeed function to effect a fundamental psychosexual reorientation in the boy. If this happens, then the couvade, as a cultural device permitting the acting out of the female role, should be unnecessary where initiation rites are practiced. And empirically, intensive couvade observances and initiation-circumcision ceremonies are seldom, if ever, found in the same society.

Although nonpsychological hypotheses have been advanced to account for the cross-cultural findings reported above (Cohen, 1964; Young, 1965), there is further research that supports the psychological interpretation. The Black Carib of British Honduras practice the couvade (Munroe, Munroe, & Whiting, 1973). Carib males observe a series of postnatal behavioral restrictions designed to protect the health of the infant. Individuals, however, differ in the number, duration, and kinds of taboos they believe it necessary to observe. If the hypothesis about the psychological meaning of the couvade is valid, the commitment of individual Carib males to the observances should be a function of their underlying sex-role typing, which in turn should be dependent on their early exposure to adult males. Specifically, Carib men who feel that intensive couvade observances are necessary should differ in two respects from those who advocate less intensive observances. First, they should have experienced a lower degree of male salience in the early years (a large proportion of men work away from home at some form of wage labor), and, second, they should give more feminine responses on tests of sex typing. A sample of Carib males who were interviewed and administered a battery of tests conformed strongly to these expectations. But in the everyday behavior of the intensive-couvade men, there was, rather than a feminine pattern, a syndrome of defensive masculinity. As rated by other members of the community, they were brave, were heavy drinkers, and tended to curse and gamble heavily in comparison to the nonintensive-couvade group. Thus even in a society in which the tendency toward feminine sex typing among the males is at an extremely high level, the most feminized males do not adopt openly female-like behavior but instead strive to match some hypermasculine ideal.

There was one aspect of behavior in which the intensive-couvade males among the Carib exhibited a definitely female pattern, but, as with the couvade itself, its feminine import was hidden from the actors. Most of the sample members experienced symptoms during their wives' pregnancies, though not necessarily the same ones as their spouses. These included vomiting, fatigue, food cravings, toothache, headache, dizziness, and fever. The intensive-couvade group reported an average of almost six symptoms per pregnancy, while among the nonintensive-couvade males the mean was about three and a half symptoms per pregnancy. The Carib did not attach any meaning to the men's symptoms despite their transparently female reference and their occurrence during a period of obvious feminine significance.

Male pregnancy symptoms are of somewhat wider interest because they have been related to feminine sex typing in a total of seven societies (Daniels, 1970; Munroe & Munroe, 1971; Munroe, Munroe, & Nerlove, 1973; Rubel & Spielberg, 1966). Furthermore, males with symptoms have regularly displayed defensive characteristics at the more overt levels, and they have reported a background of low male salience in three of the four societies in which early absence was systematically investigated. In the United States, for example, a group of males with symptoms differed covertly from nonsymptom males by completing drawings in a manner typical of females, differed overtly by making more of the decisions in the home and giving little help with housework, and differed in childhood experience by having a significantly higher frequency of father absence (Munroe & Munroe, 1971). Male symptomatology may eventually prove broadly useful as a cross-culturally valid measure of feminine sex typing, but its limitations are revealed in a case like that of the Arapesh, among whom the women themselves do not experience pregnancy symptoms (Mead, 1935). What prediction would be made about Arapesh males?

In the seven societies in which the relationship of male symptomatology to feminine sex typing has been established, there are clear societal differences in the average symptom levels. The Carib men reported an average of five symptoms each, while both Anglo-American and Mexican-American men averaged under one symptom each. It is considered more than coincidental that the couvade-practicing Carib are much more symptom prone than American men, because the institution of couvade, in any society in which it occurs, is presumed to indicate the existence of a high level of feminine sex typing among the males. Another comparison of symptom frequencies is offered by a brace of four contiguous East African societies that expose boys in infancy to conditions of low male salience and then in later childhood to a structural emphasis on males (Munroe & Munroe, 1973). Since cross-culturally this combination is associated with initiation-circumcision rites that hypothetically function to counteract the effects of the early low salience, in these four societies the level of male symptomatology should be low. Only three of the groups, however, actually observe initiation-circumcision ceremonies. For these three societies, the average number of symptoms per male ranged from one to one and a half, a frequency not far above that of the United States. The fourth society, which does not have initiation ceremonies despite the appropriate preconditions, ought to have males who still display feminine sex typing in adulthood. A small sample of men from this group averaged nearly five symptoms each, and half of them experienced something akin to labor pains during the wife's parturition. Among the seven societies, then, the reported frequency and severity of symptoms were greatest in a group with the couvade and in a group that theoretically should practice masculinizing initiation but does not do so. The interpretation of the psychological function of the institutions receives this additional support, as shown in Table 7-1.

Although institutions such as the couvade and male initiation may help to reduce the apparent anxiety and uncertainty about sex typing felt by men in many societies, numerous cross-cultural projective test findings nonetheless indicate a generally greater difficulty in adjustment to sex role for men than for women (D'Andrade, 1966). Unresolved problems are indicated behaviorally as well by the overt masculinity usually associated with male pregnancy symptoms (Munroe & Munroe, 1971; Munroe, Munroe, & Nerlove, 1973; Munroe, Munroe, & Whiting, 1973), by the greater cross-cultural incidence of male homosexuality and transvestism (D'Andrade, 1966), and perhaps by the higher male rates of alcoholism (Child, Barry, & Bacon, 1965), crime, and suicide. The analysis pursued above suggests, of course, that the problems stem primarily from the low salience of adult males in the formative years of a boy's life. But the greater anxiety and insecurity of men might also be attributable to the pancultural expectations that males must exceed females in power, dominance, and superior status—expectations that are probably fulfilled at some psychic cost (D'Andrade, 1966). Insufficient early contact with males and stringent expectations may both contribute to difficulties surrounding assumption of the male sex role. The male role, despite its worldwide social superiority, seems to be associated with heavy psychological penalties.

Females rarely lack for a same-sex adult in the critical early years, and it is predictable that they would display fewer problems of sex typing than males. The ritualized envy of the woman's role that is displayed in the couvade has no precise counterpart in female institutions. In some societies, though, the usually submissive women ceremonially dress in men's clothes, swagger, and insult men. Such a temporary status reversal occurs even in modern societies, as in the Soviet Union's annual "Women's Day," in which men prepare the meals and do all the housework (*Los Angeles Times*, 1974). But there is no

Table 7-1. Relation of early experience to adult sex typing as measured by male pregnancy symptoms

Society	Early Experience		Institutional Outcome	Adult Sex Typing	Mean Number of Pregnancy Symptoms per Male
	Male Salience in Infancy	Male Structural Dominance[a]			
Black Carib[b]	Low	Low	Couvade	Feminine	5.0*
Nilotic[b]	Low	High	None[c]	Feminine	4.7*
Bantu A[b]	Low	High	Initiation/circumcision	Masculine	0.9
Bantu B[b]	Low	High	Initiation/circumcision	Masculine	1.5
Kalenjin[b]	Low	High	Initiation/circumcision	Masculine	1.5
Anglo-American[b]	High	Low	None	Masculine	0.3
Mexican-American[d]	High	High	None	Masculine	Fewer than 1

[a]High = the presence of both strong sex differentiation and male social dominance.
[b]Munroe and Munroe (1973).
[c]Initiation-circumcision rites expected on theoretical grounds.
[d]Rubel and Spielberg (1966).
*p < .001 in comparison to symptom level for Bantu A, Bantu B, Kalenjin, and Anglo-American.

psychological evidence to the effect that women wish to usurp the central male role in these cases. As for female initiation rites, they seldom occur with the same intensity or severity as male ceremonies, and their major function seems to be control and orientation of the pubescent girl along domestic and economic lines, with sex-typing problems less central (J. Brown, 1963). This is not to say that females have hardly any adjustment problems—the use of more drugs by American women than men belies that attitude (Vils, 1974)—but the causes are less likely to be found in the early years. Men, in other words, display many sex-typing problems, some of which are probably rooted in their low exposure to adult males during childhood and some of which are probably due to the difficulties of maintaining masculine prerogatives, while women suffer from far fewer sex-typing problems, most of which are probably a reflection of the difficulties associated with their subordinate status. It is perhaps a mark of women's basic sureness of sex that their displays of envy focus less on sex attributes and more on status attributes of the male role.

For humans, as for many other animals, clear physical and behavioral distinctions between the sexes are present. Physical distinctions are genetically based. Behavioral distinctions, including a number of female- or male-only behaviors found to be similar across cultures, may be genetically influenced, may be cultural elaborations of biological differences, or, less likely, may be extensions (by tradition) of once-useful sex-distinctive practices. Cultures differ with respect to both the narrowness and the rigidity of defined sex-role behavior. Expectations of superior strength, dominance, and high status for males, coupled with the low availability of adult males as models and agents of socialization, contribute to a greater difficulty for males than for females in appropriate sex typing. Institutional solutions for difficulties with assumption of the male role include male initiation rites and the couvade. Female difficulties appear to stem more specifically from the nearly universal subordinate status assigned to women.

○

Three Cultures

The materials in Chapter One documented the differential sex-role expectations extant among the Ainu, Trobrianders, and Gusii.

As in all societies, at the adult level there is a clearly marked division of labor between the sexes, and already in adolescence the differences have begun to emerge. In socialization, the Gusii initiate an early and strong sex differentiation by applying separate terms to male and female children as they are weaned and by assigning sex-appropriate tasks from the age of 3. The Ainu provide children with sex-typed toys and induct them into differentiated tasks beginning at ages 5 to 6. The Trobrianders draw very few distinctions between boys and girls (Harrington, 1968), but from about the age of 5 onward the young boy is brought increasingly close to male activities through the maternal uncle, while for the young girl no comparable relationship and training occur. The three societies, though varying in their emphases on sex differentiation, all display the universal pattern of distinctive behaviors and expectations for men and women.

In the Western world, most infants are reared in the nuclear-family setting, and the boy therefore typically receives adequate contact with adult males in the person of his father. Among as many as 40% of traditional societies, however, conditions of low male salience prevail for a significant segment of the infant male population. According to the findings on sex typing discussed above, each society of this sort should practice either the couvade or initiation-circumcision, the outcome being dependent on male social dominance and the degree of sexual differentiation. The Ainu, Trobrianders, and Gusii expose infants to low male salience (Munroe, Munroe, & Whiting, 1973), so in all three cases an institutionalized "response" to this early experience should be forthcoming. The Ainu do not emphasize either strong sex distinctions (Harrington, 1968) or male social dominance (Munroe, Munroe, & Whiting, 1973). This lack of emphasis means that the adult males ought to retain a tendency toward feminine behavior—namely, by practicing the couvade. As described in the first chapter, the Ainu father abstains from normal activities for 12 days after the birth of a child, and for the first 6 days he observes taboos and stays wrapped up near the hearth. The Ainu observances constitute the couvade in full-blown form. The Trobrianders, as noted above, have extremely weak sex-role differentiation, but they do lean in the direction of male social dominance. The indicators are therefore ambiguous; and so too is the Trobriander institutional response. The father's birth observances are minimal (Munroe, Munroe, & Whiting, 1973) and together add up to what has been called a "semi-couvade"—perhaps making of the Trobrianders what can be called a "semi-exception." Finally, in the Gusii case, both the social dominance of males (Munroe & Munroe, 1973) and the strength of sex-role differentiation are clear, and this pattern, following the low early exposure of boys to adult males, should produce an institutionalized attempt to overcome feminine tendencies and to establish masculine sex typing in adolescent males. The Gusii, that is, should practice male initiation with circumcision, and they do so (see Figure 7-1). That the rites are effective in promoting masculine sex typing is suggested by the relatively low level of pregnancy symptoms among Gusii males—that is, one and one-half per man (Munroe & Munroe, 1973). Overall, the three societies conform well to prediction.

Chapter Eight

Social Motives

A popular stereotype holds that modern Western individuals have lost certain qualities characteristic of those who live in a simpler way. Supposedly Westerners are self-oriented, highly competitive, and constantly pushing for achievement, while non-Westerners are more group-oriented, cooperative, and accepting of things as they are. The stereotype has long persisted despite the fact that a dichotomy of this sort ignores the sharp variability among non-Western groups (Mead, 1937) and classes them all together as a type. A further problem is that generalizations about non-Westerners have typically been extrapolations from institutional arrangements to individuals—*Zuni social structure is communal; therefore the Zuni are cooperative people*— without any actual measurement at the individual level. Yet recent work surprisingly supports the stereotype, at least in broad outline. Furthermore, the source of the differences can be tentatively traced to socialization practices, and in the unusual cases in which non-Western societies' patterns of child rearing approach those of Western societies, the adult behavior pattern also approaches that of the West. Conversely, nonmodal Westerners, such as ethnic minority members and people in rural areas, tend to perform more like non-Western peoples. The major findings along these lines are discussed below under the headings of *competitiveness, achievement,* and *self-orientation.*

Numerous social motives of importance are excluded from this discussion. The particular topics chosen allow some broad comparisons, perhaps at the expense of a more careful analysis of the few well-composed cross-cultural studies. The generalizations purposefully ignore the vast differences among many of the complex and simple societies alike, go beyond the research itself, and might well be far too encompassing. But they may serve to provoke further inquiry into a set of motives so pervasive in modern life that they are implicitly accepted as proper values (for example, Hartup, 1965), if not assumed to be a part of human nature.

Competitiveness

Children like marbles, and if you put a marble in a holder attached to a string and give the other end of the string to a child, he will pull until he gets the marble. If you attach two strings to the holder and give the ends to different children, they are likely to pull against each other. What happens when the holder is designed to spill the marble if the children engage in a tug of war? Won't children quickly learn to take turns pulling so that first one and then the other can have a marble? Not if they are from urban areas (S. Kagan & Madsen, 1971; Madsen, 1967, 1971; Madsen & Shapira, 1970).What is more, competitiveness increases as children get older (S. Kagan & Madsen, 1971), and normal children are more competitive than retardates (Madsen & Connor, 1973). In other words, a normally intelligent city child becomes more and more competitive as he gets older, which is probably highly adaptive to city life in general but is not going to win him many marbles in this experimental setting.

Let us look at one of the marble studies in detail (Madsen, 1971). Mexican children from a small town and American white middle-class children from Los Angeles were both administered the marble-pull game illustrated in Figure 8-1. When two children take turns pulling the marble holder to their end of the table, they cause the marble to drop into a cup at their end on alternate trials and thereby obtain half the marbles each. But when each child pulls at the same time, the marble holder, held together by magnetic inserts, breaks apart and the marble rolls into a groove at the edge of the table. The upper part of Figure 8-1 shows this outcome. Prior to playing the game, all the children were thoroughly instructed in these conditions. Then, after they had undergone ten trials, they were asked about other possible ways to play the game. The key question was "If you wanted to get more marbles into your cup, how could you do it" (Madsen, 1971, p. 368)? Following the question, the children were instructed to alternately drop their string and let the other child have the marble. This explicit training in maximizing rewards was followed by ten more trials.

The difference between the Mexican and the American children was remarkably strong. Eight-year-old Mexicans obtained an av-

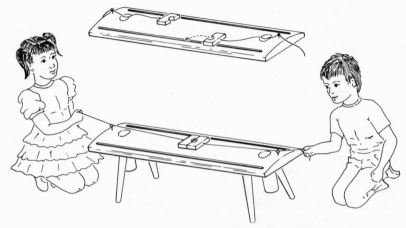

Figure 8-1. Marble-pull game. This figure from Developmental and cross-cultural differences in the cooperative and competitive behavior of young children, by M. C. Madsen, is reprinted from the *Journal of Cross-Cultural Psychology,* 1971, *2*(4), 367, by permission of the publisher, Sage Publications, Inc.

erage of 6.9 marbles during their first ten trials, and 8-year-old Americans averaged only 0.3 marbles. That is to say, the Mexicans usually cooperated, and the Americans almost never cooperated. The children were then given training in taking turns prior to the second round of trials. The Mexicans moved to perfect cooperation—a mean of 10.0 marbles—while the American children cooperated about half the time. Among 12-year-olds, the same level of difference was maintained between the Mexican and the American children, but the overall cooperation decreased in both groups. The children were undoubtedly growing wiser as they grew older because they could better verbalize the necessity of taking turns. But their competitiveness had increased, and it was maladaptive for the task of earning marbles.

Competitiveness does appear among Mexicans from urban areas (Madsen, 1967), and the same is true of urban Israeli versus kibbutz children (Shapira & Madsen, 1969) and of urban Canadians versus rural Indian Canadians (A. Miller & Thomas, 1972). At the opposite pole from urbanites are apparently found not only rural dwellers but traditional peoples as well. (For a negative instance, see Dennis, 1955.) Few examples of sharp competitiveness can be found in the ethnographic literature. One of the undoubted cases is the Kwakiutl Indians of potlatching[1] fame: "All the social relations of the Kwakiutl are keyed to the principle of rank, and each individual of any status in the community is motivated by an obsessive drive for prestige. . . .

[1]A potlatch was "a feast in which large quantities of food were consumed and great numbers of other objects given away" (Ember & Ember, 1973, pp. 129-130).

Above all, an individual gains prestige by crushing a rival" (Goldman, 1937, pp. 184-185). A rival is beaten by means of the potlatch: "Property is accumulated only to be redistributed or destroyed in a game in which prestige and self-glorification are raised to an egomaniacal pitch" (Goldman, 1937, p. 180). Perhaps the association is coincidental, but it is among the potlatching tribes that stuttering reached its greatest incidence in aboriginal North America (Johnson & Stewart, 1970). The potlatch system required formal, competitive speech rituals, which may have taken their toll in anxiety (see also Lemert, 1962).

While the Kwakiutl are a most unusual group in the traditional world, urban-industrial societies, as we have seen, produce competitiveness in abundance. Modern societies are not all alike, however, and the individuals in some seem to be even more competitive than those in others. Specifically, characterological stereotypes about four peoples—Americans, Soviets, Germans, and Japanese—contain a common element, a certain "drivenness," that may be equatable with competitiveness. These nations were the economic leaders of the world in the early 1970s (Population Reference Bureau, 1971), but they have had a good deal more in common in this century than their economic dominion. All have employed active and aggressive political tactics, and all have been very visible militarily. The syndrome extends to a nonutilitarian area like athletics: in the 1972 Olympic Games, the leading gold-medal winners were the Soviet Union (50), the United States (33), East Germany (20), West Germany (13), and Japan (13). The results were not due to advantages in sheer numbers. East Germany had less than half the population of France but won ten times as many gold medals. The competitiveness need not be individualistic; in Japan it is combined with strong familial and occupational loyalties and in Soviet society with group emphases (Bronfenbrenner, 1970), but it probably reaches a radical development when combined with personal concerns, as in the United States. Again, a purely expressive activity like athletics is revealing. The following are recent quotations from well-known American athletes and coaches:

> I go crazy when I'm introduced as the Number Two player in the world [instead of Number One].
> I just couldn't stand for anybody to be better than I was.
> You got to win and that's the only thing.
> When you win there is nothing—nothing—that can make you feel better. Not money, not anything.
> Losing is the worst pain in the world.
> Even if I fell down and died, that was better than losing.
> Losing is like death.
> Defeat is worse than death because you have to live with defeat.

The whole emphasis has been satirized by the novelist Philip Roth:

> Winning! Oh, you can't really say enough good things about it. There is nothing quite like it. Win hands down, win going away, win by a landslide, win by accident, win by a nose, win without deserving to win—you just can't beat it, however you slice it. Winning is the tops [1973, p. 287].

In all this material, the socialization variables that produce a competitive orientation are not specified, but they are likely to be closely bound up with the factors affecting achievement motivation.

Achievement

The long-term investigation of male achievement motivation by McClelland and his associates (Atkinson, 1958; McClelland, 1961; McClelland, Atkinson, Clark, & Lowell, 1953; McClelland & Winter, 1969) has provided insights at the individual, sociocultural, and historical levels.[2] The original work, experimental in character, found that subjects made to be concerned about their performance were more likely to write stories with achievement imagery in response to TAT cards than were subjects in whom a concern had not been experimentally aroused. On this basis, individuals who displayed strong TAT achievement imagery under neutral conditions—that is, without its being artificially induced—were considered to be characteristically high in achievement motivation. In daily life, the person with a strong need for achievement behaves in ways that increase the likelihood of his attaining success: he is attracted by moderately challenging tasks rather than by overly easy or high-risk tasks, he prefers personal responsibility for his job, he seeks and uses feedback on the quality of his work, and he innovates in order to improve (McClelland, 1971). These behaviors would seem particularly suited to entrepreneurial endeavors, and, in fact, the association of achievement motivation with successful economic behavior is strong. Men with high need for achievement who go into business are more likely to choose entrepreneurial positions than men with low achievement motivation (McClelland, 1965), and the men with high need for achievement seem to perform better at such occupations (Kock, 1965). High social mobility is correlated with need for achievement as well.

[2]Research on achievement motivation has yielded consistent findings for males. Studies of achievement motivation among females have been both sparse and inconsistent in findings and are not discussed here.

With historical materials, testing of individual achievement motivation is impossible, but several types of sociocultural products (folktales, children's stories in readers, and even the designs on pottery) are analyzable using the same coding systems applicable to individual fantasy productions. Because these "collective fantasies" would be widely available, known, and accepted within a given population, they seem to be usable to represent the average level of achievement concerns in any society. When this technique of measurement has been applied to historical data, it has successfully identified numerous peaks of economic attainment. The most provocative connection drawn was that between achievement motivation and the rise of capitalism. Max Weber's (1930) interpretation of market capitalism's rise as being intimately related to the Protestant Reformation's ideological emphases—especially the religious rationalization of all aspects of life and the devotion to one's vocation—was based on his observation that these doctrines had seemed to lead Protestants to work harder and to enter successfully into business more often than Catholics. McClelland argued that the relationship was probably due to the way in which the Reformation had changed the achievement-motivation level of individuals—had "put them on their toes . . . in their search for salvation" (1971, p. 16)—and that the Reformation-capitalism link was therefore only a special case of an increase in achievement motivation produced by an ideological change. Many findings demonstrate the existence of a Catholic-Protestant difference in achievement orientation or of known contributors to this orientation: (1) nonconformist Protestant sects made up only about 6% of Great Britain's population during the Industrial Revolution, but they produced about a third of the innovating entrepreneurs; (2) as of 1950, Protestant countries were well advanced over Catholic countries in economic development; (3) although no consistent differences in achievement motivation (standard measurement) could be found between present-day Catholics and Protestants in the United States (McClelland, 1971), most Protestant denominations far exceed Catholics in economic status, even when social factors like recency of immigration are controlled (Mayer & Sharp, 1962); (4) Protestant mothers in Germany subscribe less often than Catholic mothers to fatalistic statements about achievement—for example, that a man's success is already determined when he is born or that planning is not useful because one's plans hardly ever work out anyway (Wendt, 1960). And Catholic parents in the United States, as compared with Protestant parents, value obedience more highly, use more physical punishment, and do not believe it as important that a child think for himself (Lenski, 1961).

The last finding brings up the important point that a group's achievement disposition is likely to be maintained only if the child rearing is appropriately oriented. Parents of boys with high achievement motivation do show certain training and attitudinal characteristics. Parents set high standards, and mothers both interfere severely with dependency responses and try actively to foster early independence and achievement (McClelland, Atkinson, Clark & Lowell, 1953; Olsen, 1971; Rosen & D'Andrade, 1959; Winterbottom, 1958). (Also see Bartlett & Smith, 1966.) Fathers of boys who score low on achievement motivation, on the other hand, are domineering and authoritarian toward their sons (Rosen & D'Andrade, 1959). The most effective time for instilling achievement motivation is apparently from about ages 6 to 10 (McClelland, 1961). These socialization patterns hold not only for religious groups but for social classes, occupational groupings, and nations. In the United States, middle-class boys typically display higher achievement motivation than working-class boys (Douvan, 1956; Rosen, 1959, 1961), and they are exposed to parental values that should foster it (Kohn, 1969). In entrepreneurial families in the United States the mother stresses self-control and self-denial in child rearing more than the mother in bureaucratic families (D. Miller & Swanson, 1958). In nations where an authoritarian, father-dominated family structure exists, as in Brazil and Turkey, boys' achievement motivation scores are much lower than in the United States (Bradburn, 1963; Rosen, 1962; see also Ramirez, Taylor, & Petersen, 1971).

It is difficult to compare absolute levels of achievement motivation across societies, but the acceptance of authoritarian control (and primarily male-dominated family and social structures) around the world (Meade & Whittaker, 1967) suggests that child rearing in most non-Western societies is likely to be rigid and unbending enough to quell the development of strong achievement concerns.[3] By contrast, the more nearly egalitarian structures in the United States and in many other modern or modernizing societies (or segments of societies) imply the possibility of developing achievement motivation that in cross-cultural terms is both highly unusual and unusually high (LeVine, Klein, & Owen, 1967; Mussen & Beytagh, 1969). Thus the discrepancies between Western and non-Western economic development are probably a product not only of obvious cultural-historical factors but of differences in achievement motivation as well.

[3]Although non-Western societies may generally fall well below the West in average achievement-motivation levels, they are not all at an identically low level. Intersocietal variations exist, and, within this range, the McClelland formulation has successfully related frequency of achievement references in folktales to entrepreneurial activity and to childhood training for achievement (Child, Storm, & Veroff, 1958).

If the same variables are held to be operative everywhere and Western societies simply represent the farthest elaboration of achievement concerns, there ought to be identifiably high achievement motivation and appropriate child training among those few non-Western peoples who have been notably "successful" vis-à-vis other traditional societies. Two cases are available that strongly support this view. The Ibo of Nigeria have earned a reputation as perhaps the most capable and most ambitious group in sub-Saharan Africa. Prior to the recent civil war in Nigeria, their influence in economic affairs was strongly felt throughout the nation:

> Apart from [their] success in becoming a major part of the modernized professional and governing elite in Nigeria, Ibo entrepreneurs, fanning out all over the country, have also enjoyed a substantial measure of success. Ibo have a reputation for being willing to take any sort of job, no matter how menial, when they first enter a town and then working their way up, living frugally and accumulating resources until they become wealthy. Some have made the most of traditional craft specialties like blacksmithing; others have found new specialties in rubber working, automobile repair, and other occupations involving new technical skills. To a town like Calabar, containing an old Westernized Efik population, the Ibo came during the 1930's and 1940's, found economic opportunities that the Efik ignored, and soon became more powerful economically than the Efik, who were bitterly resentful [LeVine, 1966, pp. 74-75].

In the mid- and late-1960s, an unstable political situation in Nigeria was exacerbated by Ibo economic dominance. and. following a coup, there occurred a pogrom of Ibo living outside their home tribal area. Their secession and setting up of the independent state of Biafra ended ultimately in defeat in the civil war. But today the Ibo have once again begun their penetration into all areas of economic life in Nigeria.

The persistent push of the Ibo seems traceable to high achievement motivation (LeVine, 1966). Secondary-school boys from three major Nigerian tribal groups were asked to report dreams, and these were scored in the same way as TAT protocols. Ibo subjects reported a much higher percentage of dreams with achievement imagery than the Hausa, a large group in northern Nigeria, and a somewhat higher percentage than the Yoruba, another major tribal group that is relatively modernized. However, a complete reversal of tribal rankings occurred on essays written about success and scored for degree of obedience and social compliance. The Ibo *least* often saw success as linked to obedience-compliance, a dimension that appears to be negatively related to achievement motivation.

The second case involves the Manus of the Admiralty Islands, near New Guinea, who are virtually unique in the anthropological literature for having undergone profound and rapid cultural change without attendant social disruption and psychological trauma (Mead, 1956). In the 25 years from 1928 to 1953, the Manus moved from offshore pile dwellings to homes on the island, gave up G-strings and sago-leaf aprons for store-bought Western clothing, and completely dropped traditional ancestral religion in favor of church-going Christianity. The Manus were highly receptive to change and did not display the resistance offered by most peoples (Paul, 1955).

The Manus were also unusual in another way. Of all the societies rated for training in assertiveness vis-à-vis compliance by Barry, Child, and Bacon (1959), the Manus children received easily the highest score on assertiveness (achievement and self-reliance) training.[4] Their score was more than 10% above that of the closest society. The training was apparently successful, because in actual behavior the Manus children were rated as far beyond all others in exhibiting greater assertiveness than compliance. They showed no deference to parents or any other adults, performed no chores, and freely chose when to play, eat, and sleep (Mead, 1930). Initiative on the part of children was fully tolerated if not actively encouraged. Given the absence of male authoritarianism and the presence of achievement as a specific component of assertiveness training, the end result in traditional Manus society should have been, and evidently was, an adult with a strong achievement orientation. The traditional Manus, in the words of one interpreter, even had "a kind of Protestant ethic—valuing property, hard work, and financial success" (Barnouw, 1973, p. 136).

But like the premodern Ibo, the Manus were at a general techno-economic level that made indigenous development difficult. Even Japan, with early-Protestantlike values on hard work and self-denial (Bellah, 1957), did not explode economically until after contact with the West. In the West itself, the development of capitalism was aided by a series of supplementing factors, such as the rise of cities, the emergence of a middle class, the decline of Church authority, the pouring of wealth into Europe from the New World, and so on. Later, the economic growth of the United States received impetus from the Industrial Revolution and from staggering natural resources. In the same way, the Manus and Ibo achievement orientation was able to develop only when changed conditions increased the opportunities available. For the Ibo, the Pax Britannica, together with modern

---

[4]While low compliance demands during socialization also were argued to enhance cognitive development (Chapter 5), it is not expected that lower and lower demands would continue to produce higher and higher levels of cognitive functioning. Rather, when children are permitted or encouraged to exhibit a high level of assertiveness, cognitive development proceeds normally. In addition, individuals appear to be motivated strongly to achieve the goods and goals available in that society.

transportation systems, allowed secure expansion beyond the old tribal boundaries into all parts of the Nigerian colony. For the Manus, it was missionization and later the economic example set by American men and materiel in World War II that may have supplied the models for change. These facts suggest that in traditional society the most powerful achievement orientations are perhaps doomed to be overridden by cultural-historical factors, and only in special circumstances will high achievement motivation result in marked economic development. Nonetheless, Ibo and Manus achievements demonstrate the probable cross-cultural validity of the McClelland formulation.

Self-Orientation

Besides Shakespeare and me, who do you think there is?

Gertrude Stein

The rise of the "self" is recent in Western history. Concurrent with the rise has been an emphasis on the individual in economic, social, political, and spiritual matters. Not until the 17th century, for example, did self-prefixes (such as self-regard) appear in English; their introduction coincided with the growing importance of individualistic Puritanism (Bruner, 1951). Today the ascendancy of the self is taken for granted. We are unsurprised to hear a 9-year-old, beaten by an adult more than two to one in a Scrabble game, nonetheless proclaim afterward "I was brilliant," or to read that the critic Edmund Wilson would arise at 4 A.M. to read old reviews of his books (Wilson, 1971), or to learn of social science studies on self-esteem, self-perception, self-presentation, and even self-actualization.

The Western self-orientation is extreme by worldwide standards, and three major studies demonstrate it as such. In five American Southwest communities, three Western and two Indian, adult individuals were administered a carefully formulated questionnaire designed to evoke their orientations to a series of common human problems—for example, the nature of human nature, the relation of man to nature, and the relation of men to each other (Kluckhohn & Strodtbeck, 1961). For the last problem, the structured responses were sortable into one of three styles of relationship to other men—individualistic, lineal, or collateral. All three Western groups (Anglo Homesteaders, Mormons, and Spanish-Americans) felt individualistic relationships to be right, whereas Navaho and Zuni Indians chose collateral, or group-oriented, relations. The following is a typical problem from the relational sphere. Answer B was scored as *Collateral* and Answer C as *Individualistic*.

> Help in Misfortune. A man had a crop failure, or, let us say, had lost most of his sheep or cattle. He and his family had to have help from someone if they were going to get through the winter. There are different ways of getting help. Which of these . . . ways would be best?
>
> B   Would it be best if he depended mostly on his brothers
> (Coll) and sisters or other relatives all to help him out
>   as much as each one could?
>
> C   Would it be best for him to try to raise the money
> (Ind) *on his own* outside the community (his own peo-
>   ple) from people who are neither relatives nor em-
>   ployers? [Kluckhohn & Strodtbeck, 1961, p. 83]

In the Homesteader, Mormon, and Zuni communities, third-through sixth-graders were given a series of paper-and-pencil tests, and already in this middle-childhood period there were definite signs of the emerging values (Whiting, Chasdi, Antonovsky, & Ayres, 1966). On a question about magical change in status, the Western emphasis on the self could be seen in the personal-achievement responses given by Homesteaders and Mormons (48% of the two samples) as compared to Zuni (20% of the sample). In answer to a question about the worst thing that could happen to a person, Westerners showed a heightened concern over the self by their high frequency of responses like "death" or "injury" (50%) in comparison with the Zuni's responses relating to self (31%). The modal response for the Zuni on this question involved a less radical self-concern in the form of some sort of punishment.

The second study also compared white Americans with Indian Americans, only this time a single group of Anglo schoolchildren was contrasted with seven Amerindian groups of schoolchildren (Havighurst & Neugarten, 1955). From a test of moral ideology and from one of emotional response, several variables related to the self were extracted. The Anglo children scored at the top of the scale on almost all the variables, namely, individual achievement, competence, self-restraint, and self-gratification. In the concluding description, the authors depict the Anglo society as follows: "In comparison to the simpler societies of the Southwest Indians, Midwest is a self-centered society, where the individual's responsibility and the individual's feelings are given priority over his concern about the social group" (Havighurst & Neugarten, 1955, p. 198).

The third study was part of the Six Cultures Study (B. Whiting & Whiting, 1975; Whiting & Whiting, 1973). In this case, behavioral observations, not tests or questionnaires, of children aged 3 to 11 comprised the data. Twelve types of social behavior were identified, and three of these that clustered were concerned with self-seeking actions, namely, *seeking attention, seeking dominance,* and *seeking help,* and were together labeled as *egoistic* behavior. Children from three of the six societies were relatively egoistic, but the Americans scored more than 40% above even the second highest.

Findings from the three studies are in agreement, but the Six Cultures Study has gone beyond the others and asked about the sources of egoistic behavior. In addition to the American children, those in a community in India and a community in Okinawa behaved egoistically in contrast to the remaining three societies. The common factor among these communities was their relative complexity, each of the high-egoism societies displaying more in the way of occupational specialization, social stratification, political centralization, and religious specialization than the low-egoism communities. Complexity was related in turn to a small work load for mothers—where there is specialization, the mother is relieved of some of the work she would otherwise assume—and also to a low chore load for children—where the mother works less, she has less need to organize the children to help. To put it another way, cultural complexity breeds an efficiency that reduces the need for children to contribute to the family, and the result is an orientation away from the family and toward the self. In a word, the self is a luxury item that emerges in surplus economies.

Let us speculate a bit. A heightened sense of self may allow sensitivity in certain areas of experience, a sensitivity that we have come to accept as natural but that may be more or less peculiar to individuals in the developed countries. For instance, classical psychoanalysis may be impossible in groups in which verbal self-awareness is not emphasized (LeVine, 1973a), and this would include most peoples of the world. Also, an ailing self, or psychoneurosis, may appear much more frequently where the sense of self is great—civilization and its malcontents, we might say. Similarly, the experience of depression, both as pathology and in its less severe episodic form, may be more available to the highly self-oriented individual. Depression has in fact been observed less frequently in some traditional areas than in Western or highly Christianized societies (LeVine, 1961; Wittkower, 1969), and special depressive problems like the involutional melancholia occasionally associated with menopause are virtually absent in the traditional world. Even ennui can perhaps be experienced strongly only where a sharp self-orientation exists.

Another possible outcome of the treatment of the self as a discrete and important entity may be the ability to regulate one's own behavior to a marked degree, as in long-term delay of gratification, or in the application of internal moral standards rather than socially imposed controls (such as gossip or witchcraft accusations) (Grinder & McMichael, 1963). That simpler societies may function with less self-regulation of behavior is supported by the finding that mothers in these groups impose more obedience demands and are more authoritarian in their relations with children (B. Whiting & Whiting, 1975). On a completely different tack, religious mysticism, promoting loss of the self in the All, has regularly appeared in the great civilizations but not in traditional societies, and may represent a recurring cultural "solution" to the problems generated by high self-concern. Asceticism and masochism also appear more frequently in modern societies. LeVine has stated, for example, that "Africans usually cannot understand what moral virtue there can be in extreme forms of self-denial and self-punishment" (1973b, p. 143). Self-denial and self-injury are more probable where there is greater self-awareness.

Cognition might be affected by a strong self-orientation. Sharp differentiation of self from social environment should facilitate the context-free thought that is characteristic of modern man (see Chapter Five) and would be an additional factor explaining their cognitive performance in comparison with that of traditional peoples. On this point, unfound among traditional peoples are so-called idiot savants, who can perform incredible computational feats but whose defective reasoning ability leaves them unable to comprehend ordinary conversations and makes them classifiable as mental retardates. Perhaps idiot savants develop their special skills out of an awareness of social rejection and a resulting focus and pertinacity bred from their desire to gain acceptance (Fowler, 1969). The rejection could lead to a greater-than-usual concern with self, and the high self-concern might well be a necessary condition for the anomalous attainments of these individuals. The absence of idiot savants in traditional societies may reflect greater social acceptance of mental retardation and, ultimately, show evidence of less stimulation of self-concern in retardates. Along these same lines, men of genius have suffered the early death of a parent far more frequently than a chance level would predict (Albert, 1971), and, again, an experience meaningful for self-concern might be implicated as a background factor.

If the individual is sensitive to his own self, it follows that he may achieve awareness of other selves. The capacity for strong empathy—or, in psychoanalytic terms, the extension of the self—

could be dependent on the prior development of a strong self and might account in part for the stress that Westerners put on love, intimacy, and emotional attachments in interpersonal relations (Leichty, 1963; LeVine, 1973b). The existence of primary caretakers who are empathic assures some perpetuation of the self-focusing system. Even a trivial matter like concern for pets is apparently distributed differentially among Westerners and at least some non-Westerners: "The reaction of Africans to the pet-keeping practices of Britons and Americans living in Africa is usually one of astonishment and amusement at the personalized concern and affection for animals" (LeVine, 1973b, p. 142). The trauma of separation among intimates in the Western world, described below by LeVine, would be found in few traditional societies.

> We are accustomed to making strenuous efforts to avoid separating from our most intimate loved ones, to engaging in tearful departures and reunions, and to making the assumption that separation in physical residence—as when a child leaves home—has a final quality about it like a death and must be similarly mourned until the original emotional investment is irrevocably withdrawn or attenuated. These tendencies are not only widespread in our populations but are exalted in a variety of cultural forms ranging from sentimental literature and films to humanitarian ideologies with their concern about those who are rejected and abandoned . . . (1973b, p. 141).

There is, finally, still another side to this. Just as self-orientation implies the possibility of other-orientation, so empathic emotions imply the possibility not only of strong positive relations but also of strong negative relations with others. If the feelings of other selves can be understood emotionally, then great love can be generated and so, too, can great hate. Christian love is linked indissolubly with religious bigotry (Hsu, 1972): *onward Christian soldiers.* Wartime atrocities, political purges, exquisite torture methods, and acts of sadism are all more available to the self that can apprehend what other selves are feeling.

The United States and some other modern nations may lie at the far end of a scale of self-orientation, but the Six Culture findings indicate that a similar development, if not so powerful, will take place whenever there is cultural complexity. As long as the child is not needed he will focus on himself, and as the simpler traditional patterns continue to fade in the 20th century, this development of self may soon be common everywhere.

Child training in modern society discourages dependency, encourages achievement, and urges self-development. The regimen must be effective in producing individuals who can tolerate remote and impersonal means of gaining need satisfaction and of learning necessary skills—the supermarket replacing the family farm and the school system replacing the elders—because we enter just such a society. But in the United States at least, the self-reliance and independence that are so greatly valued (Hsu, 1972) are not always evident in social life. Americans are in fact highly sensitive to the opinions of others (Riesman, 1950) and enter into a relatively large number of voluntary groups and organizations (McClelland, Sturr, Knapp, & Wendt, 1958). As children they learn at an early age to act sociably (B. Whiting & Whiting, 1975) and to take the viewpoint of and offer assistance to "the other" (Boehm, 1957; Dennis, 1957). Why? Perhaps the empathic qualities generated by a heightened self-orientation can account for it. Perhaps, too, the values represent an extreme that cannot be realistically maintained, and the groupiness of Americans might be partially a compensatory mechanism. More likely than either of these possibilities, though, is that Americans are putting the group to use in the service of their motives, in this case to lend validity to the self and to support and check on their own striving behavior (Hsu, 1972; McClelland et al., 1958). Whether this proposition is correct and whether other complex societies show evidence of similar trends are matters that cannot be resolved at present. But the social motives examined in this chapter are important and deserving of continued inquiry.

Three Cultures

If strong competitiveness, achievement concerns, and self-orientation are characteristic of individuals in the modern world, then these motives should be little in evidence among the traditional Ainu, Trobrianders, and Gusii. A reading of the ethnographies confirms this expectation, but the psychological materials to document the point are unavailable. The only exception is with respect to self-orientation and the Gusii. As one of the societies in the Six Cultures Study, the Gusii can be compared with American children on the three types of social behavior making up egoism—seeking attention, seeking dominance, and seeking help. Almost one-third (32%) of the American children's behaviors belonged to the egoistic category, while less than a tenth

(9%) of the Gusii children's behaviors were so categorized (B. Whiting & Whiting, 1975). The Gusii community, like the other low-egoism groups in the Six Cultures Study, had little cultural complexity, a resulting high work load for mothers, and a high chore load for the children. The outcome should have been, and was, a low score in self-seeking behavior among Gusii children.

Conclusion

In the Introduction a general rationale for the book was presented, including an explication of the approach, an outline of convictions and biases, and a brief for the organization and presentation of findings. The various statements can be boiled down to a set of four major working assumptions, which will now be revived for a short review and assessment.

First, on the usefulness of a contrast between traditional societies and Western-modern groups, the developmental areas treated most fully in this way were cognition and the social motives of competitiveness, achievement, and self-orientation. Differences in these areas apparently have arisen from the Western child's exposure to a regimen purposefully designed to maximize his development: he is trained to be smart, competitive, and achieving, and he is expected to be self-oriented. All these facets of what might be called *developmental hypertrophy* seem to have at their root a kind of focused stimulation that is seldom found in traditional society. But in addition to the child-rearing emphasis, there is a matrix of mutually supportive rewards and controls and of special institutional arrangements that work to support the socialization practices, as in the formal educational system that spurs cognitive development and the socioeconomic institutions that help elicit competitiveness and achievement. If a traditional society happened to adopt only the narrowly appropriate socialization practices for producing hyperdevelopment in one of the developmental areas, it is not altogether certain that the outcome would be the same as in the West. The point is illustrated by the traditional Ibo and Manus (Chapter Eight), among whom intensive achievement concerns did not find full expression until opportunities were presented them via potent cultural change.

A second assumption, that early experience influences adult behavior to a significant degree, has been emphatically supported by the cross-cultural findings. But since so much of the discussion in the preceding chapters has been taken up with precisely such relationships, just a few instances will be noted. In both dependence and sex training, the imposition of early punishment seems to lead to adult anxiety about these behavior systems. The low salience of adult males in infancy and early childhood seems to lead to sex-typing problems for men. In general, it can be said that a stronger genetic contribution is probably involved in the developmental topics covered by the early chapters than in those covered by the later chapters. Early experience, then, as long as it includes ordinary environmental stimulation, typically leads to more uniform cross-cultural outcomes in the areas of physical growth, perception, affect, and language.

A third assumption was that a cross-cultural approach would enable us to extend the kinds and the range of variables available to investigation. The noncarpentered environment, a condition that is not part of the ordinary Western experience, has been proposed as the determinant of the weak susceptibility of traditional peoples to the Müller-Lyer visual illusion. The severe physical stressing of infants, again a condition that is unusual in the modern experience, apparently leads to marked increases in adult height. And the involvement of children in necessary family duties, once more an unusual event in the modern world, seems to lead to a low level of self-seeking behavior. Findings of this sort, as said above, help us to avoid assuming too much about human nature. Sometimes, though, the very absence of a broad spread of responses can be a clue to the nature of human nature. In affective development, for instance, both animal research and data from studies of institutional deprivation had suggested that there must be steady interpersonal contact during the period of infancy if the child was to become capable of developing positive and lasting affective responses toward others. Given the probability that a society comprising entirely affectively unresponsive individuals would be incapable of the cooperation and reciprocity necessary to human social life, it would have been surprising to find any group customarily treating infants as they are treated in cases of severe institutional deprivation. The fact that no society does neglect infants in this manner is a piece of evidence implying the importance—and maybe even the necessity—of a severely restricted range of infant socialization practices in the affective sphere.

Finally, the assumption was made that a cross-cultural approach could tell us whether a given relationship was valid only in the Western world or whether it held up universally. The issue, of course, involves aspects of all the preceding assumptions but goes beyond them. To take a negative case, the unassimilability of lactose by many non-Caucasoid populations sharply limits statements about the relationship between milk and resulting nutritional status. As a positive case, the linguistic generalization that children everywhere go through one-word and two-word phases in grammatical development, though still based on very incomplete evidence, appears to represent a true developmental universal—one that has weighty implications for theories of human behavior. The same question of universality must be applied to the several "grand schemes" of development: it has become clear today that the higher levels of, say, Erikson's Eight Stages or of Piaget's intellectual hierarchy sound suspiciously like modern man and no other, just as it became clear to an earlier generation that phases such as latency, adolescence, and menopausal change of life were descriptive of the experiences of only some populations and not of all. Yet the lower stages of these same theories (that is, Erikson's *basic trust* and Piaget's *sensorimotor intelligence)* point to developmental characteristics that have great cross-cultural promise. Perhaps it is here, at the primary levels of these ambitious systems, that the search for developmental universals should continue. And, perhaps, the next ambitious theoretical system will also provide greater understanding of adult humans' ingeniously diverse modes of thought and behavior.

References

Achar, S. T., & Yankauer, A. Studies on the birth weight of South Indian infants. *Indian Journal of Child Health*, 1962, *11*, 157–167.

Ainsworth, M. D. S. *Infancy in Uganda*. Baltimore: Johns Hopkins Press, 1967.

Albert, R. S. Cognitive development and parental loss among the gifted, the exceptionally gifted and the creative. *Psychological Reports*, 1971, *29*, 19–26.

Albright, R. W., & Albright, J. B. The phonology of a two-year-old child. In A. Bar-Adon & W. F. Leopold (Eds.), *Child language*. Englewood Cliffs, N.J.: Prentice-Hall, 1971. Pp. 142–146. (Originally published 1956.)

Anastasi, A. *Differential psychology*. New York: Macmillan, 1958.

Atkinson, J. W. (Ed.) *Motives in fantasy, action, and society*. Princeton, N.J.: Van Nostrand, 1958.

Ayres, B. Pregnancy magic: A study of food taboos and sex avoidances. In C. S. Ford (Ed.), *Cross-cultural approaches*. New Haven: HRAF Press, 1967. Pp. 111–125.

Bach, G. R. Father-fantasies and father typing in father-separated children. *Child Development*, 1946, *17*, 63–80.

Bacon, M. K., Child, I., & Barry, H., III. A cross-cultural study of correlates of crime. *Journal of Abnormal and Social Psychology*, 1963, *66*, 291–300.

Baker, H. J., & Stoller, R. J. Biological force postulated as having role in gender identity. *Roche Reports: Frontiers of Hospital Psychiatry*, 1967, *4*(3).

Bandura, A., & Walters, R. H. *Adolescent aggression*. New York: Ronald Press, 1959.

Bandura, A., & Walters, R. H. Aggression. In H. W. Stevenson (Ed.), *Child psychology*. The Sixty-second Yearbook of the National Society for Education, University of Chicago Press, 1963. Pp. 364–415.

Barclay, A. G., & Cusumano, D. Father-absence, cross-sex identity, and field-dependent behavior in male adolescents. *Child Development*, 1967, *38*, 243–250.

Barnouw, V. *Culture and personality* (Rev. ed.). Homewood, Ill.: Dorsey, 1973.

Barry, H., III. Cultural variations in the development of mental illness. In S. C. Plog & R. G. Edgerton (Eds.), *Changing perspectives in mental illness*. New York: Holt, Rinehart and Winston, 1969. Pp. 155–178.

Barry, H., III., Bacon, M. K., & Child, I. L. A cross-cultural survey of some sex differences in socialization. *Journal of Abnormal and Social Psychology*, 1957, *55*, 327–332.

Barry, H., III., Bacon, M. K., & Child, I. L. Definitions, ratings and bibliographic sources of child-training practices of 110 cultures. In C. S. Ford (Ed.), *Cross-cultural approaches*. New Haven: HRAF Press, 1967. Pp. 293–331.

Barry, H., III., Child, I. L., & Bacon, M. K. Relation of child training to subsistence economy. *American Anthropologist*, 1959, *61*, 51–63.

Barry, H., III., & Paxson, L. M. Infancy and early childhood: Cross-cultural codes 2. *Ethnology*, 1971, *10*, 466–508.

Bartlett, E. W., & Smith, C. P. Child-rearing practices, birth order, and the development of achievement-related motives. *Psychological Reports*, 1966, *18*, 1207–1216.

Batchelor, J. *The Ainu of Japan*. New York: Fleming H. Revell, 1895.

Bayley, N. On the growth of intelligence. *American Psychologist*, 1955, *10*, 805–818.

Bayley, N. *Manual for the Bayley scales of infant development*. New York: Psychological Corporation, 1969.

Beach, F. A. Characteristics of masculine 'sex drive.' In M. R. Jones (Ed.), *Nebraska symposium on motivation, 1956*. Lincoln: University of Nebraska Press, 1956. Pp. 1–32.

Bellah, R. N. *Tokugawa religion. The values of pre-industrial Japan*. Glencoe, Ill.: Free Press, 1957.

Benedict, R. *Patterns of culture*. Boston: Houghton Mifflin, 1934.

Benedict, R. Continuities and discontinuities in cultural conditioning. *Psychiatry*, 1938, *1*, 161–167.

Berlin, B., & Berlin, E. A. Aguaruna color categories. *American Ethnologist*, 1975, *2*, 61–87.

Berlin, B., & Kay, P. *Basic color terms: Their universality and evolution*. Berkeley: University of California Press, 1969.

Bernstein, B. *Class, codes and control* (Vol. 1). London: Routledge & Kegan Paul, 1971.

Berry, J. W. Temne and Eskimo perceptual skills. *International Journal of Psychology*, 1966, *1*, 207–229.

Berry, J. W. Müller-Lyer susceptibility: Culture, ecology or race? *International Journal of Psychology*, 1971, *6*, 193–197.

Berry, J. W. Ecological and cultural factors in spatial perceptual development. In J. W. Berry & P. R. Dasen (Eds.), *Culture and cognition: Readings in cross-cultural psychology*. London: Methuen, 1974. Pp. 129–140. (Originally published 1971.)

Berry, J. W., & Dasen, P. R. (Eds.) *Culture and cognition: Readings in cross-cultural psychology*. London: Methuen, 1974.

Biller, H. B. A multiaspect investigation of masculine development in kindergarten-age boys. *Genetic Psychology Monographs*, 1968, *76*, 89–139. (a)

Biller, H. B. A note on father-absence and masculine development in young lower-class Negro and white boys. *Child Development*, 1968, *39*, 1003–1006. (b)

Biller, H. B. Father-absence, maternal encouragement, and sex-role development in kindergarten age boys. *Child Development*, 1969, *40*, 539–546.

Bloom, B. S. *Stability and change in human characteristics*. New York: Wiley, 1964.

Blount, B. G. Aspects of Luo socialization. *Language in Society*, 1972, *1*, 235–248.

Boehm, L. The development of independence: A comparative study. *Child Development*, 1957, *28*, 85–92.

Bohannan, P. The Tiv of Nigeria. In J. L. Gibbs (Ed.), *Peoples of Africa*. New York: Holt, Rinehart and Winston, 1965. Pp. 513–546.

Bolton, R. Aggression and hypoglycemia among the Qolla: A study in psychobiological anthropology. *Ethnology*, 1973, *12*, 227–257.

Bolton, R. Michelson, C., Wilde, J., & Bolton, C. The heights of illusion: On the relationship between altitude and perception. *Ethos,* in press.

Bornstein, M. H. Color vision and color naming: A psychophysiological hypothesis of cultural difference. *Psychological Bulletin*, 1973, *80*, 257-285.

Bowlby, J. *Attachment and loss* (Vol. 1). New York: Basic Books, 1969.

Brackbill, Y. *Research and clinical work with children*. Washington, D.C.: American Psychological Association, 1962.

Bradburn, N. M. *n* achievement and father dominance in Turkey. *Journal of Abnormal and Social Psychology*, 1963, *67*, 464-468.

Braine, M. D. S. The ontogeny of English phrase structure: The first phase. *Language*, 1963, *39*, 1-13.

Briggs, J. L. *Never in anger*. Cambridge: Harvard University Press, 1970.

Brislin, R. W., Lonner, W. J., & Thorndike, R. M. *Cross-cultural research methods*. New York: Wiley, 1973.

Brockman, L. M., & Ricciuti, H. N. Severe protein-calorie malnutrition and cognitive development in infancy and early childhood. *Developmental Psychology*, 1971, *4*, 312-319.

Bronfenbrenner, U. *Two worlds of childhood: U.S. and U.S.S.R.* New York: Clarion, 1970.

Brown, J. K. A cross-cultural study of female initiation rites. *American Anthropologist*, 1963, *65*, 837-853.

Brown, J. K. A note on the division of labor by sex. *American Anthropologist*, 1970, *72*, 1073-1078.

Brown, R. *Words and things*. Glencoe, Ill.: Free Press, 1958.

Brown, R. *Social psychology*. New York: Free Press, 1965.

Brown, R. *A first language*. Cambridge: Harvard University Press, 1973.

Brown, R., & Bellugi, U. Three processes in the child's acquisition of syntax. *Harvard Educational Review*, 1964, *34*, 133-151.

Brown, R., Cazden, C., & Bellugi-Klima, U. The child's grammar from I to III. In J. P. Hill (Ed.), *Minnesota symposia on child psychology* (Vol. 2). Minneapolis: University of Minnesota Press, 1969. Pp. 28-73.

Brown, R., & Frazer, C. The acquisition of syntax. In C. N. Cofer & B. S. Musgrave (Eds.), *Verbal behavior and learning: Problems and processes*. New York: McGraw-Hill, 1963. Pp. 158-197.

Bruner, J. S. Personality dynamics and the process of perceiving. In R. R. Blake & G. V. Ramsey (Eds.), *Perception: An approach to personality*.

New York: Ronald Press, 1951. Pp. 121-147.

Bruner, J. S. On cognitive growth: II. In J. S. Bruner, R. R. Olver, & P. M. Greenfield, *Studies in cognitive growth*. New York: Wiley, 1966. Pp. 30-67.

Burton, R. V. Cross-sex identity in Barbados. *Developmental Psychology,* 1972, *6,* 365-374.

Burton, R. V. Folk theory and the incest taboo. *Ethos,* 1973, *1,* 504-516.

Burton, R. V., & Whiting, J. W. M. The absent father and cross-sex identity. *Merrill-Palmer Quarterly,* 1961, *7,* 85-95.

Caldwell, B. M., Hersher, L., Lipton, E. L., Richmond, J. B., Stern, G. A., Eddy, E., Drachman, R., & Rothman, A. Mother-infant interaction in monomatric and polymatric families. *American Journal of Orthopsychiatry,* 1963, *33,* 653-664.

Carlsmith, L. Some personality characteristics of boys separated from their fathers during World War II. *Ethos,* 1973, *1,* 466-477.

Cavalli-Sforza, L. L., & Bodmer, W. F. *The genetics of human populations.* San Francisco: W. H. Freeman, 1971.

Cazden, C. B., & John, V. P. Learning in American Indian children. In M. L. Wax, S. Diamond, & F. O. Gearing (Eds.), *Anthropological perspectives on education*. New York: Basic Books, 1971. Pp. 252-272.

Chagnon, N. A. *Yanomamo.* New York: Holt, Rinehart and Winston, 1968.

Chamove, A., Harlow, H. F., & Mitchell, G. Sex differences in the infant-directed behavior of preadolescent rhesus monkeys. *Child Development,* 1967, *38,* 329-336.

Child, I. L., Barry, H., III., & Bacon, M. K. A cross-cultural study of drinking: III. Sex differences. *Quarterly Journal of Studies on Alcohol,* Supplement No. 3, 1965, 49-61.

Child, I. L., Storm, T., & Veroff, J. Achievement themes in folk tales related to socialization practice. In J. W. Atkinson (Ed.), *Motives in fantasy, action, and society.* Princeton, N. J.: Van Nostrand, 1958. Pp. 479-492.

Chomsky, C. S. *The acquisition of syntax in children from 5 to 10.* Research Monograph No. 57. Cambridge: M.I.T. Press, 1969.

Chomsky, N. A. *Language and mind.* New York: Harcourt Brace Jovanovich, 1968.

Chopra, S. L. Measured intelligence and academic achievement as related to urban-rural residence. *Rural Sociology,* 1968, *33,* 214-217.

Clark, G., & Birch, H. G. Hormonal modifications of social behavior.I. The effect of sex-hormone administration on the social status of a male-castrate chimpanzee. *Psychosomatic Medicine,* 1945, *7,* 321-329.

Cohen, Y. A. Food and its vicissitudes: A cross-cultural study of sharing. In Y. A. Cohen (Ed.), *Social structure and personality.* New York: Holt, Rinehart and Winston, 1962. Pp. 312-350.

Cohen, Y. A. *The transition from childhood to adolescence.* Chicago: Aldine, 1964.

Cole, M., Frankel, F., & Sharp, D. W. The development of free recall learning in children. *Developmental Psychology,* 1971, *4,* 109-123.

Cole, M., Gay, J., Glick, J. A., & Sharp, D. W. *The cultural context of learning and thinking.* New York: Basic Books, 1971.

Cole, M., & Scribner, S. *Culture and thought.* New York: Wiley, 1974.

Cratty, B. J. *Perceptual and motor development in infants and children.* New York: Macmillan, 1970.

Cravioto, J., Birch, H. G., De Licardie, E., Rosales, L., & Vega, L. The ecology of growth and development in a Mexican preindustrial community. Report 1: Method and findings from birth to one month of age. *Monographs of the Society for Research in Child Development,* 1969, *34*(5).

Cutter, W. B. *Household structure, behavior, and personality in Barbados.* Unpublished honors thesis, Harvard University, 1964.

Dale, P. S. *Language development.* Hinsdale, Ill.: Dryden Press, 1972.

D'Andrade, R. G. Sex differences and cultural institutions. In E. E. Maccoby (Ed.), *The development of sex differences.* Stanford, Calif.: Stanford University Press, 1966. Pp. 174-204.

D'Andrade, R. G. Father absence, identification, and identity. *Ethos,* 1973, *1,* 440-455.

Daniels, R. E. *By rites a man: A study of the societal and individual foundations of tribal identity among the Kipsigis of Kenya.* Unpublished doctoral dissertation, University of Chicago, 1970.

Danziger, K. *Socialization.* Harmondsworth, England: Penguin, 1971.

Dasen, P. R. Cross-cultural Piagetian research: A summary. *Journal of Cross-Cultural Psychology,* 1972, *3,* 23-39. (a)

Dasen, P. R. The development of conservation in Aboriginal children. A replication study. *International Journal of Psychology,* 1972, *7,* 85-95. (b)

David, K. H. Effect of verbal reinforcement on Porteus Maze scores among Australian Aborigine children. *Perceptual and Motor Skills,* 1967, *24,*986.

Davis, K. *Human society.* New York: Macmillan, 1949.

Dawson, J. L. M. Cultural and physiological influences upon spatial-perceptual processes in West Africa—Part I. *International Journal of Psychology,* 1967, *2,*115-125. (a)

Dawson, J. L. M. Cultural and physiological influences upon spatial-perceptual processes in West Africa—Part II. *International Journal of Psychology,* 1967, *2,* 171-185. (b)

Dawson, J. L. M., Young, B. M., & Choi, P. P. C. Developmental influences on geometric illusion susceptibility among Hong Kong Chinese children. *Journal of Cross-Cultural Psychology,* 1973, *4,* 49-74.

de Lemos, M. M. The development of conservation in Aboriginal children. *International Journal of Psychology,* 1969, *4,* 255-269.

Dennis, W. Are Hopi children noncompetitive? *Journal of Abnormal and Social Psychology,* 1955, *50,* 99-100.

Dennis, W. A cross-cultural study of the reinforcement of child behavior. *Child Development,* 1957, *28,* 431-438.

Dennis, W. Causes of retardation among institutional children: Iran. *Journal of Genetic Psychology,* 1960, *96,* 47-59.

Dennis, W., & Dennis, M. G. The effect of cradling practices upon the onset of walking in Hopi children. *Journal of Genetic Psychology,* 1940, *56,* 77-86.

Dennis, W., & Najarian, P. Infant development under environmental handicap. *Psychological Monographs,* 1957, *71*(436).

Deregowski, J. B. On perception of depicted orientation. *International Journal of Psychology,* 1968, *3,* 149-156. (a)

Deregowski, J. B. Difficulties in pictorial depth perception in Africa. *British Journal of Psychology,* 1968, *59,* 195-204. (b)

Deregowski, J. B. A pictorial perception paradox. *Acta Psychologica,* 1969, *31,* 365-374.

Deregowski, J. B. Responses mediating pictorial recognition. *Journal of Social Psychology,* 1971, *84,* 27-33.

Deutsch, M. Happenings on the way back to the Forum. *Harvard Educational Review,* 1969, *39,* 523-557.

Deutsch, M., Katz, I., & Jensen, A. R. (Eds.) *Social class, race, and psychological development.* New York: Holt, Rinehart and Winston, 1968.

Devereaux, G. Institutionalized homosexuality of the Mohave Indians. *Human Biology,* 1937, *9,* 508-527.

DeVore, I. Male dominance and mating behavior in baboons. In F. A. Beach (Ed.), *Sex and behavior.* New York: Wiley, 1965. Pp. 266-289.

Dobrizhoffer, M. *An account of the Abipones.* London: J. Murray, 1822. (Originally published 1783.)

Dollard, J., & Miller, N. E. *Personality and psychotherapy.* New York: McGraw-Hill, 1950.

Doob, L. W. Psychology. In R. A. Lystad (Ed.), *The African world.* London; Pall Mall Press, 1965. Pp. 373-415.

Douvan, E. Social status and success striving. *Journal of Abnormal and Social Psychology,* 1956, *52,* 219-223.

Du Bois, C. Attitudes toward food and hunger in Alor. In L. Spier, A. I. Hallowell, & S. S. Newman (Eds.), *Language, culture, and personality: Essays in memory of Edward Sapir.* Menasha, Wis.: 1941. Pp. 272-281.

Du Bois, C. *The people of Alor.* Minneapolis: University of Minnesota Press, 1944.

Duncan, H. F., Gourlay, N., & Hudson, W. *A study of pictorial perception among Bantu and White primary school children in South Africa.* Witwatersrand: Witwatersrand University Press, 1973.

Durkheim, E. *The rules of the sociological method.* S. Solovay & J. Mueller, trans. New York: Free Press, 1938. (Originally published 1895.)

Elkind, D. Quantity conceptions in junior and senior high school students. *Child Development,* 1961, *32,* 551-560.

El'konin, D. B. General course of development in the child of the grammatical structure of the Russian language (according to A. N. Gvozdev). In C. A. Ferguson & D. I. Slobin (Eds.), *Studies of child language development.* New York: Holt, Rinehart & Winston, 1973. Pp. 565-583. (Originally published 1958.)

Ember, C. R. Feminine task assignment and the social behavior of boys. *Ethos,* 1973, *1,* 424-439.

Ember, C. R., & Ember, M. *Cultural anthropology.* New York: Appleton-Century-Crofts, 1973.

Erikson, E. H. *Childhood and society.* New York: Norton, 1950.

Erlenmeyer-Kimling, L., & Jarvik, L. F. Genetics and intelligence: A review. *Science,* 1963, *142,* 1477-1479.

Escalona, S. *Roots of individuality.* Chicago: Aldine, 1968.

Evans, J. L., & Segall, M. H. Learning to classify by color and by function: A study of concept-discovery by Ganda children. *Journal of Social Psychology,* 1969, *77,* 35-53.

Eysenck, H. J. *The IQ argument.* New York: Library Press, 1971.

Feldman, C. F., Lee, B., McLean, J. D., Pillemer, D. B., & Murray, J. R. *The development of adaptive intelligence.* San Francisco: Jossey-Bass, 1974.

Ferguson, L. R. *Personality development*. Monterey, Calif.: Brooks/Cole, 1970.

Ford, C. S., & Beach, F. A. *Patterns of sexual behavior*. New York: Harper, 1951.

Fortes, M. Social and psychological aspects of education in Taleland. In J. Middleton (Ed.), *From child to adult*. Garden City, New York: Natural History Press, 1970. Pp. 14-74. (Originally published 1938.)

Fortune, R. F. Arapesh warfare. *American Anthropologist*, 1939, *41*, 22-41.

Fouts, R. S. Acquisition and testing of gestural signs in four young chimpanzees. *Science*, 1973, *180*, 978-980.

Fowler, W. The effect of early stimulation: The problem of focus in developmental stimulation. *Merrill-Palmer Quarterly*, 1969, *15*, 157-170.

Fox, L. K. (Ed.) *East African childhood: Three versions*. Nairobi: Oxford University Press, 1967.

Freedman, D. G. The ethological study of man. In J. M. Thoday & A. S. Parkes (Eds.), *Genetic and environmental influences on behaviour*. Edinburgh: Oliver & Boyd, 1968. Pp. 37-62.

Freedman, D. G. Genetic influences on development of behavior. In G. B. A. Stoelinge & J. J. Van der Werff Ten Bosch (Eds.), *Normal and abnormal development of behavior*. Leiden: Leiden University Press, 1971. Pp. 208-233.

Freud, S. *Totem and taboo* (Standard Ed., Vol. 13). London: Hogarth, 1913.

Freud, S. *Leonardo da Vinci*. New York: Moffat, Yard, 1916.

Freud, S. *An outline of psychoanalysis*. London: Hogarth, 1938.

Freund, P. *Myths of creation*. New York: Washington Square Press, 1965.

Gardner, B. T., & Gardner, R. A. Two-way communication with an infant chimpanzee. In A. Schrier & F. Stollnitz (Eds.), *Behavior of nonhuman primates* (Vol. 4). New York: Academic Press, 1971. Pp. 117-184.

Gardner, R. A., & Gardner, B. T. Teaching sign language to a chimpanzee. *Science*, 1969, *165*, 664-672.

Garibay Patron, M. La psicología del Mexicano. *Revista Mexicana de Psicología*, 1969, *3*, 350-354.

Gay, J., & Cole, M. *The new mathematics and an old culture*. New York: Holt, Rinehart and Winston, 1967.

Geber, M. Developpement psychomoteur de l'enfant africain. *Courrier*, 1956, *6*, 17-28.

Geen, R. G. *Aggression*. Morristown, N. J.: General Learning, 1972.

Glueck, S., & Glueck, E. *Unravelling juvenile delinquency*. New York: Commonwealth Fund, 1950.

Goldfarb, W. The effects of early institutional care on adolescent personality. *Journal of Experimental Education*, 1943, *12*, 107-129.

Goldman, I. The Kwakiutl of Vancouver Island. In M. Mead (Ed.), *Cooperation and competition among primitive peoples*. New York: McGraw-Hill, 1937. Pp. 180-209.

Goodnow, J. J. A test for milieu effects with some of Piaget's tasks. *Psychological Monographs*, 1962, *76*(555).

Gordon, H. The intelligence of English canal boat children. In I. Al-Issa & W. Dennis (Eds.), *Cross-cultural studies of behavior*. New York: Holt, Rinehart and Winston, 1970. Pp. 111-119. (Originally published 1923.)

Gorer, G. *Himalayan village*. London: Michael Joseph, 1938.

Gorsuch, R. L., & Barnes, M. L. Stages of ethical reasoning and moral norms of Carib youths. *Journal of Cross-Cultural Psychology*, 1973, *4*, 283-301.

Granzberg, G. Hopi initiation rites—A case study of the validity of the Freudian theory of culture. *Journal of Social Psychology*, 1972, *87*, 189-195.

Granzberg, G. The psychological integration of culture: A cross-cultural study of Hopi type initiation rites. *Journal of Social Psychology*, 1973, *90*, 3-7. (a)

Granzberg, G. Twin infanticide—A cross-cultural test of a materialistic explanation. *Ethos*, 1973, *1*, 405-412. (b)

Greenberg, J. H. (Ed.) *Universals of language* (2nd ed.). Cambridge: M.I.T. Press, 1966.

Greenfield, P. M. On culture and conservation. In J. S. Bruner, R. R. Olver, & P. M. Greenfield, *Studies in cognitive growth*. New York: Wiley, 1966. Pp. 225-256.

Greenstein, J. M. Father characteristics and sex typing. *Journal of Personality and Social Psychology*, 1966, *3*, 271-277.

Gregory, I. Anterospective data following childhood loss of a parent: I. Delinquency and high school dropout. *Archives of General Psychiatry*, 1965, *13*, 110-120.

Greulich, W. W. A comparison of the physical growth and development of American-born and native Japanese children. *American Journal of Physical Anthropology*, 1957, *15*, 489-515.

Grinder, R. E., & McMichael, R. E. Cultural influence on conscience development: Resistance to temptation and guilt among Samoans and American Caucasians. *Journal of Abnormal and Social Psychology*, 1963, *66*, 503-507.

Guillaume, P. The development of formal elements in the child's speech. In C. A. Ferguson & D. I. Slobin (Eds.), *Studies of child language development*. New York: Holt, Rinehart and Winston, 1973. Pp. 522-541. (Originally published 1927.)

Gunders, S. M., & Whiting, J. W. M. Mother-infant separation and physical growth. *Ethnology*, 1968, *7*, 196-206.

Hampson, J. L., & Hampson, J. G. The ontogenesis of sexual behavior in man. In W. C. Young (Ed.), *Sex and internal secretions* (Vol. 2). Baltimore: Williams & Wilkins, 1961. Pp. 1401-1432.

Harlow, H. F. The development of affectional patterns in infant monkeys. In B. M. Foss (Ed.), *Determinants of infant behavior* (Vol. 1). New York: Wiley, 1961. Pp. 75-88.

Harlow, H. F. The heterosexual affectional system in monkeys. *American Psychologist*, 1962, *17*, 1-9.

Harlow, H. F. Sexual behavior in the rhesus monkey. In F. A. Beach (Ed.), *Sex and behavior*. New York: Wiley, 1965. Pp. 234-265.

Harlow, H. F. *Learning to love*. San Francisco: Albion, 1971.

Harlow, H. F., & Harlow, M. K. The affectional systems. In A. M. Schrier, H. F. Harlow, & F. Stollnitz (Eds.), *Behavior of nonhuman primates* (Vol. 2). New York: Academic Press, 1965. Pp. 287-334.

Harrington, C. Sexual differentiation in socialization and some male genital mutilations. *American Anthropologist*, 1968, *70*, 952-956.

Harrington, C. *Errors in sex-role behavior in teenage boys*. New York: Teachers College Press, 1970.

Harrington, C., & Whiting, J. W. M. Socialization process and personality. In F. L. K. Hsu (Ed.), *Psychological anthropology* (New ed.). Cambridge: Schenkman, 1972. Pp. 469-508.

Hart, I. Maternal child-rearing practices and authoritarian ideology. *Journal of Abnormal and Social Psychology*, 1957, *55*, 232-237.

Hartup, W. W. Early pressures in child development. *Young Children*, 1965, *20*, 270-283.

Havighurst, R. J., & Neugarten, B. L. *American Indian and white children: A sociopsychological investigation*. Chicago: University of Chicago Press, 1955.

Hays, D. G., Margolis, E., Naroll, R., & Perkins, D. R. Color term salience. *American Anthropologist*, 1972, *74*, 1107-1121.

Heider, E. R. "Focal" color areas and the development of color names. *Developmental Psychology*, 1971, *4*, 447-455.

Heider, E. R. Universals in color naming and memory. *Journal of Experimental Psychology*, 1972, *93*, 10-20.

Herrnstein, R. J. IQ. *The Atlantic*, 1971, *228*(3), 43-64.

Herskovits, M. *Cultural anthropology*. New York: Alfred A. Knopf, 1955.

Hess, R. D., & Shipman, V. C. Early experience and the socialization of cognitive modes in children. *Child Development*, 1965, *36*, 887-898.

Hetherington, E. M. Effects of paternal absence on sex-typed behaviors in Negro and white preadolescent males. *Journal of Personality and Social Psychology*, 1966, *4*, 87-91.

Hetherington, E. M., & Deur, J. L. The effects of father absence on child development. In W. W. Hartup (Ed.), *The young child* (Vol. 2). Washington, D.C.: National Association for the Education of Young Children, 1972. Pp. 303-319.

Hiernaux, J. Weight/height relationship during growth in Africans and Europeans. *Human Biology*, 1964, *36*, 273-293.

Hiernaux, J. Ethnic differences in growth and development. *Eugenics Quarterly*, 1968, *15*, 12-21.

Hilgard, J. R. Learning and maturation in preschool children. *Journal of Genetic Psychology*, 1932, *41*, 36-56.

Hilgard, J. R., Neuman, M. F., & Fisk, F. Strength of adult ego following childhood bereavement. *American Journal of Orthopsychiatry*, 1960, *30*, 788-798.

Hilger, M. I. *Together with the Ainu*. Norman: University of Oklahoma Press, 1971.

Hoebel, E. A. *Man in the primitive world*. New York: McGraw-Hill, 1949.

Hoffman, M. L. Father absence and conscience development. *Developmental Psychology*, 1971, *4*, 400-405.

Holmberg, A. R. *Nomads of the long bow*. Garden City, N.Y.: Natural History Press, 1969. (Originally published 1950.)

Homans, G. C., & Schneider, D. M. *Marriage, authority, and final causes*. Glencoe, Ill.: Free Press, 1955.

Hsu, F. L. K. American core value and national character. In F. L. K. Hsu (Ed.), *Psychological anthropology* (New ed.). Cambridge: Schenkman, 1972. Pp. 241-262.

Hudson, W. Pictorial depth perception in sub-cultural groups in Africa. *Journal of Social Psychology*, 1960, *52*, 183-208.

Hudson, W. Pictorial perception and educational adaptation in Africa. *Psychologia Africana*, 1962, *9*, 226-239.

Hudson, W. The study of the problem of pictorial perception among unacculturated groups. *International Journal of Psychology*, 1967, *2*, 89-107.

Husén, T. *International study of achievement in mathematics: A comparison of twelve countries* (Vol. 1). New York: Wiley, 1967.

Inhelder, B., & Piaget, J. *The growth of logical thinking from childhood to adolescence*. New York: Basic Books, 1958.

Inkeles, A. A note on social structure and the socialization of competence. *Harvard Educational Review*, 1966, *36*, 265-283.

Irwin, O. C. Infant speech: The effect of family occupational status and of age on sound frequency. *Journal of Speech and Hearing Disorders*, 1948, *13*, 320-323.

Irwin, O. C. Infant speech: Effect of systematic reading of stories. *Journal of Speech and Hearing Research*, 1960, *3*, 187-190.

Jahoda, G. Geometric illusion and environment: A study in Ghana. *British Journal of Psychology*, 1966, *57*, 193-199.

Jahoda, G. Retinal pigmentation, illusion susceptibility and space perception. *International Journal of Psychology*, 1971, *6*, 199-208.

Jakobson, R. *Child language, aphasia and phonological universals*. New York: Humanities Press, 1969. (Originally published 1941.)

Jakobson, R. Why "Mama" and "Papa"? In A. Bar-Adon & W. F. Leopold (Eds.), *Child language*. Englewood Cliffs, N. J.: Prentice-Hall, 1971. Pp. 212-217. (Originally published 1960.)

Jakobson, R., Fant, C. G. M., & Halle, M. *Preliminaries to speech analysis: The distinctive features and their correlates*. Cambridge: M.I.T. Press, 1963.

Jakobson, R., & Halle, M. Phonemic patterning. In A. Bar-Adon & W. F. Leopold (Eds.), *Child language*. Englewood Cliffs, N.J.: Prentice-Hall, 1971. Pp. 218-227. (Originally published 1956.)

Jelliffe, D. B. Infant nutrition in the subtropics and tropics. *WHO Chronicle*, 1969, *4*, 162-168.

Jensen, A. R. How much can we boost IQ and scholastic achievement? *Harvard Educational Review*, 1969, *39*, 1-123. (a)

Jensen, A. R. Reducing the heredity-environment uncertainty: A reply. *Harvard Educational Review*, 1969, *39*, 449-483. (b)

Jensen, A. R. *Educability and group differences*. New York: Harper & Row, 1973.

Johnson, W., & Stewart, J. L. Stuttering and North American Indians. In J. Akin, A. Goldberg, G. Myers, & J. Stewart (Eds.), *Language behavior: A book of readings in communication*. The Hague: Mouton, 1970. Pp. 340-346.

Kagan, J. The many faces of response. In P. Cramer (Ed.), *Readings in developmental psychology today*. Del Mar, Calif.: CRM Books, 1970. Pp. 9-15.

Kagan, J. Cross-cultural perspectives on early development. Paper presented at the Annual Meeting of the American Association for the Advancement of Science, Washington, D.C., December 1972.

Kagan, J., & Havemann, E. *Psychology: An introduction* (2nd ed.). New York: Harcourt Brace Jovanovich, 1972.

Kagan, S., & Madsen, M. C. Cooperation and competition of Mexican, Mexican-American, and Anglo-American children of two ages under four instructional sets. *Developmental Psychology*, 1971, *5*, 32-39.

Kardiner, A. Some personality determinants in Alorese culture. In C. Du Bois, *The people of Alor*. Minneapolis: University of Minnesota Press, 1944. Pp. 176-190.

Kardiner, A. *The psychological frontiers of society*. New York: Columbia University Press, 1945.

Kilbride, P. L., & Robbins, M. C. Linear perspective, pictorial depth perception and education among the Baganda. *Perceptual and Motor Skills, 1968, 27*, 601-602.

Kilbride, P. L., Robbins, M. C., & Freeman, R. B. Pictorial depth perception and education among Baganda school children. *Perceptual and Motor Skills, 1968, 26*, 116-118.

Kindaiti, K. *Ainu life and legends*. Japanese Government Railways: Board of Tourist Industries, 1941.

Kinsey, A. C., Pomeroy, W. B., & Martin, C. E. *Sexual behavior in the human male*. Philadelphia: Saunders, 1948.

Klima, E. S., & Bellugi-Klima, U. Syntactic regularities in the speech of children. In A. Bar-Adon & W. F. Leopold (Eds.), *Child language*. Englewood Cliffs, N.J.: Prentice-Hall, 1971. Pp. 412-424. (Originally published 1966.)

Klingelhofer, E. L. What Tanzanian secondary school students plan to teach their children. *Journal of Cross-Cultural Psychology, 1971, 2*, 189-195.

Kluckhohn, F. R., & Strodtbeck, F. L. *Variations in value orientations*. Evanston, Ill.: Row, Peterson, 1961.

Kock, S. W. *Management and motivation*. Unpublished doctoral dissertation, Swedish School of Economics, Helsingfors, Finland, 1965. Cited in D. C. McClelland, *Motivational trends in society*. New York: General Learning, 1971, P. 23.

Kohen-Raz, R. Scalogram analysis of some developmental sequences of infant behavior as measured by the Bayley Infant Scale of Mental Development. *Genetic Psychology Monographs, 1967, 76*, 3-21.

Kohen-Raz, R. Mental and motor development of kibbutz, institutionalized and home-reared infants in Israel. *Child Development, 1968, 39*, 489-504.

Kohlberg, L. A cognitive-developmental analysis of children's sex-role concepts and attitudes. In E. E. Maccoby (Ed.), *The development of sex differences*. Stanford, Calif.: Stanford University Press, 1966. Pp. 82-173.

Kohlberg, L. Stage and sequence: The cognitive-developmental approach to socialization. In D. A. Goslin (Ed.), *Handbook of socialization theory and research*. Chicago: Rand McNally, 1969. Pp. 347-480. (a)

Kohlberg, L. *Stages in the development of moral thought and action*. New York: Holt, Rinehart and Winston, 1969. (b)

Kohlberg, L. The child as a moral philosopher. In P. Cramer (Ed.), *Readings in developmental psychology today*. Del Mar, Calif.: CRM Books, 1970. Pp. 109-115.

Kohn, M. L. *Class and conformity*. Homewood, Ill.: Dorsey, 1969.

Labov, W. The logic of non-standard English. *Georgetown Monograph on Languages and Linguistics 22*. Washington, D.C.: Georgetown University Press, 1969. Pp. 1-22.

Lambert, W. W., Triandis, L. M., & Wolf, M. Some correlates of beliefs in the malevolence and benevolence of supernatural beings: A cross-cultural study. *Journal of Abnormal and Social Psychology, 1959, 58*, 162-169.

Landauer, T. K. *Psychology: A brief overview*. New York: McGraw-Hill, 1972.

Landauer, T. K., & Whiting, J. W. M. Infantile stimulation and adult stature of human males. *American Anthropologist,* 1964, *66,* 1007-1028.

Landor, A. H. S. *Alone with the hairy Ainu.* London: John Murray, 1893.

Leichty, M. M. Family attitudes and self concepts in Vietnamese and U. S. children. *American Journal of Orthopsychiatry,* 1963, *33,* 38-50.

Lemert, E. M. Stuttering and social structure in two Pacific societies. *Journal of Speech and Hearing Disorders,* 1962, *27,* 3-10.

Lenneberg, E. H. Understanding language without ability to speak: A case report. *Journal of Abnormal and Social Psychology,* 1962, *65,* 419-425.

Lenneberg, E. H. *Biological foundations of language.* New York: Wiley, 1967.

Lenski, G. *The religious factor.* Garden City, N.Y.: Doubleday, 1961.

Lester, B. M., Kotelchuck, M., Spelke, E., Sellers, M. J., & Klein, R. E. Separation protest in Guatemalan infants: Cross-cultural and cognitive findings. *Developmental Psychology,* 1974, *10,* 79-85.

LeVine, R. A. Gusii sex offenses: A study in social control. *American Anthropologist,* 1959, *61,* 965-990.

LeVine, R. A. Africa. In F. L. K. Hsu (Ed.), *Psychological anthropology.* Homewood, Ill.: Dorsey, 1961. Pp. 48-92.

LeVine, R. A. Child rearing in sub-Saharan Africa: An interim report. *Bulletin of the Menninger Clinic,* 1963, *27,* 245-256.

LeVine, R. A. *Dreams and deeds.* Chicago: University of Chicago Press, 1966.

LeVine, R. A. *Culture, behavior, and personality.* Chicago: Aldine, 1973. (a)

LeVine, R. A. Patterns of personality in Africa. *Ethos,* 1973, *1,* 123-152. (b)

LeVine, R. A., Klein, N. H., & Owen, C. R. Father-child relationships and changing life-styles in Ibadan, Nigeria. In H. Miner (Ed.), *The city in modern Africa.* New York: Praeger, 1967. Pp. 215-255.

LeVine, R. A., & LeVine, B. B. Nyansongo: A Gusii community in Kenya. In B. B. Whiting (Ed.), *Six cultures: Studies of child rearing.* New York: Wiley, 1963.

Lévi-Strauss, C. *The elementary structures of kinship.* Boston: Beacon Press, 1969. (Originally published 1949.)

Lévy-Bruhl, L. *How natives think.* New York: Washington Square Press, 1966. (Originally published 1910.)

Lindzey, G. *Projective techniques and cross-cultural research.* New York: Appleton-Century-Crofts, 1961.

Littenberg, R., Tulkin, S., & Kagan, J. Cognitive components of separation anxiety. *Developmental Psychology,* 1971, *4,* 387-388.

Lloyd, B. B. The intellectual development of Yoruba children: A re-examination. *Journal of Cross-Cultural Psychology,* 1971, *2,* 29-38.

Lloyd, B. B. *Perception and cognition: A cross-cultural perspective.* Harmondsworth, England: Penguin, 1972.

Longabaugh, R. Mother behavior as a variable moderating the effects of father absence. *Ethos,* 1973, *1,* 456-465.

Los Angeles Times. Russ women—royalty for a day. March 9, 1974. Part I, p. 14.

Lynn, D. B., & Sawrey, W. L. The effects of father-absence on Norwegian boys and girls. *Journal of Abnormal and Social Psychology,* 1959, *59,* 258-262.

MacArthur, R. S. Sex differences in field dependence for the Eskimo: Replication of Berry's findings. *International Journal of Psychology*, 1967, *2*, 139-140.

Maccoby, E. E. (Ed.) *The development of sex differences*. Stanford, Calif.: Stanford University Press, 1966.

Maccoby, M., & Modiano, N. On culture and equivalence: I. In J. S. Bruner, R. R. Olver, & P. M. Greenfield, *Studies in cognitive growth*. New York: Wiley, 1966. Pp. 257-269.

Madsen, M. C. Cooperative and competitive motivation of children in three Mexican subcultures. *Psychological Reports*, 1967, *20*, 1307-1320.

Madsen, M. C. Developmental and cross-cultural differences in the cooperative and competitive behavior of young children. *Journal of Cross-Cultural Psychology*, 1971, *2*, 365-371.

Madsen, M. C., & Connor, C. Cooperative and competitive behavior of retarded and nonretarded at two ages. *Child Development*, 1973, *44*, 175-178.

Madsen, M. C., & Shapira, A. Cooperative and competitive behavior of urban Afro-American, Mexican-American, and Mexican village children. *Developmental Psychology*, 1970, *3*, 16-20.

Malcolm, L. A. Growth and development in New Guinea—A study of the Bundi people of the Madang district. *Monograph Series, 1*. Madang: Institute of Human Biology of Papua and New Guinea, 1970.

Malinowski, B. *The sexual life of savages*. New York: Harcourt, Brace & World, 1929.

Malinowski, B. *Coral gardens and their magic*. (2 vols.). New York: American Book Co., 1935.

Malinowski, B. *Sex and repression in savage society*. New York: Meridian Books, 1955. (Originally published 1927.)

Marler, P., & Hamilton, W. J. *Mechanisms of animal behavior*. New York: Wiley, 1966.

Mayer, A. J., & Sharp, H. Religious preference and worldly success. *American Sociological Review*, 1962, *27*, 218-227.

McClelland, D. C. *The achieving society*. Princeton, N. J. : Van Nostrand, 1961.

McClelland, D. C. *n* achievement and entrepreneurship: A longitudinal study. *Journal of Personality and Social Psychology*, 1965, *1*, 389-392.

McClelland, D. C. *Motivational trends in society*. New York: General Learning, 1971.

McClelland, D. C., Atkinson, J. W., Clark, R. A., & Lowell, E. L. *The achievement motive*. New York: Appleton-Century-Crofts, 1953.

McClelland, D. C., Sturr, J. F., Knapp, R. H., & Wendt, H. W. Obligations to self and society in the United States and Germany. *Journal of Abnormal and Social Psychology*, 1958, *56*, 245-255.

McClelland, D. C., & Winter, D. G. *Motivating economic achievement*. New York: Free Press, 1969.

McCord, J., McCord, W., & Thurber, E. Some effects of parental absence on male children. *Journal of Abnormal and Social Psychology*, 1962, *64*, 361-369.

McCracken, R. D. Lactase deficiency: An example of dietary evolution. *Current Anthropology*, 1971, *12*, 479-517.

McNeill, D. The development of language. In P. H. Mussen (Ed.), *Car-*

michael's manual of child psychology (Vol. 1, 3rd ed.). New York: Wiley, 1970. Pp. 1061-1161.

Mead, M. *Coming of age in Samoa.* New York: William Morrow, 1928.

Mead, M. *Growing up in New Guinea.* New York: William Morrow, 1930.

Mead, M. *Sex and temperament in three primitive societies.* New York: William Morrow, 1935.

Mead, M. (Ed.) *Cooperation and competition among primitive peoples.* New York: McGraw-Hill, 1937.

Mead, M. *New lives for old.* New York: William Morrow, 1956.

Mead, M. *Continuities in cultural evolution.* New Haven: Yale University Press, 1964.

Mead, M. Foreword. In T. R. Williams, *Introduction to socialization.* St. Louis: C. V. Mosby, 1972. Pp. ix-xi.

Mead, M., & Macgregor, F. C. *Growth and culture.* New York: Putnam's Sons, 1951.

Meade, R. D., & Whittaker, J. O. A cross-cultural study of authoritarianism. *Journal of Social Psychology,* 1967, *72,* 3–7.

Menyuk, P., & Bernholz, N. Prosodic features and children's language productions. *Quarterly Progress Report,* No. 93. Cambridge, Mass.: M.I.T. Research Laboratory of Electronics, 1969. Pp. 216-219.

Meredith, H. V. Change in the stature and body weight of North American boys during the last 80 years. In L. Lipsitt & C. Spiker (Eds.), *Advances in child development and behavior* (Vol. 1). New York: Academic Press, 1963. Pp. 69-114.

Meredith, H. V. Body size of contemporary groups of eight-year-old children studied in different parts of the world. *Monographs of the Society for Research in Child Development,* 1969, *34*(1). (a)

Meredith, H. V. Body size of contemporary youth in different parts of the world. *Monographs of the Society for Research in Child Development,* 1969, *34*(7). (b)

Meredith, H. V. Body size of contemporary groups of one-year-old infants studied in different parts of the world. *Child Development,* 1970, *41,* 551-600.

Metheny, N. Y., Hunt, F. E., Patton, M. B., & Heye, H. The diets of preschool children: 1. Nutritional sufficiency findings and family marketing practices. *Journal of Home Economics,* 1962, *54,* 297-303.

Miller, A. G., & Thomas, R. Cooperation and competition among Blackfoot Indian and urban Canadian children. *Child Development,* 1972, *43,* 1104-1110.

Miller, D. R., & Swanson, G. E. *The changing American parent.* New York: Wiley, 1958.

Miller, G. A., & Chomsky, N. Finitary models of language users. In R. D. Luce, R. R. Bush, & E. Galanter (Eds.), *Handbook of mathematical psychology* (Vol. 2). New York: Wiley, 1963. Pp. 419-492.

Miller, N. E. Liberalization of basic S-R concepts: Extensions to conflict behavior, motivation and social learning. In S. Koch (Ed.), *Psychology: A study of a science* (Vol. 2). New York: McGraw-Hill, 1959. Pp. 196-292.

Miller, R. J. Cross-cultural research in the perception of pictorial materials. *Psychological Bulletin,* 1973, *80,* 135-150.

Minturn, L., Grosse, M., & Haider, S. Cultural patterning of sexual beliefs and behavior. *Ethnology,* 1969, *8,* 301-318.

Minturn, L., & Lambert, W. W. *Mothers of six cultures*. New York: Wiley, 1964.

Mischel, W. Sex-typing and socialization. In P. H. Mussen (Ed.), *Carmichael's manual of child psychology* (Vol. 2). New York: Wiley, 1970. Pp. 3-72.

Montagu, M. F. A. *Prenatal influences*. Springfield, Ill.: C. C. Thomas, 1962.

Moore, T. Language and intelligence: A longitudinal study of the first eight years. *Human Development*, 1967, *10*, 88-106.

Moss, H. A. Sex, age, and state as determinants of mother-infant interaction. *Merrill-Palmer Quarterly*, 1967, *13*, 19-36.

Mundy-Castle, A. C. Pictorial depth perception in Ghanaian children. *International Journal of Psychology*, 1966, *1*, 289-300.

Mundy-Castle, A. C., & Nelson, G. K. A neuropsychological study of the Knysna forest workers. *Psychologia Africana*, 1962, *9*, 240-272.

Munroe, R. L., & Munroe, R. H. Male pregnancy symptoms and cross-sex identity in three societies. *Journal of Social Psychology*, 1971, *84*, 11-25.

Munroe, R. L., & Munroe, R. H. Psychological interpretation of male initiation rites: The case of male pregnancy symptoms. *Ethos*, 1973, *1*, 490-498.

Munroe, R. L., Munroe, R. H., & LeVine, R. A. Africa. In F. L. K. Hsu (Ed.), *Psychological anthropology*. (New ed.). Cambridge, Mass.: Schenkman, 1972. Pp. 71-120.

Munroe, R. L., Munroe, R. H., & Nerlove, S. B. Male pregnancy symptoms and cross-sex identity: Two replications. *Journal of Social Psychology*, 1973, *89*, 147-148.

Munroe, R. L., Munroe, R. H., & Whiting, J. W. M. The couvade: A psychological analysis. *Ethos*, 1973, *1*, 30-74.

Murdock, G. P. *Our primitive contemporaries*. New York: Macmillan, 1934.

Murdock, G. P. Anthropology as a comparative science. *Behavioral Science*, 1957, *2*, 249-254. (a)

Murdock, G. P. World ethnographic sample. *American Anthropologist*, 1957, *59*, 664-687. (b)

Murdock, G. P. Cross-language parallels in parental kin terms. *Anthropological Linguistics*, 1959, *1*(No. 9), 1-5.

Murdock., G. P., *et al.* Ethnographic atlas. *Ethnology*, 1962-, *1-*.

Murdock, G. P., Ford, C. S., Hudson, A. E., Kennedy, R., Simmons, L. W., & Whiting, J. W. M. *Outline of cultural materials* (4th ed., 3rd printing, with modifications). New Haven: HRAF Press, 1967.

Mussen, P. H. Early sex-role development. In D. A. Goslin (Ed.), *Handbook of socialization theory and research*. Chicago: Rand-McNally, 1969. Pp. 707-731.

Mussen, P. H., & Beytagh, L. A. M. Industrialization, child-rearing practices, and children's personality. *Journal of Genetic Psychology*, 1969, *115*, 195-216.

Mussen, P. H., Conger, J. J., & Kagan, J. *Child development and personality* (3rd ed.). New York: Harper & Row, 1969.

Naroll, R. *Data quality control*. New York: Free Press, 1962.

Needham, R. *Structure and sentiment*. Chicago: University of Chicago Press, 1962.

Neimark, E., Slotnick, N. S., & Ulrich, T. Development of memorization strategies. *Developmental Psychology*, 1971, *5*, 427-432.

Nerlove, S. B. *Trait dispositions and situational determinants of behavior among Gusii children of southwestern Kenya*. Unpublished doctoral dissertation, Stanford University, 1969.

Okonji, O. M. A cross-cultural study of the effects of familiarity on classificatory behavior. *Journal of Cross-Cultural Psychology,* 1971, *2,* 39-49.

Olsen, N. J. Sex differences in child training antecedents of achievement motivation among Chinese children. *Journal of Social Psychology,* 1971, *83,* 303-304.

Olson, D. R. *Cognitive development: The child's acquisition of diagonality.* New York: Academic Press, 1970.

Omari, I. M., & MacGinitie, W. H. Some pictorial artifacts in studies of African children's pictorial depth perception. *Child Development,* 1974, *45,* 535-539.

Osofsky, J. D., & Danzger, B. Relationships between neonatal characteristics and mother-infant interaction. *Developmental Psychology,* 1974, *10,* 124-130.

Patterson, G. R., Littman, R. A., & Bricker, W. Assertive behavior in children: A step toward a theory of aggression. *Monographs of the Society for Research in Child Development,* 1967, *32*(5).

Paul, B. D. (Ed.), with W. B. Miller. *Health, culture and community.* New York: Russell Sage Foundation, 1955.

Pelto, P. Psychological anthropology. In A. Beals & B. Siegel (Eds.), *Biennial review of anthropology.* Stanford, Calif.: Stanford University Press, 1967. Pp. 140-208.

Peluffo, N. Culture and cognitive problems. *International Journal of Psychology,* 1967, *2,* 187-198.

Peterson, D. R., & Migliorino, G. The uses and limitations of factor analysis in cross-cultural research on socialization. *International Journal of Psychology,* 1967, *2,* 215-220.

Piaget, J. *The psychology of intelligence.* New York: Harcourt, Brace, 1950.

Piaget, J. *The origins of intelligence in the child.* London: Routledge & Kegan Paul, 1953.

Piaget, J. *The child's construction of reality.* London: Routledge & Kegan Paul, 1955.

Piaget, J. *The mechanisms of perception.* New York: Basic Books, 1969.

Piaget, J., & Inhelder, B. *Le développement des quantités chez l'enfant.* Neuchâtel: Delachaux et Niestlé, 1941.

Population Reference Bureau, Inc. *1971 world population data sheet* (Rev. ed.). Washington, D.C.: Author, 1971.

Porteus, S. D. *The psychology of a primitive people.* London: Edward Arnold, 1931.

Porteus, S. D. *Primitive intelligence and environment.* New York: Macmillan, 1937.

Premack, D. Language in chimpanzee? *Science,* 1971, *172,* 808-822.

Price-Williams, D. R. A study concerning concepts of conservation of quantities among primitive children. In D. R. Price-Williams (Ed.), *Cross-cultural studies.* Harmondsworth, England: Penguin, 1969. Pp. 201-210. (Originally published 1961.)

Price-Williams, D. R., Gordon, W., & Ramirez, M., III. Skill and conservation. *Developmental Psychology,* 1969, *1,* 769.

Provence, S., & Lipton, R. C. *Infants in institutions: A comparison of their development with family-reared infants during the first year of life*. New York: International Universities Press, 1962.

Rabin, A. I. *Growing up in the kibbutz*. New York: Springer, 1965.

Ramirez, M., Taylor, C., Jr., & Petersen, B. Mexican-American cultural membership and adjustment to school. *Developmental Psychology*, 1971, *4*, 141-148.

Ray, V. F. Human color perception and behavioral response. *New York Academy of Sciences, Transactions*, 1953, *16*, 98-104.

Rebelsky, F. G. Infancy in two cultures. *Nederlands Tijdschrift voor de Psychologie*, 1967, *22*, 379-385.

Rebelsky, F. G. First discussant's comments: Cross-cultural studies of mother-infant interaction. *Human Development*, 1972, *15*, 128-130.

Rebelsky, F. G., Starr, R. H., & Luria, Z. Language development: The first four years. In Y. Brackbill (Ed.), *Infancy and early childhood*. New York: Free Press, 1967. Pp. 289-357.

Rheingold, H. L. The measurement of maternal care. *Child Development*, 1960, *31*, 565-575.

Rheingold, H. L. The effect of environmental stimulation upon social and exploratory behavior in the human infant. In B. M. Foss (Ed.), *Determinants of infant behavior* (Vol. 1). New York: Wiley, 1961. Pp. 143-171.

Ricciuti, H. N. Malnutrition, learning and intellectual development: Research and remediation. In F. F. Korten, S. W. Cook, & J. I. Lacey (Eds.), *Psychology and the problems of society*. Washington, D.C.: American Psychological Association, 1970. Pp. 237-253.

Riesen, A. H. Stimulation as a requirement for growth and function in behavioral development. In D. W. Fiske & S. R. Maddi (Eds.), *Functions of varied experience*. Homewood, Ill.: Dorsey, 1961. Pp. 57-80.

Riesman, D., with Glazer, N., & Denny, R. *The lonely crowd*. New Haven: Yale University Press, 1950.

Roberts, D. F. Race, genetics and growth. *Journal of Biosocial Science, Supplement*, 1969, *1*, 43-67.

Roberts, J. M., & Sutton-Smith, B. Child training and game involvement. *Ethnology*, 1962, *1*, 166-185.

Rodgers, W. B., & Long, J. M. Male models and sexual identification: A case from the Out Island Bahamas. *Human Organization*, 1968, *27*, 326-331.

Rohner, R. P. Parental rejection, food deprivation, and personality development: Tests of alternative hypotheses. *Ethnology*, 1970, *9*, 414-427.

Rohner, R. P. Parental acceptance-rejection and personality development: A universalist approach to behavioral science. In R. W. Brislin, S. Bochner, & W. J. Lonner (Eds.), *Cross-cultural perspectives on learning*. Beverly Hills, Calif.: Sage/Halsted, in press.

Rohner, R. P., & Rohner, E. C. *They love me, they love me not*. New Haven, Conn.: HRAF Press, in press.

Rosen, B. C. Race, ethnicity, and the achievement syndrome. *American Sociological Review*, 1959, *24*, 47-60.

Rosen, B. C. Family structure and achievement motivation. *American Sociological Review*, 1961, *26*, 574-585.

Rosen, B. C. Socialization and achievement motivation in Brazil. *American Sociological Review*, 1962, *27*, 612-624.

Rosen, B. C., & D'Andrade, R. The psychosocial origins of achievement motivation. *Sociometry*, 1959, *22*, 185-218.

Rosenberg, B. G., & Sutton-Smith, B. *Sex and identity*. New York: Holt. Rinehart and Winston, 1972.

Roth, P. *The great American novel*. New York: Holt, Rinehart and Winston, 1973.

Rowell, T. E., & Hinde, R. A. Vocal communication by the rhesus monkey *(Macaca mulatta)*. *Proceedings of the Zoological Society of London*, 1962, *138*, 279-294.

Rubel, A., & Spielberg, J. Aspects of the couvade in Texas and northeast Mexico. *Summa anthropologica en homenaje a Roberto J. Weitlaner*. Mexico: Instituto Nacional de Antropología e Historia, 1966. Pp. 299-307.

Rumbaugh, D. M., Gill, T. V., & von Glasersfeld, E. C. Reading and sentence completion by a chimpanzee (Pan). *Science*, 1973, *182*, 731-733.

Sade, D. S. Inhibition of son-mother mating among free-ranging Rhesus monkeys. *Science and Psychoanalysis*, 1968, *12*, 18-38.

Santrock, J. W. Paternal absence, sex typing, and identification. *Developmental Psychology*, 1970, *2*, 264-272.

Sapir, E. Language and culture. *American Anthropologist*, 1912, *14*, 226-242.

Schaffer, H. R. Objective observations of personality development in early infancy. *British Journal of Psychology*, 1958, *31*, 174-184.

Schaffer, H. R. *The growth of sociability*. Baltimore: Penguin Books, 1971.

Schaffer, H. R., & Emerson, P. E. The development of social attachments in infancy. *Monographs of the Society for Research in Child Development*, 1964, *29*(3).

Scribner, S., & Cole, M. Cognitive consequences of formal and informal education. *Science*, 1973, *182*, 553-559.

Scrimshaw, N. S. Malnutrition, learning and behavior. *American Journal of Clinical Nutrition*, 1967, *20*, 493-502.

Scrimshaw, N. S., & Gordon, J. E. (Eds.) *Malnutrition, learning, and behavior*. Cambridge: M.I.T. Press, 1968.

Scott, J. P. *Early experience and the organization of behavior*. Monterey, Calif.: Brooks/Cole, 1968.

Sears, P. S. Doll play aggression in normal young children: Influence of sex, age, sibling status, father's absence. *Psychological Monographs*, 1951, *65*(6).

Seemanova, E. A study of children with incestuous matings. *Human Heredity*, 1971, *21*, 108-128.

Segall, M. H., Campbell, D. T., & Herskovits, M. J. *The influence of culture on visual perception*. Indianapolis: Bobbs-Merrill, 1966.

Senden, M. V. *Raum-und Gestaltauffassung bei Operierten Blindgeborenen vor und nach Operation*. Leipzig, Germany: Barth, 1932.

Shapira, A., & Madsen, M. C. Cooperative and competitive behavior of kibbutz and urban children in Israel. *Child Development*, 1969, *40*, 609-617.

Shirley, R. W., & Romney, A. K. Love magic and socialization anxiety. *American Anthropologist*, 1962, *64*, 1028-1031.

Siegman, A. W. Father absence during childhood and antisocial behavior. *Journal of Abnormal Psychology*, 1966, *71*, 71-74.

Skeels, H. M. Adult status of children with contrasting life experiences. *Monographs of the Society for Research in Child Development*, 1966, *31*(3).

Slobin, D. I. Universals of grammatical development in children. In G. B. Flores d'Arcais & W. J. M. Levelt (Eds.), *Advances in psycholinguistics*. New York: American Elsevier, 1970. Pp. 174-184.

Slobin, D. I. Grammatical development in Russian-speaking children. In A. Bar-Adon & W. F. Leopold (Eds.), *Child language*. Englewood Cliffs, N. J.: Prentice-Hall, 1971. Pp. 343-348. (Originally published 1965.)

Slobin, D. I. Children and language: They learn the same way all around the world. *Psychology Today*, 1972, *6*(2), 71-74, 82.

Slobin, D. I. Cognitive prerequisites for the development of grammar. In C. A. Ferguson & D. I. Slobin (Eds.), *Studies of child language development*. New York: Holt, Rinehart and Winston, 1973. Pp. 175-208.

Sonstroem, A. K. On the conservation of solids. In J. S. Bruner, R. R. Olver, & P. M. Greenfield, *Studies in cognitive growth*. New York: Wiley, 1966. Pp. 208-224.

Spiro, M. E. *Kibbutz: Venture in Utopia*. Cambridge: Harvard University Press, 1956.

Spiro, M. E. *Children of the kibbutz*. Cambridge: Harvard University Press, 1958.

Spiro, M. E., & D'Andrade, R. G. A cross-cultural study of some supernatural beliefs. *American Anthropologist*, 1958, *60*, 456-466.

Spitz, R. A. Hospitalism: An inquiry into the genesis of psychiatric conditions in early childhood, I. *The Psychoanalytic Study of the Child*, 1945, *1*, 53-74.

Spitz, R. A., & Wolf, K. M. Anaclitic depression: An inquiry into the genesis of psychiatric conditions in early childhood, II. *The Psychoanalytic Study of the Child*, 1946, *2*, 313-324.

Stephens, W. N. *The Oedipus complex*. Glencoe, Ill.: Free Press, 1962.

Stephens, W. N. *The family in cross-cultural perspective*. New York: Holt, Rinehart and Winston, 1963.

Stephens, W. N. A cross-cultural study of modesty. *Behavior Science Notes*, 1972, *7*, 1-28.

Stoch, M. B., & Smythe, P. M. Does undernutrition during infancy inhibit brain growth and subsequent intellectual development? *Archives of Diseases of Childhood*, 1963, *38*, 546-552.

Sutton-Smith, B., Roberts, J. M., & Rosenberg, B. G. Sibling associations and role involvement. *Merrill-Palmer Quarterly*, 1964, *10*, 25-38.

Talmon, Y. Mate selection in collective settlements. *American Sociological Review*, 1964, *29*, 491-508.

Tanner, J. M. *Growth at adolescence*. Springfield, Ill.: C. C. Thomas, 1955.

Tanner, J. M. *Education and physical growth*. New York: International Universities Press, 1961.

Tanner, J. M. Earlier maturation in man. *Scientific American*, 1968, *218*, 21-27.

Tanser, H. A. *The settlement of Negroes in Kent County, Ontario, and a study of the mental capacity of their descendants*. Chatham, Ont.: Shepherd Publ., 1939.

Tizard, B. IQ and race. *Nature*, 1974, *247*, 316.

Tomlinson-Keasey, C. Formal operations in females from eleven to fifty-four years of age. *Developmental Psychology*, 1972, *6*, 364.

Tuddenham, R. D. Soldier intelligence in World Wars I and II. *American*

Psychologist, 1948, *3*, 54-56.

Tulving, E. Theoretical issues in free recall. In T. R. Dixon & D. L. Horton (Eds.), *Verbal behavior and general behavior theory*. Englewood Cliffs, N.J.: Prentice-Hall, 1968. Pp. 2-36.

Turnbull, C. *The forest people*. Garden City, N.Y.: Doubleday, 1962. (Originally published 1961.)

Underhill, R. M. *Social organization of the Papago Indians*. New York: Columbia University Press, 1939.

Velten, H. V. The growth of phonemic and lexical pattern in infant language. *Language*, 1943, *19*, 281-292.

Vernon, P. E. *Intelligence and cultural environment*. London: Methuen, 1969.

Vetta, A. Conservation in Aboriginal children and "genetic hypothesis." *International Journal of Psychology*, 1972, *7*, 247-255.

Vils, U. Why do women take more drugs? *Los Angeles Times,* March 10, 1974, Part X, p. 1.

von Frisch, K. *The dance language and orientation of bees*. Cambridge: Harvard University Press, 1967.

Ward, M. C. *Them children: A study in language learning*. New York: Holt, Rinehart and Winston, 1971.

Warren, N. African infant precocity. *Psychological Bulletin*, 1972, *78*, 353-367.

Watson, J. S. Operant conditioning of visual fixation in infants under visual and auditory reinforcement. *Developmental Psychology*, 1969, *1*, 508-516.

Weber, M. *The protestant ethic and the spirit of capitalism*. New York: Scribner, 1930. (Originally published 1904.)

Wegner, R. N. Die Quruñgu'a, ein neuentdeckter Stamm primitivster Kultur ohne artikulierte und grammatikalische sprache in Ostbolivien. *Phoenix, Zeitschrift Deutsche Geistesarbeit für Südamerika*, 1928, *14*, 369-384.

Wendt, H. W. On information, season and religion as pre-verbal determinants of some later risk-taking. Unpublished manuscript. Mainz: Joh. Gutenberg Universitat, 1960. Cited in D. C. McClelland, *The achieving society*. Princeton, N.J.: Van Nostrand, 1961. P. 449.

Werner, E. E. Infants around the world: Cross-cultural studies of psychomotor development from birth to two years. *Journal of Cross-Cultural Psychology*, 1972, *3*, 111-134.

Werner, E. E., & Bayley, N. The reliability of Bayley's revised scale of mental and motor development during the first year of life. *Child Development*, 1966, *37*, 39-50.

Werner, H. *Comparative psychology of mental development* (Rev. ed.). Chicago: Follett, 1948.

Wheeler, L. R. A trans-decade comparison of the IQ's of Tennessee mountain children. In I. Al-Issa & W. Dennis (Eds.), *Cross-cultural studies of behavior*. New York: Holt, Rinehart and Winston, 1970. Pp. 120-133. (Originally published 1942.)

Whiting, B. B. (Ed.) *Six cultures: Studies of child rearing*. New York: Wiley, 1963.

Whiting, B. B. Sex identity conflict and physical violence: A comparative study. *American Anthropologist*, 1965, *67*, (Special publication), 123-140.

Whiting, B. B., & Edwards, C. P. A cross-cultural analysis of sex differences in the behavior of children aged three through 11. *Journal of Social Psychology*, 1973, *91*, 171-188.

Whiting, B. B., & Whiting, J. W. M. Task assignment and personality: A consideration of the effect of herding on boys. In W. W. Lambert & R. Weisbrod (Eds.), *Comparative perspectives on social psychology*. Boston: Little, Brown, 1971. Pp. 33-45.

Whiting, B. B., & Whiting, J. W. M., in collaboration with R. Longabaugh. *Children of six cultures: A psycho-cultural analysis*. Cambridge: Harvard University Press, 1975.

Whiting, J. W. M. Cultural and sociological influences on development. In *Maryland child growth and development institute*, 1959, 5-9.(a)

Whiting, J. W. M. Sorcery, sin, and the superego: A cross-cultural study of some mechanisms of social control. In M. R. Jones (Ed.), *Nebraska symposium on motivation*. Lincoln: University of Nebraska Press, 1959. Pp. 174-195.(b)

Whiting, J. W. M. Comment. *American Journal of Sociology*, 1962, *67*, 391-393.

Whiting, J. W. M. Methods and problems in cross-cultural research. In G. Lindzey & E. Aronson (Eds.), *The handbook of social psychology* (Vol. 2, 2nd ed.). Reading, Mass.: Addison-Wesley, 1968. Pp. 693-728.

Whiting, J. W. M. *The place of aggression in social interaction*. Paper presented at the Annual Meeting of the American Anthropological Association, New Orleans, November 1969.

Whiting, J. W. M. Masculine and feminine cognitive styles. n.d. (mimeo)

Whiting, J. W. M., Chasdi, E. H., Antonovsky, H. F., & Ayres, B. C. The learning of values. In E. Z. Vogt & E. M. Albert (Eds.), *People of Rimrock*. Cambridge: Harvard University Press, 1966. Pp. 83-125.

Whiting, J. W. M., & Child, I. L. *Child training and personality*. New Haven: Yale University Press, 1953.

Whiting, J. W. M., Landauer, T. K., & Jones, T. M. Infantile immunization and adult stature. *Child Development*, 1968, *39*, 59-67.

Whiting, J. W. M., & Whiting, B. B. *Progress report*. Nairobi: Child Development Research Unit, University of Nairobi, 1970.

Whiting, J. W. M., & Whiting, B. B. Altruistic and egoistic behavior in six cultures. In L. Nader & T. W. Maretzki (Eds.), Cultural illness and health. *Anthropological Studies*, 1973, *9*, 56-66.

Willerman, L. Review of H. J. Eysenck, *The IQ argument*. *Contemporary Psychology*, 1972, *17*, 585-586.

Willerman, L. Reply to Eysenck's letter. *Contemporary Psychology*, 1973, *18*, 246.

Willerman, L., Naylor, A. F., & Myrianthopoulos, N. C. Intellectual development of children from interracial matings. *Science*, 1970, *170*, 1329-1331.

Williams, T. R. *Introduction to socialization*. St. Louis, Mo.: C. V. Mosby, 1972.

Wilson, E. *Upstate: Records and recollections of northern New York*. New York: Farrar, Straus, & Giroux, 1971.

Winick, M., & Rosso, P. Head circumference and cellular growth of the brain in normal and marasmic children. *Journal of Pediatrics*, 1969, *74*, 774-778.

Winterbottom, M. R. The relation of need for achievement to learning experiences in independence and mastery. In J. W. Atkinson (Ed.), *Motives in fantasy, action, and society*. Princeton, N. J.: Van Nostrand, 1958. Pp. 453-478.

Witkin, H. A. A cognitive-style approach to cross-cultural research. *International Journal of Psychology*, 1967, *2*, 233-250.

Witkin, H. A., & Berry, J. W. Psychological differentiations across cultures: A theoretical and empirical integration. *Journal of Cross-Cultural Psychology*, 1975, *6*, in press.

Witkin, H. A., Dyk, R. B., Faterson, H. F., Goodenough, D. R., & Karp, S. A. *Psychological differentiation*. New York: Wiley, 1962.

Witkin, H. A., Goodenough, D. R., & Karp, S. A. Stability of cognitive style from childhood to young adulthood. *Journal of Personality and Social Psychology*, 1967, *7*, 291-300.

Witkin, H. A., Lewis, H. B., Hertzman, M., Machover, K., Meissner, P. B., & Wapner, S. *Personality through perception*. New York: Harper, 1954.

Witkin, H. A., Oltman, P. K., Raskin, E., & Karp, S. A. *A manual for the Embedded Figures Test*. Palo Alto, Calif.: Consulting Psychologists Press, 1971.

Wittkower, E. D. Perspectives in transcultural psychiatry. *International Journal of Psychiatry*, 1969, *8*, 811–824.

Wober, M. Sensotypes. *Journal of Social Psychology*, 1966, *70*, 181-189.

Wober, M. Adapting Witkin's field independence theory to accommodate new information from Africa. *British Journal of Psychology*, 1967, *58*, 29-38.

Wohlford, P., Santrock, J. W., Berger, S. E., & Liberman, D. Older brothers' influence on sex-typed, aggressive, and dependent behavior in father-absent children. *Developmental Psychology*, 1971, *4*, 124-134.

Wolf, A. P. Childhood association, sexual attraction, and the incest taboo: A Chinese case. *American Anthropologist*, 1966, *68*, 883-898.

Wolf, A. P. Childhood association and sexual attraction: A further test of the Westermarck hypothesis. *American Anthropologist*, 1970, *72*, 503-515.

Wright, G. O. Projection and displacement: A cross-cultural study of folk tale aggression. *Journal of Abnormal and Social Psychology*, 1954, *49*, 523-528.

Yarrow, L. J., & Pedersen, F. A. Attachment: Its origins and course. In W. W. Hartup (Ed.), *The young child* (Vol. 2). Washington, D.C.: National Association for the Education of Young Children, 1972. Pp. 54-66.

Young, F. W. *Initiation ceremonies*. Indianapolis, Ind.: Bobbs-Merrill, 1965.

Zelditch, M., Jr. Role differentiation in the nuclear family: A comparative study. In T. Parsons & R. F. Bales (Eds.), *Family, socialization and interaction process*. Glencoe, Ill.: Free Press, 1955. Pp. 307-352.

Zigler, E., & Child, I. L. Socialization. In G. Lindzey & E. Aronson (Eds.), *The handbook of social psychology* (Vol. 3, 2nd ed.). Reading, Mass.: Addison-Wesley, 1969. Pp. 450-589.

Author Index

Subject Index

178